www.ThePassionDrivenLife.com

"The Butterfly Effect"
and Your Life Transformation

Life is not about our 'time management',
But our management of the quality of our life.

It's been said that the flapping of the wings of a butterfly in Brazil can change the weather system in China. The idea is based on research by physicist Edward Lorenz in his study of the behavior of systems that are highly sensitive to initial conditions --- this sensitivity is known as "the butterfly effect." The flapping butterfly wings represent a small change in the initial condition of atmospheric patterns surrounding the butterfly and which can cause a chain of events leading to large-scale weather alterations elsewhere.

A real-life application of 'the butterfly effect' theory is that a casual meeting with a new acquaintance or a new idea can lead to large-scale and long-term effects in our life, and that *small changes* in our belief patterns can lead to long-term transformational life alterations.

Imitate the butterfly. The reason for choosing the butterfly as the symbol for The Passion-Driven® Life is that *the butterfly transforms itself from an unsightly and common looking creature to an uncommon and inspiring creation of beauty.* We can transform our lives through hope, divine inspired guidance, and by small changes in our beliefs and circumstances that can cause large changes in our life outcome. These small vibration changes (flapping of the wings) and minor conscious and sub-conscious heart, soul and mind changes in our everyday life can have wide spread effects not only on our future, but affect and touch the lives of others throughout the world.

∞

Prelude To
The Passion-Driven® Life

Thank you for accepting the invitation to seek, dig, unearth and unleash meaningful success, balance and enjoyment in your life! In this journey you'll discover your hidden talents and tap into the divine source of purpose and passion. And you'll discover empowerment, the power of commitments and intention, what really matters in life, how to overcome setbacks and obstacles, how to develop great relationships, and formulate meaningful goals. You'll also discover:

- How to go from mundane to great.
- The 21 Secrets of Business Success.
- The Alchemy of Life Success.
- What's replaced the "Unique Selling Proposition" adage?
- How to accomplish more without burning out.
- The Top 10 Reasons dreams slowly die.
- How to harness the power of the mind.
- How ordinary people have made extraordinary differences.
- The 9 Ancient Secrets of Wealth.
- Proven simple tools for lasting change & self-improvement.
- Why "faster" in life is no longer always better.
- Powerful processes to find passion and purpose in life and business.
- Why life's really not all about you (sorry to disappoint you).
- The source of unshakeable faith and hope in life.

The secrets to life success you'll soon find out do not lay in ancient laws, talent requirements, intelligence, and personality traits, or "systems" hawked in late night infomercials. Rather, they lie with an ability to harness your true calling and strengths, seek and harness God's role in your life, accept and love who you are in the moment, an ability to take action and appropriate risks at the right time, and being able to unleash a passion-driven purpose that moves you. It is in that process that you will be able to transform and inspire your heart, soul and mind, and create deep impactful changes as you journey onward in life.

∞

PRAISE FOR
THE PASSION-DRIVEN® LIFE

"To go to the 'Next Level', you need awareness, passion, drive, and persistence. Louis shows you how to keep your desires white-hot and that success can look effortless and easy."
~ **MARK VICTOR HANSEN**, #1 NY Times best-selling author of 85 books (154 million sold) including Chicken Soup for The Soul® series. Personal transformation guru.

"This book shows you how to unleash your energies and creativity to do wonderful things with your life."
~ **BRIAN TRACY**, #1 NY Times best-selling author of 47 books (22 million sold), including The Psychology of Achievement and 100 Absolutely Unbreakable Laws of Business Success. Speaker. Personal/organizational development expert.

"In The Passion-Driven® Life Louis F. Vargas reveals the secrets, principles, and tools that allow you to transform dreams into personal success. It inspires us to believe there is greatness in all of us, if we are willing to search for it and let it develop."
~ **RICHARD PAUL EVANS**, #1 NY Times best-selling author of 23 books (26 million sold) including The Christmas Box, Grace, The Five Lessons a Millionaire Taught Me: About Life and Wealth, and The Gift.

"This book resonates with the belief that every individual and organization has the potential to achieve and sustain greatness, and leave impacting legacies. The Passion-Driven Life has the principles needed for everyone to achieve their purpose and passion. A must read!"
~ **ROBERT G. ALLEN**, #1 NY Times best-selling author of eleven books (10 million sold) including Creating Wealth, Multiple Streams of Income, co-author Cracking the Millionaire Code and The One Minute Millionaire.

"The Passion-Driven Life distills how to create purpose and success in life and business. It is a tale of how to triumph over tragedies and a call to create meaning beyond just making money."

~ **DANIEL H. PINK**, NY Times & BusinessWeek best-selling author of A Whole New Mind. Former White House speechwriter for Vice-President Al Gore.

"This book represents a new approach to living life. If you are looking for total purpose and total prosperity in your life, then read it and apply its principles of balanced living!"

~ **RICK FRISHMAN**, NY Times best-selling author of ten books (over 400, 000 sold), including Where's Your WOW and Networking Magic. Marketing and publicity expert.

"Inspiring and uplifting. The Passion-Driven Life introduces the world to concepts and ideas that are profound and will have an impact upon the lives of those desperately searching for a turning point in their life."

~ **MARSHALL SYLVER**, best-selling author of Passion, Power & Profit. Success expert and authority on subconscious programming.

"I am now thoroughly convinced that the ONLY life worth living is a 'Passion-Driven Life.' This marvelous book shows you how to create one!"

~ **GREGORY J. GODEK**, #1 best-selling author of 1001 Ways to Be Romantic and Enchanted Evenings (3.1 million books sold).

"Awesome, enjoyable, and a refreshing look at how to live a passionate life. The Passion-Driven Life shows you how to experience total fulfillment and enjoy life at a much higher level."

~ **PEGGY McCOLL**, NY Times best-selling author of Your Destiny Switch and The 21 Distinctions of Wealth. CEO of Destinies, Inc.

"A motivating and innovative approach of how to define one's passions and purpose in life. This book can help you to make meaningful change in all areas of life."

~ **DEBBIE ALLEN**, best-selling author of Confessions of Shameless Self Promoters. International speaker, business trainer, featured in the motivational movie The Compass.

"An absolute must read for business executives to completely balance effectiveness and impact in their Work/Business Life, Personal Life, and other areas of life. The Passion-Driven Life has a lasting contribution to personal and organizational development. It makes us realize that there is the possibility to lead and live a life of balance, while unleashing our Divine purpose."

    ~ **JOHN CHILDERS**, author of John Childers on Think and Grow Rich. Founder The Wealth Academy.

"I've been a businessman for fifty years and former Chairman of a $100+ million company. I know what it takes to go 'the Next Level'. I've been up and way down; and I know what it takes to be successful, lead people, and make a difference in life. This book is the premier guide to be and do just that!"

    ~ **DONALD F. FORD**, President & CEO National Enterprises, one of the largest evaporative cooler distributors & service providers.

"Sharing from his own experience as an immigrant turned millionaire, Louis opens our eyes to possibility—the real possibility of rising above personal tragedy, pain, and loss, and attaining a life filled with purpose, power, and passion. He is a fighter, and he inspires us to persevere while letting us in on the secrets to achieving success in the key areas of life. Read The Passion-Driven Life and be prepared to have an inextinguishable fire awakened in your heart!"

    ~ **DUDLEY C. RUTHERFORD**, author and senior pastor of the 10,000 member Shepherd of the Hills Church in Porter Ranch (Los Angeles), CA.

"If you're ready to get up out of your seat in life and live... to connect or re-connect with the thing that fills your heart with passion... first get some coaching from The Passion-Driven Life. It will be time very well invested!"

    ~ **PRIOLEAU ALEXANDER**, author of Want Fries With That? A White-Collar Burnout Experiences Life at Minimum Wage. Marketing consultant & speaker.

"WOW! In The Passion-Driven Life Louis F. Vargas opens a powerful door to creating deep happiness and meaningful success by unleashing your passion and deep commitment. This easy-to-read book offers a spiritual call to action for individuals and businesses, challenging all to work at extraordinary levels of service and purpose. A must-read for leaders from large or small companies!"

~ **Dr. LINNE BOURGET, Ph.D.**, author of four books, including From Old Power to New Power and Dr. Linne's Leadership Series. Corporate consultant, leadership, and management expert.

"Ever wondered what it takes to win in life? Ever searched for meaning and passion? The Passion-Driven Life guides you to answers to your life questions. You learn how to win, you identify your meaning and passion, and you discover your motives for making the choices you make. Be inspired, HAPPY, passionate, and be balanced. That's what the world needs right now. Buy this book."

~ **ANITA JEFFERSON**, author of Climb Every Obstacle: Find Your Purpose, award-winning speaker, personal development/corporate leadership expert.

"It explains clearly what is important to all of us. The author enlightens us with a description of G.R.O.W.T.H. and what it is to be H.A.P.P.Y. The book was an eye-opener and a life changer for me!!"

~ **GREP P. SOFIO**, author of Honey, I Quit My Job!

"The Passion-Driven Life embodies the principles required to succeed in business and life and become an individual whose life is exhilarating at every turn. This is more than a book; it is a step-by-step life instruction manual on how to turn your aspirations and dreams into reality, and live life with passion and purpose in the process."

~ **ALLEN STARCZYK**, President White Star Enterprises, Inc., leading business software, and IT consulting firm.

≈

The
PASSION-DRIVEN® *Life*...

The *Secrets* of Success, Balance & Fulfillment in The 9 Key Areas of Life™

LOUIS F. VARGAS

www.ThePassionDrivenLife.com

New York

The Passion Driven Life
The Secrets of Success, Balance & Fulfillment in the 9 Key Areas of Life

Author photo by Ralph Auletta

Softcover ISBN: 978-1-60037-721-1
Hardcover ISBN: 978-1-60037-722-8

Library of Congress Control Number: 2009937982

MORGAN · JAMES
THE ENTREPRENEURIAL PUBLISHER

Morgan James Publishing
1225 Franklin Ave., STE 325
Garden City, NY 11530-1693
Toll Free 800-485-4943
www.MorganJamesPublishing.com

In an effort to support local communities, raise awareness and funds, Morgan James Publishing donates one percent of all book sales for the life of each book to Habitat for Humanity. Get involved today, visit **www.HelpHabitatForHumanity.org**.

The author gratefully acknowledges permission to use the following:

Scripture quotations from The Holy Bible, New International Version
Copyright © 1973, 1984 International Bible Society.
Used by permission of Zondervan Publishing House.

The Shawshank Redemption copyright © 1996 Universal Studio Pictures.
Used by permission of Universal Pictures, Inc.

The *Andrew Cherng* story copyright © 2008 Los Angeles Business Journal
Associates. Used by permission of the Los Angeles Business Journal.

It's a Wonderful Life copyright © 1946 RKO Pictures.
Used by permission of Warner Brothers Pictures, Inc.

Anthony Robbins quote copyright © 2000 Anthony Robbins Holdings,
LLC. Used by permission of Anthony Robbins.

Richard Paul Evans quote copyright © 2000 Richard Paul Evans, Inc.
Used by permission of Richard Paul Evans.

Slow Dance poem copyright © 2001 David L. Weatherford.
Used by permission of David L. Weatherford.

Dudley C. Rutherford quote copyright © 2005 Joy Comes in the Morning
Productions. Used by permission of Pastor Dudley C. Rutherford.

What's Important story copyright © 2008 Focus on the Family.
Used by permission of Focus on the Family and Cindy Sigler Dagnan.

FOREWORD

My passion, and what has driven me since 1979, is to heed the Lord's command to love Him, give of oneself, and make a difference in the life of individuals. Feed the Children does exactly that by providing basic living essentials to children and their families who are suffering hardship. Through that we provide not only sustenance, but hope.

We live in an age where the common dogma is to pursue financial success at whatever cost. For most people the notion of seeking a purpose and unleashing it with passion is lost amid the hustle and bustle of modern-day living.

The Passion-Driven® Life is an awakening call to the world to seek spiritual strength in God and to realize that it is possible to live life with proper balance. Its proposition is that all can live a passion and purpose-driven life. That we all must face head-on the various personal, relational, financial, health or business challenges we may face in life, make the necessary choices, and implement the changes needed in order to live a life with impact and meaning.

It is a refreshing and delightful read. More importantly, it is a call for the world to seek a Godly destiny and to be change-agents in various areas of life.

Larry Jones
President & Founder
Feed The Children
Oklahoma City, Oklahoma

ACKNOWLEDGMENTS

At times our own light goes out,
And is rekindled by a spark from another person.
Each of us has cause to thank with deep gratitude,
Those who have lighted the flame within us.

~ Albert Schweitzer

The English poet John Donne wrote, "No man is an island unto himself." Therefore, I did not accomplish anything by myself. Above all, I give thanks to God for providing me the eternal hope. Things fell apart into a million pieces in my life, but He put them back together, and opened doors of possibility. My heartfelt thanks to:

To all the authors and experts who honored me by endorsing this book, you are all awesome, and were a great inspiration and help.

Mark Victor Hansen, my friend and mentor, my deepest and sincere thanks for your encouragement, help, listening heart, and for being an ambassador of possibility.

Robert G. Allen thanks for being my friend, an inspiration, and a mentor. *Brian Tracy*, for helping out and believing early on. *Rick Frishman*, the greatest P.R. man in the business --- thanks for your advice and support. *John Childers,* your training was invaluable.

Larry Jones, for accepting Mark's invitation. *Greg Godek*, you were a patient God-send in the very beginning. *Marshall Sylver*, for teaching success with harmony.

My dear friend and mentor, *Donald "The King" Ford*, you are a living example of personal/business success, passion, and loving people without condition. Thank you for being my friend.

To my wonderful publicist *Suzanna Gratz* and team at *Morgan-James Publishing*. Many thanks to my marketing team: *Jay Abraham, Rich Schefren, Steve Harrison, Yanik Silver, Peggy McColl, Bob Baker* and *John Kremer*. My editor: *Dr. Charlotte Evans* --- thanks for your wonderful effort.

To my departed mentors and friends Max and Aaron from whom I learned lessons in humility and life and *Dottie Walters*, the dame of communication skills.

And everyone who allowed me the privilege of sharing a story or a quote: the *Carlson's, Richard Paul Evans, Dick & Rick Hoyt, Universal Pictures, Los Angeles Business Journal, Warner Brothers Studios, David L. Weatherford, Werner Berger, Mark Victor Hansen, Anthony Robbins, Gabriel Garcia Marquez, Pastor Dudley C. Rutherford* and *Cindy Sigler Dagnan*. Without you the message would have never been the same.

DEDICATION

Love is the only universal currency
That costs us nothing.
It can be freely exchanged and
Has the ability to make us all happy.
It leaves behind the most of cherished gifts:
Eternal true wealth and
Memories beyond measure.
Love is far more precious than what
Money could ever buy or leave behind.

~ Louis F. Vargas

To my loving wife. Thank you for love, faith, patience, and support. You are a wonderful wife, friend, and mother. I love you.

For my adorable twin daughters, "The Twinkies" (aka "Copiecitas"). Because of you I made the choices and changes that took our lives in a new and wonderful direction. To Chris and Ricky, two sons of whom I am proud of the decisions you made in your lives. Thanks for serving our country in the Navy and Marines! I love you.

To all those individuals who feel as if they have no direction, purpose, or passion in their lives. Though life may seem broken, there is a way to put it all together again. There is hope, never give up. Quitting is never an option. There is a better tomorrow, and the possibility to live a purposeful and passion-driven life that rocks your world.

Lastly, to the memory of many family, friends, and acquaintances whose lives on earth were cut short and a void was left in our hearts: my mother, my aunt Leonor, my aunt Rosalva, my step-mother Elena, my sister Estella, my cousins: Little Jorge Vargas, Jr., Guillermo Barrera, Jairo Triana. And my friends Debbie Pabon, Michael Schevetsky, Sam Comouche, Andrea Denbrowski, Brenden Foster, Ron Carlson, Darren Reynolds, Pastor Joshua Weaver, Carol Francisco, Meredith and Jason Morgan, Teo Gamboa, and Ralph Curtis. So painful to see all you leave us so soon.

The Alchemy of Life Success

Love, connect to & trust God.
Love, connect to & trust yourself.
Forgive & love yourself.
Forgive & love others.
Believe in your dreams.
Empower your faith.
Empower yourself.
Inspire your heart & soul.
Believe in your dreams.
Cultivate your mind power.
Focus on what is possible.
See the opportunities
And the possibilities
Amidst the challenges,
Take the action needed.
Then, let go ---
Grow, and let powerful
Transformation unfold....

TABLE OF CONTENTS

PART IV: THE KEY QUESTIONS
THAT REVEAL THE SECRETS

PART V: THE SECRETS TO THE NEXT
LEVEL IN LOVE, LIFE & BUSINESS

Twenty years from now
You will be more disappointed
By the things you didn't do,
Than by the things you did.
So throw off the bowlines,
Sail away from the safe harbor.
Catch the trade winds in your sail.
Explore.
Dream.

~ Mark Twain

∞

Hold fast to dreams
For if dreams die,
Life is but a broken-winged bird that cannot fly.
Hold fast to dreams
For when dreams go,
Life is but a barren field of frozen snow.

~ Langston Hughes

PART I

GETTING PREPARED FOR THE JOURNEY

Success is not a place at which one arrives,
But rather the spirit with which one
Undertakes and continues the journey.

~ Alex Noble

---

www.ThePassionDrivenLife.com

THE QUESTIONS
What's Life Really All About?

I know of nothing more despicable and pathetic,
Than a man who devotes all waking hours
To the making of money for money's sake.
If you want to succeed you should strike out on new paths,
Rather than travel the worn paths of accepted success;
Singleness of purpose is one of the essentials for success in life,
No matter what may be one's aim.

~ John D. Rockefeller

---

*C*an you have a life filled with passion, happiness and significance? Are you imbalanced in life? Is your life plain vanilla? Feeling unfulfilled by material success? Trapped in an unsatisfying dead-end job or business? Do you live life with laser beam focus? How can you turn life around to make it count? Do you desire to reach the next level in love, life and business?

There is hope. Living a purpose filled and passion-driven life is possible as you ask, "What's life really all about?" It requires that you discover and use the keys to The Secrets. God has a divine purpose and destiny for you. Life needs to be more than just "getting by." If you are able to transform your heart, soul and mind you will then be able to transform your life and live it with purpose, power and passion!

The stories throughout this book, including that of the author's personal, financial and emotional struggles, failures and successes, quotes, principles and tools of self-improvement and business success, will inspire the soul and spirit, touch the heart, and move your mind. They will spark faith and hope in the lives of individuals who have lost passion and purpose. It will hit home to others who have placed their family and personal life "on hold" in order to pursue success without realizing the pain and costs paid. It doesn't have to be that way though.

Each chapter has practical insights and advice that will guide you in the process of discovering the secrets and realizing the importance of having successful balance in The 9 Key Areas of Life™ --- Spiritual Life, Love Life, Family Life, Health Life, Business/Work Life, Personal Life, Financial Life, Social & Relationships Life, and Community Life.

Asking the questions found in *The Passion-Driven® Life* and seeking the answers can transform the way you live, think, play, work, interact, worship, connect to others and give back to the world. You'll find the answers and define the kind of life you desire and dream of when you dig deep in your soul, seek uncommon and new paths, and take the steps to become successful in *all* areas of life. Doing so will enable you to become a better person, a better spouse, a better friend, a better executive, manager, leader, employee, and help you embrace life fully.

≈

THE CHALLENGE

Finding Passion & Purpose for the Soul

If you're to be used by God,
He will take you through a multitude of experiences
That are not meant for you at all.
They're meant to make you useful in His hands,
To help you understand what transpires in the souls of others
So that you'll never be surprised by what you come across.

~ Oswald Chambers

---

*T*o *be successful in life we must be willing to be, do and tackle uncommon things in the face of pressures to be common! And that's not at all easy to be or to do, yet it is one of the fundamental keys of true success, balance and fulfillment in all areas of our life --- to be willing to go against the flow of commonness in our world.*

Uncommon courage to accept mistakes, uncommon faith and trust in God, uncommon acceptance of our flaws while making improvements in our character, uncommon decisions to get the most out of our life, uncommon choices to heal the wounds of our past and move on. An uncommon love to build lasting and loving relationships, uncommon ways to lead and respect others, uncommon personal empowerment where we no longer base self-worth on our accomplishments or upon the opinions of others, uncommon action that leads to major breakthroughs and milestones.

An uncommon refusal to compromise and be mundane, and uncommon choices to create greatness in our personal, business and work life. All achievers of success in life throughout the ages have been willing to be uncommon --- are you willing to be passionate, uncommon and create meaningful change in yours?

Have you wondered why it seems hard to focus on positive change in our lives? Why it's so hard to change our inner chatter and put a stop to limiting thoughts in our heads?

Why do we make New Year's resolutions with all our feeling and good intentions only to see very little happen during the year to make them a reality? And it goes on and on....

We ask so many questions when things aren't going the way we want them to: Why is fear paralyzing me? Why am I afraid to take action? Why am I not living the life I want? Am I living my divine purpose? Why am I not happy? Why do I have to go through so many tough times in my life? Why can't I get my company's staff to believe in what we do? Why isn't my company growing? And on and on it goes....

We chase and desire so many things because we believe they will somehow bring us happiness and make us feel better: More money. A nicer car. A bigger house. Bigger profits. More clothes. More jewelry. A new spouse or partner. A new look. And on and on it goes....

Ever noticed that these things don't really make you happy at all in the long run? Why is that? It's because those changes and chasing after things are superficial. They're only temporary. You soon become bored, depressed or overwhelmed once again by life.

According to recent research, in the United States forty million adults will suffer from depression and anxiety at least once in their lifetime. We're not talking about having a depressing day or a depressing week. No, this is diagnosed long-term depression and anxiety. In fact, according to the World Health Organization by the year 2020 the world will see depression become the second most important health issue, after heart disease, as a burden or cause of serious illness.

More people becoming unhappy at a time when we have the highest prosperity the world has ever seen. We have more stuff but that does not necessarily mean we have a better life or that we make a difference in our personal life, let alone the world.

So to truly make a difference in our lives we've got to look below the surface. We've got to dig deep into our soul, into our spiritual being, past our fear and limiting thoughts. We must connect with God and we must do it with all our heart, mind, and soul. We have

to go to a spiritual and sub-conscious level. That is where true transformation and meaningful changes will take place in our lives. It is where we come face-to-face with ourselves on a deep level, and where we come to love and embrace our being.

Life passes us by quite quickly. When we were young we couldn't wait for our birthday or Christmas to arrive. The days in between were filled with impatient waiting. The days and weeks seemed like an eternity.

Once we hit twenty-one, though, life just seemed to pass us by in a flash. We no longer have "markers" to measure our life. At least, we don't have many of them. And we're no longer waiting for our next birthday with anxious anticipation. We don't exactly look forward to middle age as we looked forward to our teenage years or our twenty-first birthday. Past the age of thirty, many people wished the time clock would break or at least malfunction. But no life just goes on. So either we get busy living or we wait impatiently for life to end!

What if we challenged our soul and spirit? What if we changed things around? Wouldn't we have a renewed hope, divine happiness, and a life filled with purpose and passion? Wouldn't each week, each month, look different? Couldn't we expect amazing things to be accomplished in our lives? Couldn't we really "wow" our heart and soul, and establish a different measuring *marker* in our lives?

The challenge we have is not to measure our life by our age, but by how passionate we are about life, the purpose we are living out, and the passion by which we demonstrate it through love. Life's really too short *not* to do this.

What if you found out that you only had one year to live? Wouldn't you stop worrying about the insignificant stuff in life and concentrate on the bigger picture: the re-awakening, meaningful transformations, and *connections* you would need to make during that year --- spiritual connections, family connections, love connections, personal connections, social connections, and community connections?

So live life as it matters, because it does! To do that we need to rewire our heart, our soul, and our minds so that we can indeed create meaningful and empowering beliefs, launch our dreams, renew our hope, and make changes that leave a lasting legacy. Despite what we hear or see daily, in reality, life's not just about seeking to pleasure ourselves all the time.

After awhile the race for it all, the glitter and luster all fade away. If you embrace that idea, I assure you, a ton of societal pressure "to keep up" will come off your shoulders. Think about others and ask how you can better their lives first; in the process you will become a better person.

You can unleash the passion in your soul and align it with your divine purpose. You can heal from within all the past hurts, love unconditionally, overcome obstacles, have breakthroughs, reduce stress, accept your greatness, find inner calm, and peace, create abundance in all areas of life, embrace your power, transform your life, and empower your future. You can create balance and harmony where chaos and confusion exist in daily or weekly life; you can create meaning in life where doubt and self-centeredness may abound.

The challenge you and I face today is to confront the fears and worries that hold us back. To seek, find, and unleash the passion and purpose from deep within our soul; to connect with passion and purpose to God. Passion is that beautiful thing in life that when experienced is magical.

Passion is an inspiring and uplifting energy, a power and divine illumination in our life. It can bring meaning and purpose to how and who we love, what we do in life and how we go about doing it --- from our personal relationships to our work, to our spiritual walk to our personal pursuits, and to our community involvement.

Living with passion is not a-hard-to-reach-concept, available only to a select few. You can unleash passion in your life when you decide to inspire, when you decide to act from a deeper level of commitment, and when you decide to *connect* your spirit and soul to the daily miracles that God plants in our lives: from creation itself where we embrace its awesomeness and beauty; to little things like a kiss from a child, the simple pleasures of life like a stroll along the beach, a mountain or lake; to feeling and giving true love.

Finding and unleashing your divine purpose creates transformation, and it is the way we declare to ourselves and the world that life has significance. When you follow that purpose with passion, you find meaning. It is then that we can live life fully out loud in all key areas of life with joy, fulfillment and happiness.

To me, the sad part is that so many people in the world decide not to live this way. Don't let your life slowly pass you by. In the dark and foggy nights when your soul is downcast, look up and accept the challenge; decide to re-connect and dig deep in your heart and spirit for the passion and purpose in your soul. The goal then is to break out of our lethargy and experience the activity and life God wants for us in ways that renews our soul and our passion!

A person may simply wake up one day and find himself or herself lost and adrift without a purpose. The poet Dante Alighieri said of this situation: "In the middle of the road of my life, I awoke in a dark wood, where the true way was wholly lost." You will find your way to a new life when you seek success and fulfillment based on purpose and passion that move your soul.

So many people in the world, especially "type A" success-driven personalities, hide their personal brokenness, perceived inadequacies, past hurts, longing for recognition and/or disappointments behind a wall of either titles, degrees, accomplishments, achievements, material possessions, or successes ---- all the while hurting deeply inside and longing for that intangible "something" which can move their soul to a point of tears. Their level of personal passion is dismal. Whether or not you are in this category, I encourage you to face what's not working in your life and accept the challenge: the search for that inner passion and divine purpose that will move you and inspire the world, and exhilarate you weekly, if not daily.

≈

in the face of them. Yes, challenges and times of difficulty, such as we are experiencing now, are unavoidable. That's life.

The Encarta dictionary defines *crisis* as "a situation or period in which things are very uncertain, difficult, or painful, especially a time when action must be taken to avoid complete disaster or breakdown."

The American Heritage dictionary defines it as "a crucial or decisive point or situation; a turning point."

The words of Miyazawa's ring true, though they are very difficult to embrace or believe in while we are in the midst of pain and our soul is downcast. The greater the pain, the less we need to focus on ourselves and instead on a greater purpose and a greater passion in our life. It is by focusing on the purpose and passion, rather than on our present state of pain, that we can transcend that pain, elevate our thoughts, dig deep in our inner core, and reach out to God for answers, and through hope see the light at the end of the tunnel. However, if we are mired in pain and deep in self-pity we get nowhere and accomplish nothing except going deeper into depression and into lonesome thoughts.

So what should you do when, for example, a personal life crisis, a business crisis, a work crisis, a love crisis, or a health crisis hits? What should you do when fear and worry hit you separately or all at once? The aim should not be to avoid them --- that's impossible --- but to: (1) hang on and brace for them as best as possible; (2) seek God's comfort, wisdom and insight immediately during them; (3) be open to the journey they'll take us towards and the character they will mold in us; (4) accept the fact that we can become better and stronger due to them; (5) not get stuck as a result of them; (6) accept where we are and take appropriate actions and steps today that will shape our tomorrow; and (7) move on to the next facet of your life after them. Doing so enables us to live an empowered life.

I believe that the purpose of a crisis is to move us from acting as a "victim of life" to a "victor in life." Where we empower ourselves and no longer ask, "Why is this crisis [i.e. a divorce, a business failure, a health crisis, a spiritual crisis, a loss of a loved one, etc.] happening to me?", and ask instead, "What can I learn from this?" I have asked both sets of questions. The latter is the best to ask as it empowers your soul and allows you to move on in life to the next level.

We should no longer fear crises; instead we should see them as opportunities for positive changes in the present that will shape our future. You should not believe that "Lady Luck" or your "wish-bone" will get us out of them. The 1st century Roman philosopher Seneca said it best about preparation versus luck: "Luck is what happens when preparation meets opportunity." So instead of believing in luck and "crossing your fingers" as your safe passage out of crises in life, be prepared for the storms that inevitably will come your way and learn the lessons they bring to you, and the character they'll mold in you. At first, I wasn't prepared for my crises, however, I learned rather quickly as I was battered about in my storms of life.

Our aim during times of crises is to learn from and embrace them, no matter how *ugly* they appear, and indeed are, at the time; and to move through them so that at the end we can understand that we were made stronger and resilient because of them. There is a reason for times of crises in our life. They can point the way to critical decisions and turning points that must be made and taken to get to the next level. We must hold firmly onto faith, hope, and persistence in our soul as we're in the midst of storms and crises.

That is what *The Passion-Driven® Life* is about --- emphasis on divine faith, personal empowerment, massive action, an acceptance of who you are in life, the process of transformation, and a shift in your soul and mind to a new realm of believing what is possible. In all, in this journey together I want to inspire you to enjoy the simple things in life, to make a difference, to increase your level of personal and business productivity, and at the same time create more personal freedom as you build quality relationships. Above all, to live a life filled with abundance, blessings and confidence. For that to manifest in your life change must take place.

I've had many personal and business successes where I hit the bulls-eye target dead-center; personal and financial successes; some professional recognition, and congratulatory pats-on-the back. I've had many ups and many downs. Broken dreams and, thankfully, many dreams fulfilled. I've experienced many a moment of victory, accomplishment, and an exhilarating feeling of fulfillment on "top of the mountain."

And I've also had many a crisis, failure, and cataclysmic storms along the way, that loom in the shadows and recesses of my memory, but which shaped me and guided me towards the light at the end of the tunnel. I've had long and dreary moments of pain while living in the valleys of life.

Hurt and briefly down, I did not counting myself out but got back up with skinned knees and a skinned heart, then crawled and clawed my way up the mountain of obstacles that faced me. All along I continued on with faith and God-inspired strength; I made it back to the mountaintop. I've had soap opera-like twists and turns that I overcame because of spiritual faith, immense fortitude and a fighting spirit.

During and after the time of a *life crisis,* I made the changes within my soul and mind, made turning point decisions and then created the breakthroughs necessary towards living fulfilled and appreciative of all of God's blessings. You can do the same in your personal life, work life, love life, and spiritual life.

Otherwise, if you do not, it is probable that you shall live distant and adrift in the sea of disillusion and alone with your hidden dreams; never having reached the shores of fulfillment, abundance, and the opportunity to witness and experience the fullness of the promises God has in store for your life.

This book contains the wisdom and strategies that allowed me to bounce back from failure and become successful in my personal and business life. It also contains the experiences and advice of individuals who are living, or who lived, a fulfilling life filled with spiritual abundance, balance, harmony, and meaning in all areas of life, not just financial success. There is more to life than money. It comes and it goes. Trust me on that one as I'm proof of that. One bad decision, one bad economic cycle, one serious illness, a divorce or any other crisis and "poof" --- it can evaporate. This book is about achieving a true *abundant* and *successful* personal life.

What matters in life are the transitions and changes we make in our character, our spiritual life, our family life, our health life, our love life, our personal life, and the legacy we leave the world, as we are in the process of transformation. I now have a deeper understanding of balance, harmony, meaning, purpose and passion in *The 9 Key Areas of Life* which I shall share with you. The stories in this book, I hope, will paint a broader panorama of the beauty of life that can be filled for you with promises and possibilities.

No love, no friendship
Can cross the path of our destiny
Without leaving some mark on it forever.

~ Francois C. Mauriac

My mentors and friends, Mark Victor Hansen and Robert G. Allen, undoubtedly have left a mark in my life. They knew my stories of overcoming obstacles and crises, and had for a long time encouraged me to share them with the world. I resisted. I thought they mattered only to me, so I just kept on doing my own thing in the shadows. I never sought to go under the spotlight or scream from the mountain-top, "Hey, here I am look at me. See what I've been through and accomplished, you can make it too!"

Mainly, I just focused on how I could continue my own climb. Bob and Mark continued to encourage me every chance they could. I finally saw their vision that by sharing my story, life lessons, and life principles that I learned, it was not really about me but about reaching out to others and helping them in their own struggles. So they could be inspired from the stories contained in this book and could pick themselves up and continue onward, despite whatever set-backs or difficulties in their life, never giving up, and thereby being able to implement a positive change in their lives.

So here we are! This book does address the "How Can I Succeed?" question that is most often asked, but more importantly to me answers the deeper question, "How Can I Go From Financial Success to Personal Success and Have Significance?"

One of the frequent questions asked of me comes from people who are who are either stuck in the valleys of despair and don't believe there's a way out or from people looking to go the "next level" in their life is, "How'd you do that?" "That" being me going from an immigrant living in tough Los Angeles neighborhoods to being awarded multiple academic scholarships to a prestigious university, becoming a young millionaire as a Wall Street municipal bond and stock-broker, then spiraling downward to being beyond broke, without a job, and without freedom, then afterwards persisting onward until I eventually established several businesses, including an award winning multi-million dollar *Inc. 500* company.

The Passion-Driven° Life contains the principles, strategies, lessons, knowledge, secrets, and divine wisdom that I learned from life, the school of hard-knocks and from many mentors which I used and implemented, just as one uses a special tool to accomplish a specific task, to rise above my circumstances of defeat, pain, difficulty, and disappointments beginning from early childhood onward.

Maybe you are already accomplished in life and feel you need no direction or tips on how to become financially successful; you're there already but feel empty. If you're like I was, you've hit the wall and realize you've sacrificed too much in lost love, relationships, personal time, or even health for that success you strived so hard to get and maintain ---then you're in the right place. You realize that you need to get to the next level in other areas of life which will bring you, in the short and long run, deeper satisfaction and a broader and deeper sense of life accomplishment, above and beyond making money.

This is *not* an autobiography. I share many stories of individuals from various walks of life, from the financially poor ones, but wealthy in their soul and spirit, to multi-millionaires, and even a billionaire. From an 11 year old cancer patient who has since passed away but who left an endearing example of love and compassion, to an 88 year old that lived a life filled with purpose and passion, despite major childhood heartaches. These are people who decided to life fully, give unselfishly back to the world, and chose to rise above their circumstances. Their stories, I trust, will touch your heart, give you amazing perspective, fuel your hope, affirm and uplift your own vision, and unleash your passion and purpose for life. I hope that the quotes contained here will also allow you moments of reflection and insight on a variety of topics ranging from money, to success, to love, to fame, to a simple life, to family, and to God.

My life has been an interesting colored canopy of experiences. I'm an immigrant from Colombia who grew up in very challenging neighborhoods with a disciplinarian for a father. He provided for and loved us, but at times in my early childhood years he was physically abusive to my mother and us kids. That made me a fighter from day one. My growing up fights and battles with street thugs were all too common and at times a concern for my parents. However, I focused on a goal and dream in my heart and mind; and after many obstacles and crises, I was admitted to an exclusive private university, from which I am proud to say I am an alumnus having graduated with honors and a triple major.

My growing up experiences got me ready to fight later in life because after graduate school I had to learn to swim amidst and fend off the sharks I encountered on Wall Street as a municipal bond trader and stockbroker in Beverly Hills. I had other successes after Wall Street in a couple of businesses ranging from real estate development, finance, to legal services, healthcare, marketing, and management consulting. Sandwiched in between my many accomplishments, yet never forgotten, were major battles and fights not in the streets but in the halls of the court system which were the catalyst for both my personal and financial demise. Nonetheless, by God's grace and blessing, I rose up from the ashes of defeats just like the mythic creature the Phoenix.

It is no irony that God allowed me to graduate from the University of Southern California (USC) whose motto is, quite appropriate, "Fight On!" All I have ever accomplished in my life has been a blessing from the Lord, who kept me in his safe in his bosom while the world around me burned, storms battered me about and who gave me that indomitable spirit to fight on during the times of crises.

The *Passion-Driven® Life* is meant to encourage and inspire you to seek your personal potential, enhance your spiritual connection, and unleash personal success in all facets of your journey in life. If need be for you to fight for and claim what's yours --- like I had to! It is about living a life where you create purpose and meaning; and about living in such a way your legacy, no matter your age, speaks volumes for you. That it would say in your absence that you lived boldly and courageously, made the right choices, overcame challenges, and made a difference in the world.

One thing I have realized is that our life purpose and life passion are unique. Don't follow someone else's version of it. Not your parents, not your teachers, not your spouses or friends. By all means, seek their wisdom, if any wise wisdom or advice is offered, in the meantime with prayer and meditation seek the correct road to take, accept yourself with all the imperfections, create a vision of where you want to go, begin to assemble an action plan, and then just let go of the anchor and sail onward.

In every step God will reveal the opportunities, relationships, and your purpose and passion. In the search for your unique possibilities, your unique potential, and your unique breakthroughs, you will find them if you persist.

Ask yourself: Am I living the life I want? Does the work I do matter to me? What is my purpose in life? Do I have abundance? Am I living life with amazing passion? Am I ready to go to the next level in all nine areas of life?

It is not death that a man should fear.
A man should fear never beginning to live.

~ Marcus Aurelius

Pray. Search. Dream. Focus. Forgive. Accept. Listen. Learn. Laugh. Love. Find. Unleash. Live your purpose. Live your passion. There is only one lifetime on earth, so make it count. Keep in mind though that success *is* not just about money. Whatever *your* definition of success is, choose to search for it and make it a reality it in your life. In the process of searching for answers and overcoming crises we find more than what we sought in the first place --- we find our true inner essence and our inner strength --- and that alone is a thing of beauty to discover.

Follow the advice of the ancient Roman philosopher Cicero and, "spend your life well." Remember that the *choices* we make *and changes* we take in life are what will ultimately determine our destiny --- more than the *chances* we do or do not take. Therefore: *Choose* passion. *Choose* meaning. *Choose* to love yourself. *Choose* the less traveled road. *Choose* purpose. *Choose* to love others. *Choose* to serve. *Choose* charity. *Choose* to make each day worthwhile. *Choose* a new destiny. *Choose* to make a difference.

Live life without excuses --- no matter what's happened to you in the past; no matter how ugly, how bad, or how tough your story is, just move on. Past failures cannot have a strangle hold on how you live in the present. When you do that you will empower your life, your future, your hope, your purpose, your passion, and empower others in the process.

Choose to be a decision maker and pro-active, rather reactive. Therefore, grab the wheel of life and go where you dream of going. Go where God has destined and desired for you to journey. Stop the "wishing" and focus on the *future-stances* of the journey ahead. Focus on the new direction you will decide to head towards, rather than continuing on that familiar and worn-out road behind you filled with never ending *excuses* and *circumstances*. Make your new life happen now ... no matter what!

The joy of the Lord is my strength.

~ Nehemiah 8:10

With God as your source of strength, *choose* to rise above your circumstances in life. I did. Others have and so can you. The stories contained through the passages of *The Passion-Driven® Life* prove that. They convey what I believe are messages of hope and possibility, of the ability of people to rise up from difficult crises and circumstances --- even terrible ones people have suffered --- such as poverty, prison, Nazi concentration camps, total financial meltdown, loss of loved ones, physical and mental disabilities, and terminal illness. There is hope. You are here to serve God and others. The rest will all take care of itself, if you just take the right steps to improve your life, prepare to leap, and move to the next level.

Our past does not define us as individuals. Even though we are products of our past and our good and bad decisions, we must not allow the past to haunt us forever. We must not allow it to limit us or define us in the present, or what we intend to become in the future. My past legal and financial experiences or difficulties certainly did *not* define my future nor limit me in my circumstances. In fact, they opened a new meaning in my life and allowed me to view opportunities where others saw mostly difficulty and impossibility.

The storms, obstacles, and tough times molded me into a better person; they humbled me and made me realize that I was not in control of anything. That idea may be hard for many to accept but that's just how it is with life --- *if* we choose to accept our storms of life in that way. Too many people in this world lose their purpose and lose their passion for life; especially nowadays in the wake of so much economic bad news, personal storms and crises.

I had an aunt and a friend who committed suicide. How one can lose hope was amazing to me, but it happened to them. Amidst their storms and crises, they lost hope, faith, purpose, and passion, and thought life was just too hard, and instead of reaching out they quit altogether.

For other people in the world they also lose hope, faith and passion and do "check out" not by killing themselves, but by killing their dreams, relationships and purpose in life, and merely existing day-to-day.

If I can inspire and prevent just one person from quitting in life and instead to move past their storms, keep their dreams alive and empower their hope, then my personal storms, struggles, crises and pain, despite being hard to endure, would have been worth it.

Life is far too fragile not to live it fully with every breath we have. I'm reminded of Psalm 90:12: "Teach us to number our days and recognize how few they are; help us to spend them as we should." Remember, God is a God of second chances. Never give up on your dreams, never give up on yourself, never give up on God, and never give up on life. It's never too late for a second chance at life. It's never too late to *choose* to live life with purpose, take steps to go to the next level in life, and *choose* to live passion-driven. Blessings on your unique soul journey…

Louis F. Vargas

The Crossroads

**Choose a Road
Upon Which Your
Dreams, Prayers, Desires, and
Plans Will Be Unleashed;
And Upon Which You Will
Fulfill Your Divine Purpose
And Destiny.
Do Not Stay Stuck at
The Crossroads of Life...**

INTRODUCTION

The Power of Fully Embracing Life

It is a brief period of life that is granted to us,
But the memory of a well-spent life never dies.

~ Marcus Tallies Cicero

Faith, hope, and desire are missing in a lot of people these days. My desire is simply to inspire. To have others *see* what's possible in their lives, get the vision of hope, move past the hard times, believe in themselves, live the dreams of their heart, and fulfill God's role and purpose in their lives. The life lessons in *The Passion-Driven® Life* are intended to bring hope, inspiration, and possibility to those who believe these things are no longer around in their life. There are no excuses to leading a life of purpose and a life of success. You can fully embrace life!

Beyond being just about life and business success, my purpose in undertaking this project was also to give a perspective on what truly matters in life. Our life shouldn't just be all about attaining financial success or making a comfortable living, while we forsake living in the moment, and forgo enjoying life's simple pleasures.

What I have accomplished came also about because I was passionate and hungry for what I was seeking to accomplish. I suppose that like so many other immigrants and passion-driven people, I had the genes of persistence, street smarts, school smarts, a deep desire, and drive all imbedded in my DNA. Having grown up at an early age in less than desirable neighborhoods for a while I was accustomed to exchanging blows with thugs to survive. This served me later as I had to fight and wrestle it out with sharks, alligators, and piranhas in business, as well all the well-oiled resources of the federal government.

"Fight On!" baby, no matter what life throws at you. That DNA strand of persistence and unwillingness to let defeats become permanent, fueled along by my faith in God's providence and protection, became more important in my survival and success than any MBA or graduate school education I could have ever attained. Moreover, love and support from family and true friends were essential keys to keep from going off the deep end. All these also combined to propel me back from the abyss into which I fell.

> *Most men lead lives of quite desperation,*
> *And go to the grave with the song still in them.*
>
> ~ Henry David Thoreau

Don't let the *song* in your heart die with you totally unsung. Get up, shake off whatever's going on, dig deep, and unleash passion. As you pursue those things which you deem or believe will bring you happiness, don't put off living and being happy in the moment. No one knows how long we have been gifted by God to live our years on this earth.

We tend to think and plan "long-term" towards our golden years of retirement and we seem invincible; that is until tragedy or difficult storms arrive, and our worlds are jolted and jarred. We put off many small or big things that could enhance our life today on a shelf and we bribe our psyche and our spirit into accepting the mantra, "Don't worry I'll get to that one day." That "one day" may never arrive. I've witnessed that too many times already. Don't look back and regret those things you wish you could have done years ago. It is what it is, so my advice is just start a clean slate and move on.

The secrets, keys, and lessons I cover are applicable to your personal life and work environment, and are designed for you to have a well-rounded and fulfilling life. The message is simple: life should not be just an endless chasing after victory, success, money, or whatever "thing" you chase after. Instead, we must stop and appreciate the little victories and small things in our life now. Then we can move on, plan, reach, and achieve higher goals and dreams, all along never lose sight of the fact that we must make a difference each month and each year of our lives.

The basic premise of living a passionate and purpose-filled life is to understand the fact that God created all of us with brilliance which we must use for the greatest good, and to live with divine purpose and passion. God is my guidance, strength, and eternal hope.

This book is a guide to help you define and live a personal and spiritually meaningful life. It is a guide on how you can achieve a life of balance, abundance, and live a life that has intention, purpose, and value.

Happiness is a healthy mental attitude,
A grateful spirit,
A clear conscience, and
A heart full of love.

~ Anonymous

I never had anything handed to me. My daddy was not a multi-millionaire who built a business and then gave me the secrets and the keys to the kingdom. Heck, I had to go looking for them on my own. My dad was a former banker and entrepreneur in Colombia who immigrated here in search of the American dream for all of us. He was forced to adjust to menial labor right away that was far different from having a chauffeur-driven car and use of company country clubs. Instead, he worked as a painter at USC, a photographer, print shop owner, and a slew of other work culminating as a realtor. He accomplished some things he was proud of but in the end he died flat broke, alone despite being married six times, and seeking spiritually meaning. At least he died knowing his family cared and loved him.

My mom was a licensed nurse in Colombia who couldn't practice here due to language barriers. She died very young from a brain tumor, with sadness about many things, including not living a life of total fulfillment. Both of my parents, nonetheless, left a rich legacy to their six children. Their legacy of hope, a fighting spirit and example of being able to make lemonade from the occasional lemons that life gave them --- propels us to this day.

No sir. Every success I have has been hard earned and fought for. I've gone from rags-to-riches-to-rags and back to riches during my journey. I've been blessed to learn many life lessons and secrets along the way about what does and doesn't work.

In a business career spanning twenty-three years, I've started companies with nothing more than an idea, little if no money, and through sheer determination made them succeed. As an immigrant I faced immense social and educational obstacles growing up. My successes sound great but I also had failures that cost me. I've been sued for millions, lost millions, been indicted by the federal government, lived to see the inside the walls of prison, and started again at the bottom of the pile with nothing more than a smile on my face, tons of hope and determination, and unending perseverance.

Many are the plans in a man's heart,
But it is the Lord's purpose that prevails.

~ Proverbs 19:21

I have had to face immense personal and family health issues --- things which I could never have overcome without the love and hand of grace of almighty God. He was there for me, and he's there for you too. Believe it.

Despite all my trials and tribulations I never lost faith, hope, love, or perspective. I've learned many lessons about adversity, faith, fortitude, persistence, the value of family, purpose and making a difference. Through all these ups and downs, I have been blessed with marriage to the same loving, supportive and loyal woman since 1990.

I have also had many mentors whose loving advice has given me assurances that things could always be worse. Two of the most memorable have been Max and Aaron, both Holocaust survivors, who I met at my condo complex in Encino. We had many a stoic moment of late night chat about life when I was a budding Wall Streeter.

From them I learned many happy stories as well as soulfully sad tales. There were many pearls of wisdom I learned during my encounters with them. Aaron said to me one night, in his thick German accent, as I was complaining about my work challenges, "No matter what happens to you in your young life, you need to remember that quitting is never an option! You hear me?" That advice has stayed in my heart and mind to this day.

My roller-coaster ride has taught me of the need to reinforce and adopt that philosophy in our hearts and minds. Stop the whining about one thing or another and get on with it.

Sports, I think, can provide a good analogy for life. You are either one of three types --- (1) a *participant* in the game: risking, getting bruised here and there, and no matter the outcome you gave it your all; (2) a *referee*: calling out others mistakes and living disinterested in the outcome; or a (3) a *spectator*: sitting on the side-lines watching others live.

My hope is that you get in the game of life and give it your all. Not only that you dream big, but that you launch those ideas or passions you have hidden within your soul.

When you get into a tight place
And everything goes against you,
Till it seems as though
You could not hang a minute longer,
Never give up,
For that is just the place
And time that the tide will turn.

~ Harriet Beecher Stowe

It doesn't matter where you are right now in life, or where you've been. I've been down and out, as it were. Yet by God's grace, I have been picked up from the mess and given renewed hope. I dusted off the dirt and got back into the game.

What's important is where you want to go, what want to achieve. To get to where you dream of going, you must overcome the challenges in your life through prayer, hope, faith, vision, and

action. You must align with Divine providence and believe that change is possible. Forget about your circumstances. Resolve in your heart and mind to change and transform. Then move on.

Feeling as if life has no greater purpose? Feeling as if life has passed you by? Feeling that the words "passion" or "purpose" sound nice, but appear to be lacking in your life or your business? Stressed beyond measure because of work, business or family responsibilities? Have a desire to go to the next level in your life? Have a desire to make a difference in the world? Or have your dreams just flat-lined? If you are feeling the frustration of being "stuck", then this book is for you! Beginning today all the excuses that keep holding you back will stop. Move onward no matter what! Live the empowered life.

In our journey together we'll look at these types of questions, how you can create a new you and a new life. It will be rewarding only if you apply the steps revealed and the secrets of how you can go to the next level in love, life and business.

Adopt the belief that any regrets you may have should and need to be left in the past and stop thinking that the future is fearful. That is only true for individuals who lack forgiveness, have no action plan, and look to the future without possibility and hope. There is power in the now, *only* if you decide and really move towards change what is meaningful and impacting.

In *The Passion-Driven® Life* we'll look at crucial mind, spirit, soul and issues, and the secrets to some areas such as:

- Attitude, Achievement and Action.
- Balance, Beliefs, and Breakthroughs.
- Challenges, Choices, and Changes.
- Dedication, Destiny, and Dreams.
- Faith and Fortitude.
- Giving, Godly Guidance, and Greatness.
- Inner Power, Imagination, and Inspiration.
- Harmony, Healing, and Hope.
- Possibility, Planning, and Prayer.
- Satisfaction, Service, and Success.

The Lord is my shepherd,
He restores my soul.
Even though I walk through the valley
Of the shadow of death,
I will fear no evil,
For you are with me.

~ Psalm 23:1-4

The 9 Key Areas of Life ™

Living a purpose-driven **and passion-driven** life is possible. It requires that you discover **and use the** keys that unlock the secrets. God has a divine destiny for you. There is more to life than merely existing. Focus on your dreams, your desires, and happiness, then design who you want to be in the future, then take the steps in the present that will allow you to get there and lead and enjoy a life without excuses and with fulfillment!

Unblock yourself from what is holding you back mentally and spiritually. When you "unblock" your soul and mind, amazing love, power, and brilliance will flow from within and from above which will transform you in all key areas of life.

Being empowered in life is about weathering the storms and challenges we face, the choices made during those challenges, and the changes we enact because of them. Life is about our willingness to fight for what we want. Life is about connecting to God; about making a difference. It is about fully living empowered and alive in all areas of life.

The secrets, strategies, and steps, which I cover in *The Passion-Driven® Life* all relate to living life fully in all aspects of our daily living. We should not concentrate just on a couple areas and ignore the rest --- that is, where we compartmentalize our life or place major emphasis on one over the others. The result, if we do that, is imbalance, loss, harmony, and imbalance in the rhythm of life.

Your destiny, passion, and purpose fulfilled life await you in *The 9 Key Areas of Life* ™. They are:

1. **Spiritual Life** --- our connection to God, prayer and quite time.
2. **Love Life** --- our personal love relationships.
3. **Family Life** --- our family connections and interactions.
4. **Health Life** --- our body, health vitality and living habits.
5. **Business or Work Life** --- our profession, our company or our work.
6. **Financial Life** --- our money and finances.
7. **Personal Life** --- our hobbies and personal pastimes.
8. **Social Relationships Life** --- our social connections/networks and friends.
9. **Community Life** --- our connection to our community/ volunteering/charity.

My goal is for you to no longer be an uncertain, scared, or passionless person. You have the power to face challenges, to make choices, and to create internal and external changes to go to the next level.

There is plenty of lost passion and lost hope in the world. There are millions who have lost purpose. There are millions who have lost meaning. There are millions who have lost the road map for life. There are millions paralyzed by fear, unsure what to do next.

Through this book I want to challenge you so that you connect to your heart and your dreams; so that you have a life filled with deep meaning, joy, faith, and hope. It is possible to enjoy *living* rather than merely existing.

Live a life so you stop being part of the problem. Wake up, shake it off. Get busy with the business of living!

God created us and gave us hope. Nonetheless, doubts, fears, and excuses pop into our minds and hold us back. If you don't know how to go about fulfilling your purpose in life or how to achieve a balance between work and family life, that's okay; you're in the right place by reading this book. Or you may know that God indeed has a purpose for your spiritual life, but you simply have no idea how to connect that spiritual side with everyday living and don't have a roadmap for the journey, then that's okay too. We'll move on and by the end of this journey they should be clear to you.

I want to kindle your heart, touch your soul and expand your mind so you can live a life filled with total passion, total purpose,

total meaning, total love, total peace and total prosperity. Have you lost that kind of passionate living? Are you actively looking for them? If "No", why not?

When we lose something of value we start looking for it with immense determination! All our focus and energy at that time is directed in the search for the item lost. We persist in our search. We never give up the search. We work to find it.

When, and if we find what we've lost, we embrace it and reflect upon its importance in our lives.

Why is it then that we do not do the same with our dreams, our hopes, our aspirations, our goals, our purpose, or our passions? We lose them, and instead of beginning the search for them, we seem indifferent. We are unmoved by their loss in our life.

We say, "I know something is missing in my life." Yet we do not bother to do anything about it. Apathy sets in. We merely exist. All along we despair as to what life has become. I speak from experience. *The Passion-Driven® Life* came about as a result of personal and business challenges in my life when I asked: What is my purpose and what am I passionate about? How can I do something that really matters?

Asking those questions was the catalyst for my realization that while I was building a successful multi-million dollar company, I was sacrificing too much in my family life, health life, and personal life. I began the quest and I realized that it is *possible* to have success, and a fulfilling family and personal life without sacrificing one over the other. However, I had to make major *choices and changes!* I had to make it happen without excuses.

We all have potential and possibility perched in our hearts which we call "hope." That hope was placed there by an almighty God. It is up to each of us to search for that hope through wisdom, meditation, prayer and faith.

We dare to dream because of the hope in our hearts. We dare dream things are possible in our lives because divine providence allows us to believe in a better life. We dare to envision a life of meaningful purpose because we seek to act upon that providence. We act upon those dreams *only* if we choose to believe we have a mission in life.

> ## *Choose this day whom you shall serve.*
> ### *~ Joshua 24:15*

In the search for our dreams and in the process of unleashing our unique purpose we make *choices* and take *action* because we are passionate about life. Believe in God's power for your life. Be unique. Search for hope. Have meaning in life. Make a difference. *Choose* to live.

Focus intensely in the search for that unique and meaningful purpose you were created to follow. Don't wait another day to start the search. Dig. If you have what you believe is your purpose or calling, then don't wait any longer, and unleash it with greater passion.

I Want to Buy More Time

A rich old man lies dying on his bed. He has been slowly ebbing away the past few months from an incurable disease. He is mad at the world, at God and complains to whomever is around about everything and everyone. The rich old man is surrounded by what appear to be his many friends.

His life has been driven by making money. In that he succeeded. Yet, his personal life is a different story. Failed marriages and disconnected relationships. Strained relations with his family; too proud, he never bothered to mend the broken bridges to their lives. That is the reason they are not at his deathbed.

His "friends" stand a distance away from his bed, defeated. After a while the old man musters all his strength and thanks them for coming to bid him farewell. He tells them not to be down. He tells them that he thinks he has lived a "good life."

One of the visitors finally looks straight at him, gets close to the old man, and says to him, *"You don't understand, we have not come here in honor of you. We cry not tears of sorrow for you, but for us. We have come here not to celebrate how you lived your life or to celebrate your many business accomplishments. We come here sad because you failed at the*

---

meaning of life. We are deeply sad, because you never allowed us be a part of your life. We stand here crying because with you, we die as well. We tried to be a part of you, but you would not have us. We are your relationships with God and your family, your divine purpose, your true love, your forgiveness, your charity, your life legacy, and your passion for life. We all die with you. We are sad, for we shall never be expressed, nor allowed to blossom. We die unfulfilled in your life."

The old man then looks at each of his visitors as they leave his side one-by-one. He feebly reaches out to them and whispers, *"Wait, wait, I want to buy more time. Help me buy more time, so I can accomplish that."*

The last visitor slowly replies as he leaves, *"There's no more time. Even now you don't understand the true meaning of life. We never wanted your money, nor could your money ever buy those things. We merely wanted you to share your heart and soul with God and the world."*

He now finds no comfort in his accomplishments. Finally, he realizes that he has indeed missed his opportunity. He is now alone. His mind races for answers but find none. He cries silently with no one to see or ease his pain, his anguish or to comfort him. The old man closes his eyes sobbing as he mutters, "What did I do?"

If money is not your servant,
Then it will be your master.
Of the greedy man
It cannot be said that he possesses wealth,
But that is possesses him.

~ Francis Bacon

≈

PART II

THE POWER IN SEEKING ANSWERS & MAKING DECISIONS IN LIFE...

Trials teach us what we are;
They dig up the soil,
And let us see what we are made of.

~ Charles Spurgeon

---

www.ThePassionDrivenLife.com

<u>The Bridge</u>

**Search
For the Bridge of Faith and
The Bridge of Hope
That Will Take You Safely
Over the Raging Waters,
Difficulties and Crises of Life...**

CHAPTER ONE

The Power of Living Life Without Excuses ... No Matter What

Everyone has the power for greatness,
Not for fame, but greatness,
Because greatness is determined by service.

~ Martin Luther King, Jr.

I envision this to be a journey, a toolbox, and a guide along the road of your life. My desire is that it gives hope to those who have "hit the wall" and are losing, or have lost, their passion or purpose. For those who may feel an insignificance in what they are doing. As a continuous reminder to you that there are no excuses in life for you to pursue your dreams or aspirations! Pray, plan, persist, and just go for it --- no matter what.

Picture this: I'm sitting in heavy Los Angeles early morning commuter traffic, so far I'm not telling you anything that won't surprise you; anyway, I'm en route to my corporate headquarters (an hour and half away) of my *Inc. 500* multi-million dollar company where I'm President, Chairman and co-founder of, and a thought races through my head: "Is this going to be my life for the next 10 to 15 years; being stuck in grid-lock traffic and hurriedly going from one meeting to the next, and living life at a dizzying speed that is zapping me?" I pondered that thought in the back of my mind for a long time and for many months afterwards it lingered, quietly, and sometimes loudly, humming in my brain.

As I mentioned, I'm the President, Chairman, and co-founder of an *Inc. 500* multi-million company. In 2007, my company was featured in *Inc.* magazine as one of the fastest growing private companies in America. My company was on the leading edge as an English and Spanish language advertising agency, marketing consulting and sales training company. I engineered a merger and acquisition in 2006, and as a result we were on target for $10 million in the first fiscal year.

The milestone was both bittersweet. It was sweet because it validated my abilities as an entrepreneur and executive. It was a good morale booster for the company staff as well. Bitter because it took a lot of time away from my family and home. Was I elated to get there? Was the sacrifice worth the pay-off? Yes and no. To me, if you consider what I had to give up: my personal life balance, harmony, health, major milestone memories with my children and wife. There was just too much, in my opinion, to continue to give up for the sake of business and the sake of making money.

A man should never neglect his family for business.

~ Walt Disney

So back to being stuck in traffic, I'm getting nowhere as I drive to the office and I'm thinking to myself that there had to be a better way for me and my business where I could have an alternative that would be a win-win for everyone. I began to question why I was doing what I was doing and asking, "For what purpose?" I began to envision of a lot of other ways to make a great living and not die in the process, and leave behind a trail of tears, unfulfilled dreams, a heart-broken wife and children.

I have plenty of time to think as I drive, crawl along is more like it in my German luxury import: I think to myself, "Let's see I usually work 10-12 hour days and fight traffic for about easy 3 hours each day; that comes to a daily total of 12 to 15 hours engulfed by work. Subtract that from a 24 hour day, and I have roughly 9 good hours left to sleep, eat, relax (ha-ha), enjoy and actually see my twin daughters and wife. Take away at least six to seven for sleep, and you can see the major problem and issue I'm facing here: No time, except work time!" Sound familiar?

I hit the wall and said forget it! Today, I am no longer the Chairman, President, and co-founder of that company. Guess what? I couldn't be more relieved and happier. Why? As you can now imagine, I was sacrificing too much for it. It was draining me. I had no life beyond this company. The trade-offs in my personal life versus business growth were too much beyond what I was willing to endure. To experience the life we dream and desire we face: Choices, Challenges, and Changes. The Secrets to Life lie in how we answer each accordingly.

I faced my challenges in my life, made the decisions, and changes to experience it fully. Because of the challenges I faced, the choices and changes I made, I was able to reassess, refocus, recharge, and unleash my passion and redefine my purpose in life. I reconnected with my family, and as a result, I was able get my life back!

It was in the process of searching for the secrets of going to the next level in life, after having experienced a financial meltdown in my life in the 1990s, serious legal difficulties, and conducting in-depth research and introspection that I realized that in our quest of living life in our modern world, almost all of us have created an amazing cottage industry of "busyness" --- defined as fully and always occupied, and unavailable to live life.

Everywhere in the industrialized nations we have crafted an art of somehow always being "busy." Some people carry it around as a badge of honor and proud of constantly stating to others, "Gee, I'm so busy. Can talk now, I've got to go!" While I believe in productivity, there is a major difference between being productive and just being busy for the sake of it. Activity or motion is not productivity.

In the meantime, rarely do we do anything to slow the pace about being so busy. It is no small irony that the levels of stress, heart attacks, depression, anxiety and dissatisfaction with life have dramatically increased over the past thirty ears.

"Busyness" rarely pays great dividends. It instead extols a heavy price on us: constantly being physically tired while it further taxes our mind, heart, spirit and soul. When you run so fast to get somewhere, we miss half the fun of getting there. So, I resolved to walk, not to run as much, and enjoy the scenery along the way of life. I decided to help my family and myself by placing "busy-all-the-time" on the shelf before it placed *me* in a pine box. Now I get to still be in the business arena, yet I can now take a lot of time to enjoy my family and my twin toddlers.

> ### *The highest level of charity,*
> ### *Is helping others help themselves.*
>
> ~ Maimonides

At one time in my life I was where perhaps many of you are presently: hopeless, poor, in trouble, looking for answers, and just plain sick and tired of being sick and tired. In my search though for a better life, I came to the realization that I could live in, what Marshall Sylver refers to as an *"and"* world. Rather than having to choose between either one thing or another, you can have both!

You can have a world of success *and* a world of great family life *and* personal interests. I realized that I needed to stop worrying about aspects of *running* and *owning* a business. I realized I could own a business, and not be bogged down with daily administration issues, and still reap the benefits that come with being an entrepreneur.

There is no question that the company I co-founded was on the fast track, but I was on the slow track in my health, my relationships, and my overall quality of life. I had lost the passion for continuing onward for a multitude of reasons. After awhile it was no longer about a vision to merge the company with an even larger one, but to get my sanity, my life and my peace of mind back --- that is, believe me, priceless!

It was looking myself daily in the mirror and realizing that I could not continue with the same rhythm. That I had to choices to make. So I changed the business model and paradigm to fit my personal vision, life desires, dreams, purpose and passions for life.

We all have choices we must make without excuses. The difference is that some of us decide to take a leap of faith when we make them. We decide to follow our heart, to seek wisdom, and pray about the choices. We know that in doing so we can live life again.

Yet, so many others refuse to confront the reality or refuse to make the choices needed to regain a passion. They refuse to live out purpose. Instead they toil away with a burden in their heart, never looking to change the circumstances or to get past hurts or issues that have been holding them back.

A lot of you can relate. Perhaps you are a workaholic whose career or business seems to be more important than connecting with family, spouse, children, relatives, or friends. Perhaps you are someone who has lost, or is losing, passion and purpose in areas of personal relationships. Perhaps you are a mom who is constantly busy running from one place to the next and overloaded with "stuff" and you sometimes question the meaning of it all as you feel overwhelmed and sometimes unappreciated.

Or maybe you are someone who simply feels something is missing in your life. You could be a business person wondering: "What can I do to get me away from this situation that is causing me so much stress and heartache?"

> *99% of the failures come from people*
> *Who have the habit of making excuses.*
>
> ~ George Washington Carver

There are no excuses for not having personal or financial success *and* a great spiritual relationship with God that uplifts you and builds others. There are no excuses for not having dynamic family, personal or social relationships. There are no excuses for not having a balanced life where you enjoy the "small things", rather than merely focus on the large picture. There are no excuses for living an abundant life.

I've had to face social, family, economic, and legal struggles to make it in life. Growing up, I experienced first-hand back breaking work. I had no choice when I was young, as I was forced by my father to work, unpaid mostly, long hot summer days and weekends alongside him in various manual intensive tasks such as a car mechanic, construction assistant, machinery mechanic, painter, delivery person, and a printer. It was at my Dad's print shop, when I was just twelve, in an industrial accident that I almost severed my hand. I had to undergo multiple surgeries and years and years of physical and emotional pain afterwards. That ended my days of forced manual labor.

After that episode two things became pretty clear to me: 1) I appreciated hard work and doing a job well and; 2) I hated any kind of manual labor! It also sold me on the concept that I needed to get a college degree to create a better life for myself and seek to fulfill my American Dream. With no trust fund in sight I decided that I was better off heading for the books instead of back to the mean streets.

Refuse to be average.
Let your heart soar as high as it can.

~ A.W. Tozer

Despite my upbringing and challenges, I fought on and was blessed to attend a college. I faced my challenges and unloaded my personal baggage from my rough upbringing, made choices and early on in my life changed my direction. I created breakthroughs and turning points to the next level. So for you there should no excuses in life.

I know what it is to struggle. But I also know what it is to experience success. In my thinking there are no excuses. I've had ups and downs just like an elevator. Despite everything, I persevered onward, blessed by God, and with an unbending spirit to succeed. I've faced my mountains of obstacles and got busy moving upward and onward to climb them.

This book came about as a result of personal lessons and inspiration from experiences I had from years of starting various successful businesses. In the process of my business career, at times I also did not place proper boundaries and priorities in my family, personal or social life. I suppose it was an unbending drive to have the type of lifestyle and financial freedom I never experienced as I was growing up.

It was only until confronted recently with the fact that I was repeating the same pattern once again, and that it was affecting my family life, did it strike me that I could not continue on like that anymore. There sometimes is a price that is paid. At the end of it all with the *Inc. 500* company I realized that I was not living a harmonious life. The balance had been lost in my life while pursuing to build another business. I was not enjoying the process, or my company's success.

For all the success, I was *not* having fun nor did I believe that I was really making a difference. As I mention later in the 21 Laws of Business, having fun and being passionate about what you do is one of the most important criteria. I had to contend with boring administrative matters and internal struggles, along with grueling daily commutes of 3.0 to 3.5 hours. These highly stressful work days extended into late evenings and quite often to weekends.

It placed emotional strains on myself and my wife, and affected the quality of time I could spend with her and my adorable newborn twins. It had created an imbalance. I was paying a heavy price. Something had to change. I had choices to make.

I wanted to explore new frontiers. I wanted to reconnect with my personal interests, my family life, and my dreams. I needed to recharge, reenergize, redirect, refocus and disengage from all that was toxic in my business life that was engulfing me personally. I too needed to refuel my heart and spirit. It was time for a change --- no more excuses.

The toxicity and stresses of my business life affected my passion in the other core areas of my life. It began to affect my passion for living life fully. I longed to recapture the passion of being a part of something that was more significant to me than just growing a company.

Just as I had toxic imbalance in my business life that affected my personal life, the same could be occurring in your life. Examine yours and the areas of toxicity that could be spilling from one area of life into others such as your personal life, spiritual life, family life, or love life.

During a recent period of challenge in my life vis-à-vis the company and future I came across the book *Want Fries With That?* which captured my attention as it detailed the author's escape from being an advertising executive into various blue-collar jobs. He did so as a way of searching for his meaning and reconnecting with himself without the stresses and strains of corporate life. The book caught my eye because the author, like me, had been engulfed by his business and had lost touch with the passion of his personal and family life.

My hope is that *The Passion-Driven® Life* touches your heart and soul and that it helps you unravel the secrets of how to get to the next level in areas you wish to excel in, for example, your

personal life, love life, business or work life, spiritual life, social life, or health life. For you to find, redefine and redesign your life, and assist you in unleashing your purpose and passion in all areas of life. It's never too late to start and you're never too young to begin. As you shall see there are no excuses or past experiences, no matter how deep and painful, as to why you should not do so.

From my growing up years I realized there was a lot of baggage I was carrying that I had to unload to lighten the burden. Therefore, I decided to dump it on the side of the road before I could get on with my new journey in life. Do the same, if you are still carrying baggage from year's gone bye. There are no excuses!

There should be no excuses for you to capture and unleash the dreams you harbor in your heart and soul. That is the major purpose of this book. It's about how you have the inner power given by God to propel yourself to a new level of meaning, purpose and passion.

Life is too short and too precarious not too. As far back as I can remember, tragic or sudden death has surrounded my life from a very early age and shaped, to a major extent, how I value the gift of life. It is why I choose to appreciate life it in its totality.

When I was nine, my maternal grandmother died from an aneurism, when I was about 11, an aunt committed suicide. At twelve, a forty-one year old very close family friend died from a heart attack while cutting his lawn and an elementary school friend died from leukemia. When I was sixteen, my mother died from a brain tumor; at age eighteen a college friend died in a moped accident and shortly after another aunt died from stomach cancer. When I was twenty-one, my two year old cousin died from a fall. Toiling away at USC at twenty-two, I found out a cousin disappeared --- he was never found to this day. At twenty-four, another young cousin died from appendicitis. At twenty-five a friend committed suicide; and at twenty-eight, I witnessed and helped in a massive-rear accident in which a female passenger died in the flames. When I was thirty, my step-mother died at the young age of fifty-nine. And at thirty-six, I witnessed another serious car accident where the driver died in my arms. Within the last year four family members (my father, sister, mother-in-law and a cousin) and three close family friends passed away.

These tragedies or deaths haven't made me cynical. They served to remind me that living is about capturing small and big moments, and turning each experience into fabulous memories. To remind me that there is hope of living a life that counts. And that a life of greater passion and purpose must be lived. No one in the world has guarantees as to how long our life will be, so don't put it off --- no excuses.

We are indeed given a purpose here on earth by God; to connect with Him and life passionately. To connect with our hopes, our passions, and our dreams before it is too late. To connect with our family and friends, and to create relationships that touch people's hearts and make a difference. There are no excuses.

If you want to be happy,
Set a goal that commands your thoughts,
Liberates your energy,
And inspires your hopes.

~ Andrew Carnegie

What We Will Learn Together.

In this journey together through *The Passion-Driven® Life* I will drive you down the road of passion in life with the top down, wind blowing clarity of exhilarated belief. You will feel alive, free, and connected to life again as we search together for your unique passions and purpose in life. Some of the topics we will also explore together:

- The Top 10 Reasons Dreams Slowly Die.
- How Can I Excel in The 9 Key Areas of Life?
- What Stops Me From Enjoying A Life of Passion?
- The 9 Secret Keys to Balance & Financial Success.
- How to Create Happiness, Life Success and Harmony.
- What is The Secret Alchemy of Passion?
- How Can I Unleash Hope and Purpose?
- The Secret and Power of Spiritual Connectedness.

- The Secret and Power of Choices and Change.
- The Secret and Power of Planning and Action.
- The Secret and Power of Living Passionately Inspired.
- How Can I Live a H.A.P.P.Y. Life™?

In the book *"Under the Tuscan Sun"*, the protagonist undertakes a radical change in her life. She finds her passion, hidden deep within, not yet extinguished, and brings it to the surface. She dreams big and takes major steps. Her passion drives her. As a result she finds fulfillment in recreating herself. In her search she finds new purpose, new meaning, and passion. She fulfills a dream and moves to Italy to experience a new life. She knows she's been missing out. A little bold, but that is life on the edge. Define and unleash yours!

We were created to make a difference in our lives. How are we to be a great living example of life, if we have chosen to allow the pressures of life to suppress our dreams and passion for living it to the fullest?

As a result of me examining the imbalances in my life, I learned how to balance my life, to engage passion in all that I do in all areas of my life, not just business. I learned how to embrace the fullness of who I am, and how to make a passionate difference in my life.

You can live the life you want. You can have the life you dream about, it just requires the proper tools, the proper attitude, the proper actions and the proper focus. In this journey you will find those tools.

The Secret to Unleashing Passion & Purpose

There is a secret to recharging your dreams. It requires a different perspective, and for you to be open to the possibility and opportunity of creating a new you. It requires connection to spiritual principles. It requires a turning point from where you are *and* action, so that you can get to where you dream of being. Passion comes from the heart and gives us motive to move on despite difficulties. It puts our desires into action. Change how you harness your passion and your purpose, and you will change your circumstances. Doing so will change your life!

The inner thought coming from the heart represents
The real motives and desires...
These are the cause of action.

~ Dr. Raymond Holliwell

Life is not easy. But neither is living a life that is not fulfilling. I would rather have obstacles while pursuing living a life of my dreams than die slowly because I dared not venture out from my "comfort zone."

I know the difficult task we face in this country and around the world. So many ask questions such as: "How can I maintain a positive outlook when the news is teaming with negative information about the economy?" or "When is it ever going to get better because I can't take this anymore?"

But asking negative questions will only get you negative results. The quality of our answers in life is established by the quality of the questions asked. We will delve into detail later about a proper mind-set and how that can change your circumstances.

There are countless businesses and entrepreneurs who are thriving in this economy. It's just that we don't hear about that them daily, if at all. Look for possibility in your life amid these difficult times. Don't buy into the belief that "it's too late to make it." Difficult times can be a time for opportunity and possibility. Countless successful businesses were started during the Great Depression.

If you focus on negativity you will never be able to see what can be possible for your life. You will never emerge a different person, nor will you be prosperous or successful. In short, focus on negativity and you limit the likelihood that you will lead a passion-driven life.

Change is Tough

For a lot of people change is difficult. I understand it is easier to want to stay within what feels comfortable, especially when the wave of bad news bombards us almost daily. I know it is an almost knee-jerk response to want to maintain the status quo in your life.

It is *precisely* when things appear to not be going as you planned that you must take time to analyze what change is required in your life.

The changes required in my life were not easy for me either. However, I decided that for my sake and that of my family I had to enact them to have a quality of life and cease to neglect them for the sake of the company. I speak from experience about embracing change and embracing possibility. So, embrace challenges in your life instead of wallowing in misery of your dire circumstances.

God wants us to lead a life driven by meaning, purpose, and greater passion. Whatever you do in life do not stay mired in the circumstances that are causing or creating misery in your life. Change is hard if done all by yourself, but you are not alone as you will see throughout *The Passion-Driven® Life*.

One thing is pretty clear: the types of questions asked, having faith, and the things you focus on will ultimately determine your actions. Your actions will then determine the results. The results, in turn, will reflect how passionately you live your life.

You too have a choice to choose your *attitude* in light of your present circumstances. I accepted the challenge to redefine my life, go to the next level and unleash passion in all areas of my life.

I'm once again in the cancer department where chemo-therapy is administered and I'm editing the final portion of this book surrounded by several cancer patients of varying ages, 18 to 69, and cancer stages. I'm here with my nanny/housekeeper of fifteen years, whose is only forty-two, and is being treated for terminal Stage 4 colon, liver and lung cancer, that was just diagnosed a couple of months ago. One day she was working as usual and otherwise in great health, and the next she was rushed to the hospital with excruciating abdominal pain. After several hours and multiple tests the dreaded words from the doctor's diagnosis were uttered to her, "You have a major tumor which we think is cancerous."

I have been driving 1.5 hours each way to be with her for all her oncology consults and tests to support her and assist as best I can with all the raw medical data and information the doctors relay to her. This for her is a new, unexplored, and difficult journey. My wife speaks to her almost on a daily basis. The medical prognosis is dismal and, at best, they give her one year to live. It saddens me and brings to me flashbacks of the many family and friends who have been stricken by this disease.

Despite the pain she's undergoing I, however, see and hear in Tonia strength, perseverance, and Godly faith. Though naturally she's scared by what looms ahead she moves forward into the unknown. Her faith and attitude light her path. She's determined to face what looms ahead --- without excuses. We must be and do the same when situations pop into our life we did not expect. Move on with faith, power, and commitment, no matter what, and without excuses.

My mission as the author in *The Passion-Driven® Life* is to plant the seeds of choice, personal inspiration, spiritual discovery, and transformation in love, life, business and in *9 Key Areas of Life*, whether in individual's lives and in businesses or organizations.

It is possible to have a balanced personal life and a business life that embody compassion, purpose, passion, creativity, collaboration and meaning. It is possible to have a shift in our hearts, souls, and minds that result in balance and breakthroughs in life. The rewards include our personal empowerment and fulfillment, increased corporate responsibility, productivity, profits, and meaningful community service.

So let's see *The Secrets* that life has taught and revealed to me that I used to redefine my dreams, recharge hope, unleash greater passion, and create meaningful purpose in life. And how you can do the same, so that with every breath of air you breathe you move closer and closer to living a life of abundance and a life of meaning in which you call forth your very best whether in your personal and business life.

≈

The Harmony of Life

**Life has ---
A Harmony,
A Balance,
A Purpose,
A Passion.
Find it in Yours…**

CHAPTER TWO

The Power in Facing Tough Times &
The Secret of "Keep on Keeping On"

Men must live and create.
Live to the point of tears.

~ Albert Camus

The Secret to Persevering Despite the Storms. These are uncertain, trying and difficult times emotionally and financially worldwide. Emotionally, the uncertainties, hopelessness, lack of dreams, perhaps a lack of purpose, or a lack commitment to something bigger than oneself drives many to depression, feeling frustrated, sad, apathetic, fatigued, stressed, or just plain unhappy.

The United States *National Center for Health Statistics* reported adult use of antidepressants almost tripled between 1988 to 1994 and 1999 to 2000. Ten percent of women 18 and older and 4% of men now take antidepressants. Prescriptions for antidepressants, among others, increased significantly between 1996 and 2002. The economic impact of depression on companies is over $48 billion a year in the form of reduced productivity; that figure even excludes disability costs.

The *National Health and Nutrition Examination Survey* found a 13-percent increase between 1988-1994 and 1999-2000 in the proportion of Americans taking at least one drug and a 40% jump in the proportion taking three or more medicines. Forty-four percent reported taking at least one drug in the past month and 17% were taking three or more in the 2000 survey.

Drug use, divorce and rates of suicide also increased during these same periods, which also coincided with one of the largest economic booms in history from 1987 to 2005. The use of legal prescription drugs for depression and usage of illegal drugs among ordinary folks has increased dramatically. Not feeling too happy about life? No problem, go to your doctor and he or she will just medicate it and you'll be fine. More often than not the usage of these drugs has come about as a result of the emotional upheaval life throws people and they find that as a coping mechanism. If we're supposed to be happier as a society, how come we're more depressed and disconnected?

I'm not ridiculing the diagnosis of a lot of patients. Under many circumstances there are people who are in need of medical treatment and require usage of prescriptions for their mental condition. I know as I have a schizophrenic nephew and have had two friends with this disease. Other people, it seems, fail to dig for the reasons for their situation and rely on drugs to make it all better; this is like putting your head into the sand when the storms are about to blow in, and hope they just go away.

No doubt you believed that the world was supposed to be "happier," given increases in per capita incomes in every developed country in the last twenty-five years and all the fabulous technological advances in our time. What happened? In some cases, the opposite has happened. We as families are no longer like those depicted on TV that reflected societal norms and values at the time such as the 1970s show *The Brady Bunch* or the 1950s show *Leave It to Beaver*. Instead, too many families have become dysfunctional, disconnected, and depressed.

Why are we in general not as happy?

Famous celebrities' overdoses and admitted drug or alcohol abuse are now accepted as common and, seemingly, a rite of passage. The deaths of stars such as singer Kurt Kobain, actor Brad Renfro, model Anna-Nicole Smith, actor Health Ledger, and singer Michael Jackson reflect a sad commentary on supposedly "finding happiness".

Many in the world still believe that if we find fame and fortune, we'll be happy --- that is why so many, in fact, make the huge sacrifices to chase these things. Alert, alert: I have news for you --- the dream life doesn't exist --- unless you have grounded yourself with God and a have harmonious balance, will you not find happiness.

Money does not buy happiness. It just can buy the nice things that make life easier and a lot more enjoyable, but it can't get you true happiness --- believe that! It's not the end of the rainbow many think it to be. More money in your life does not equal more happiness. So stop chasing the pie-in-the-sky dream that you'll be "happy" if you can just have more money.

We do not succeed in spite of our obstacles and challenges. We succeed precisely because of them.

~ Richard Paul Evans

Financially, these are trying and difficult times as well. One day the stock markets are up, and another day, they are down. The value of most of our wealth, stocks, and real estate has declined alarmingly. The values of retirement savings, investments or pensions for millions have shrunk drastically. Hundreds of thousands of people have lost their homes. Many wonder if their job or company is next on the chopping block.

These are times that require hope.

Many Americans and people worldwide are asking themselves, "What's going to happen to me, my job, and my company?" These are times, for many, of struggle, of doubt, of hopelessness. These are indeed times of difficulty for a lot of people in the world. However, hope must remain in your heart. Trust that things will get better in your life and move forward, as hard as it may be some times, towards making each day or week a little better, one small step at a time. Some are getting depressed as the days wear on. Some are just frozen in inaction.

I fully understand these emotions and these thoughts. Though I have never ever used drugs of any kind to cope with my emotional difficulties, I have indeed lived through times of difficulty. I know what it is to have cars repossessed, homes foreclosed, investments and savings evaporated. I know what it is ask yourself, "How in the world am I going to pay for basic needs?"

I know what it's like to close a company due to lack of business. I know what it is to be sued for millions. I know what it is to be jobless, penniless, and massively distraught. I know what feeling helpless is when doctors tell you news you don't want to hear, don't want to believe, and can't do anything about. From my mother, father, sister, cousins, mother-in-law to friends, and my own daughter, I've had to deal with and embrace the moments of shear tragedy when it comes to sudden death, tragedy and medical problems.

When my twins were born, it was one of the happiest days of my life. They were indeed a miracle brought to us by God. Yet, at the same time they were also a test of our faith and fortitude. They were born premature. At birth, for all intents and purposes, they were born healthy. However, two days after their birth, their pediatrician was conducting a routine exam and noticed a condition in one of them; he said nothing to my wife and me as he picked up the phone in the room and called the Neonatal Pediatric Intensive Care Unit and ordered a "stat" on one of the twins.

Within seconds our world buzzed and our hearts sank as he then told us that she had a collapsed lung, that it was very serious. He explained that undetected and left untreated, a severe pneumo-thorax could lead to death within minutes! He also said that she would undergo non-invasive therapy and treatment which he hoped would work. Otherwise, surgery would be the only option to save her life.

It was a reality check for our faith when we saw our newborn hooked to IV's, a breathing machine and all kinds of electrodes hooked up to her tiny little body. It is such moments that every single ounce of faith you have in the Lord is tested --- in the fire of turmoil and tribulation. The thought of this little angel having to undergo a delicate surgery was heart-wrenching.

I visited her three or four times during the day and always at night to "put her to sleep" and pray over her while my wife stayed home, recuperating and nursing the other twin. During one of those routine visits, I got off the elevator and was buzzed into ICU. I made my way around the corner and as I turned and headed towards my little baby girl's incubator it was empty --- panic and fear set in. The attending nurse saw my shocked face, and unknowingly made it worse, as she stated, "I'm sorry Mr. Vargas, we should have called to warn you."

In my mind and in my aching heart, I cried out to God, "Please, no, no. no." My baby girl had fought the good fight early in her life, won some rounds and by God's grace He had carried her through. It turns out she no longer needed to be in front of the nurses' station for constant visual observation and had been moved to a different part of Pediatric ICU.

This scene later reminded me of my niece, Destiny, who years earlier was born two months premature and with immense complications. She underwent multiple surgeries and spent over two and a half months in ICU. We all cried and prayed for a miracle. It did arrive and she pulled through. Today, she is strong and a vibrant little girl. However, those indeed are the type of moments and times that try one's soul.

These are times that require faith.

I've lived through many trying and difficult times. I know what it is to suffer in times such as these. I know what it is to feel scared what the next day may bring upon you. I know what it is to suffer death close to you. I know what it is to have economic meltdown; to be stressed to the ultimate degree, and depressed. I've lived through tough economic storms and legal crises.

Through the years, I have befriended and been mentored by many special people in my life who've endured some of the worst things life can throw at you. From their experiences as well as mine I learned that the bottom line common in these experiences is that to emerge victorious one must have intense divine faith in of testing during times of trials and tribulations.

In the end, after the trials and storms subside you emerge a better person from the challenges. You are refined in the fire of testing, like just like gold is refined of its impurities. With God's guidance you can emerge an individual who sees possibility where others see "doom", opportunity where others see "crisis", purpose where others see "meaningless", love where others see "hate", and hope where others see "despair."

The Lord is my rock, my fortress and my deliverer,
He is my stronghold, my refuge and my savior.

~ 2 Samuel 22:3

The world needs to continue to trust God in and through the storms of life. He is the *real* Secret and *power* to all of life's issues, problems and struggles. We need to trust Him and move on. We also desperately need to reawaken the passion and hope within ourselves. To pick ourselves up and reaffirm that we can beat what's going on. Whatever your politics might happen to be, there is no denying the fact that Ronald Reagan loved his country and that he embodied a sense of ruggedness and "Can Do" spirit of America. He brought hope and possibility to the forefront of the hearts and minds of the people. Because of his bold actions and firm commitments, history judges him as one of the best presidents ever. He was willing to step forward in the face of criticism, challenges and difficulties for principles he believed in.

We must do the same in our lives. Whatever is facing you at the moment and is holding you back financially, emotionally or spiritually, you must boldly encounter head-on and overcome. No mountain or obstacle is ever high enough that we cannot climb to the top. I came from a pretty difficult upbringing, what I have been able to achieve and create I have done so because of God's providence and my willingness to work hard. I've been blessed by a supportive and dedicated wife and mother. No amount of excuses suffice for me, I've experienced, seen or heard just about all of them. *You* can achieve what it is you seek or dream of --- go for it, without any excuses.

When one door closes, another door opens;
But we so often look so long
And regretfully upon the closed door,
That we do not see the ones which open for us.

~ Alexander Graham Bell

It is time to reawaken a passion and purpose to create a better life, a better family environment, and better work place attitude and ethic. It is time to refrain from being a subscriber to the 'gloom and doom' theory. To banish from your brain thoughts that it will never get better. It is time to be a passion-driven, a hope bearing, possibility thinking, and faith laden individual.

These are times that require purpose.

It is now the time for us to embrace an attitude of gratitude. It is time for us to approach our work with zest and vitality. To put our 100% effort in what we do. It is time for employees and employers to cease the game of competition and enroll into the concept of being "team players." It is time for them to see their roles not as adversaries, rather as collaborative partners with a goal in mind that can benefit everyone involved.

At one point in my life, after I lost my business and a ton of money, and reemerged from massive financial and legal problems. I was earning $1,200 a month as a negotiator at a personal injury law firm. I was humbled. I used to spend that much money on just one car payment --- which, of course, was repossessed. Nonetheless, I did not approach that job as just a temporary thing until I could get something better.

Instead, I poured my entire spirit, skill, and positive attitude into that position. I stayed there two years! Why? Because I was offered that job by a friend back when no one else would willingly and openly do so without a hassle. I learned a lot about the healthcare, legal and insurance industries.

As a result of my attitude and production, my boss accepted a business plan I had previously presented to him on health care collections. That "job" ended up being my life-jacket to getting back a financial footing. Where most would have chosen to see despair and hopelessness, I got a shovel and dug for any gold among the pile of rocks. I saw opportunities amidst the serious setbacks.

An optimist sees the opportunity in every difficulty.

Winston Churchill

As we reconnect with each of our individual and organizational goals and passions, we create a new synergy, a new wave of possibility. I have much faith that we can and will reawaken that unbeatable spirit of: "Yes, we CAN!" There are no excuses.

Be solution-minded, goal orientated, leadership and passion-driven problem solvers, not problem creators. Believe it or not, there is a boom of business out there for those companies and individuals who look beyond the daily bombardment of bad news.

There is hope of a better tomorrow. Believe that. There is a bright future bright for all of us. We must choose to leave our children and their children a better way of living and thinking about life. So when they reflect back on our generations legacy and times of difficulty they can say, "Wow, they sure were facing difficulties, yet they overcame them. They refused to bow down to defeat, to times of trouble and be swallowed up by them. They were fighters that had faith, hope and love. They were driven to succeed."

The world in which we live can be changed for the better. Each one of us has the key to impact the lives of others and make a lasting difference. They say success leaves clues. The same can be said of a passion-driven individual. They leave clues and evidence of living with love, zeal, purpose and passion.

In times of difficulty there are always new frontiers of possibility to be conquered – individually, socially, politically, and professionally. Frontiers of possibility crave new approaches and new leadership. It's broken and it's now time to fix it. Fix your life. Break bad habits. Get rid of toxic people and environments. You can only do so much and if they don't share the same values, spiritual beliefs, and sense of hope and possibility, then bid them farewell with love. Move on.

> *The key is to keep company only with people who uplift you,*
> *Whose presence calls forth your best.*
>
> ~ Epictetus

Faith, passion and hope are the best medicines for a weary soul. Today the world is quite weary. Many have lost the passion for living life at its fullest. It is time to discover, ignite and propel the passion in your life, within your company or organization, and the halls of government so that together we all look at tomorrow with an undeniable ray of hope.

These are times that require persistence.

The world faces difficult times, it is up to all the passion-driven mothers, fathers, business leaders, political leaders, pastors, community leaders, and students, led by a love of what they do, devotion to giving, commitment to making a difference, a love for humanity, and their dream of creating a better world for future generations, to lead the way in search of opportunities amidst difficult times. To lead in their families, organizations, businesses, parties, campuses and churches.

You, just like me, are capable of making a masterpiece out of the million broken pieces of your life and situation. You can transcend despair and move beyond difficulties facing us. You can reconnect to God and the faith and hope He offers. As a result, we can bring faith and hope to those around us. There is renewed hope. There is a better way and a better life ahead.

We will succeed despite the times of difficulty because we allow our passion, faith, drive, and focus to manifest the answers. The difficult times are what mold us into better persons who appreciate the small things in life. Life is not always about the "big" moments or things but about those little moments or little things that embrace us and, in turn, we embrace them back and that eventually create impressionable memories for us.

These are the times that require passion.

Our passion draws to us a divine source of faith and strength that will propel us past our challenges and difficult times. Our passion, purpose, prayers and persistence will not allow defeat.

Though there are small battles that may be lost, we still endure in spite of them. Passion and hope are indeed a medicine to cure the weary soul. I know that certainly did. We know and believe in the core of our being that the best is yet in store for us because of the faith, passion and hope God has placed within our hearts, minds and soul to do something about our situation in life.

The most difficult thing is the decision to act,
The rest is merely tenacity.
The fears are paper tigers.
You can do anything you decide to do.

~ Amelia Earhart

We know then that we will see a new dawn and that millions will continue onward blazing a trail of love, a legacy of giving, and a legacy of passion. Grab a hold of the promise, act, then unleash the passion and hope *you* have within your bosom!

Ask Yourself:

1. Why do I do what I do?
2. Am I happy doing it or just do it to "survive?"
3. What matters most to me?
4. Is my life all about me?
5. Am I seeking more meaning in life?
6. Am I convinced God has a purpose for my life?
7. What life dreams are hidden in my heart?
8. What life passion(s) do I have waiting to be unleashed?

<u>Observation/Reflection</u>: Living life is about giving and creating relationships: With God, family, in marriage, business, in social relationships and with friends. Build passion-driven relationships that have purpose and meaning. Build relationships that honor God. Build relationships that allow for open and honest communication. No hidden agenda, just love.

With faith, hope and close relationships we can get through tough times. Times are tough right now. Create and treasure rich relationships. That is one of the best legacies we can leave. Money is certainly a blessing, but only when we have the proper perspective and use as a tool with which to enjoy life and bless others.

<u>Sail On</u>

What Are You Waiting For
To Live Out Your
Unique Purpose?
To Experience The
Passion of Life?
To Live Your Dreams, and
Unleash Your Divine Destiny?
Set Sail Towards Them,
Without Excuses,
No Matter What...

CHAPTER THREE

The Secret Alchemy: The Power of Faith, God & Moving On!

Cherish your visions; cherish your ideals;
Cherish the music that stirs in your heart,
The beauty that forms in your mind,
The loveliness that drapes your purest thoughts.
For out of them will grow delightful conditions,
All heavenly environments;
Of these if you but remain true to them,
Your world will at last be built.

~ James Allen

The Real Secret to Life's Challenges: America and the world are scared. Scared of what may or may not happen. These are tough times we are living through right now. However, we cannot stay frozen in a hypnotic trance. We must take action to improve our situation, to seek and find the passion that defines us. To dig for a purpose that enlivens us and gives us meaning. We need to break free and access the one and only universal truth, the creator of all known and unknown secrets and power in the world: God

There is a disconnection for many weary souls from hope. There is also a spiritual disconnection from God. Break free from these circumstances and face the challenges, then make the choices. Hope can be found in the solace of our heart and faith only in God. We can and will get past these times of economic difficulty. It requires a belief in many things, but above all, a belief and trust in God.

For many in this world, God has been put on the back-burner as they have gone on about with materialistic quests. Too busy to rely on anything or anyone else, we only relied on "us." As a society, therefore, the lines of love, truth, honor and commitment got moved as we separated ourselves from doing what was correct, honorable and right.

This is what is sad when one contemplates human life,
That so many live out their lives in quiet lostness...
They live away from themselves and vanish like shadows.
Their immortal souls are blown away,
And they are not disquieted by the question of its immortality,
Because they are already disintegrated before they die.

~ Soren Kierkegaard

I have known many people who lived through times of economic and personal difficulties. From overcoming major obstacles such as the Great Depression, the Holocaust, the loss of loved ones, loss of a job, failure of a company, divorce, complete financial meltdown, serious health issues, being indicted, as I was, and even prison. The one single common denominator to making it through and endure these travails is trusting in God. No matter how tough and how difficult it is you surrender your hold on and control in life, let go and then let God take over. There is no such thing as being the captain of your ship in life; all that will take place is a shipwrecked life! It did for me.

All who persevere through storms of life have a strong spiritual connection. For some it is hidden it in the recesses of our life as we go about busy lives, until a particular difficult situation or catastrophic moment enveloped us. Then we search and dig for it. It's there in each one of us.

God is always there. It's plain and simple that we cannot pretend to begin to lead or search for a life of passion and meaning, if we live disconnected from a spiritual connection to God. We can no longer be a society that says we can make it without God. It's, in my belief system, pure nonsense and arrogance. God is there to help us in the "digging" process within our hearts and our souls as we navigate along the valleys of life.

Spend time alone and reflect upon God and his goodness. Dig for meaning amid the rubble of your life, if that is where you happen to be. Seek and you will reap the rich rewards given to those who connect with God.

For the overworked mother, the busy business person, or individual who at the end of each day wonders where time went and operates in the realm of "stretched" to exhaustion, this may seem impossible. It is, however, possible to operate on a different level of living life in which enjoyment, satisfaction, peace, prosperity, and purpose flow. It just requires different approaches. Not impossible, just different.

If you are one that needs a new beginning or realize the current course of your life has resulted in meandering through a desert of dried up hopes and aspirations. There is possibility. Believe it and see it within you and seek it through God. Connect to the spiritual power that resides in the universe created by an almighty that loves you and wants the best for you.

The times of difficulty in which we ask questions as to what direction to take in our lives, are not moments of weakness. Rather they are moments in life where we realize that we can no longer go at it alone. They are moments of power as we begin the search for the hope, faith, love, meaning, passion or purpose that is buried deep within our hearts and souls that is clamoring to come alive and be fully expressed. The answer to begin the journey in life is: Pray. Seek. Dream. Inspire. Believe. Dig.

Begin to dig the well that dried up in your Spiritual Life and you will begin to see the rich rewards bubble up from a spring of living water. See the beauty that flows from the blessings that God will bestow upon you when you dig with all your heart and soul.

Life is sometimes like a game of chess. If you lose your queen you should not panic or give up, instead continue to stay in the game and modify your game plan, if you persist you'll get your "queen" back. Things will fall back into place, just keep the faith and dig without ceasing.

Therefore, commit to getting your passion and purpose back. Continue to be involved in making your life the best now, not tomorrow. Refuel your soul. Redesign your dreams. Live in the here and now, not in the past. Look to the future with hope and passion, not anxiety. Be confident of the rich rewards and abundance you will have bestowed by God as a result of the decisions you make and the actions you take. Be bold. Boldness has its rewards.

We Need A Refueling of the Heart and Soul

The story of the rich old man may be familiar to us all in some way or another as we have either known, heard or read about such a person. They appear to have all the trappings of great success, yet internally they are miserable, isolated, lost and angry individuals. Why?

Because they do not place proper priorities in their life: personal relationships, family connections, a spiritual connection to God, and a desire to leave a lasting legacy. So many of us desire to have such great financial success and make sacrifices that are not wise or healthy. I was one of them. Wealth is a tool, a blessing, and can be wonderful if used for unleashing our passion, our purpose, and making a difference in the lives of others.

Success is the ability to go from failure to failure,
Without losing enthusiasm.

~ Winston Churchill

We need a refueling! In our personal lives we need to refuel the heart, soul and the spirit of man. We need to refuel through our faith in God, prayer, purpose-living, and passion-living. We need a spirit of persistence, a spirit that fights onward. We need minds and hearts that make wise, moral and decisive decisions, and take actions that benefit the greater good of humanity. We need innovation, inspiration and dedication to bettering our world.

Simply Love: For Sure, For Sure

Ron Carlson lived a life that was simple by most accounts. He was a hard-working man from the San Fernando Valley in California, who grew up in Santa Monica, CA. He had changed careers from a computer programmer to general contractor awhile back.

He chose to live a simple life. He could have lived in a fancy home, yet he lived in a comfortable and modest 1950's era single story house.

He loved to encourage or punctuate points in his conversations with statements such as: "For Sure, For Sure" and "Ain't Nothing to It, But Do It."

This was a man and friend who truly loved his family, had empathy for the suffering of those around him, a love for animals, and a great passion for collecting classic cars. He was a man who was generous to others with his heart, time and money.

He died from pancreatic cancer at a fairly young age. At his life celebration family, friends and acquaintances came to honor the memory of a person who was for many there larger than life. A young woman said that Ron had given her the love, re-assurance, comfort and encouragement that her own alcoholic, mentally and physically abusive father had not. Ron filled the gapping void in her heart.

A family of five brothers from Mexico spoke about he had worked side-by-side with them, and how he had "adopted" them as sons. All five brothers were at his side when he died. Another woman recounted how Ron dedicated his time and money to several dog rescues.

Even when he knew of his terminal condition, under pain and discomfort, he would make the trek down to the shelter and place treats in his pockets and pet his favorite dogs behind the ears. He would say to his daughter, "Who else is going to come here and love them, when I'm gone?" He felt obligated to do that as long as he was alive.

Ron's story and life legacy is a lesson in offering simple love, simple encouragement; simply living with a heart of passion for family, friends, and strangers.

Are you sick and tired of being sick and tired? If you are struggling in your personal life, if you are seemingly unsure of which direction to go, then take heart there is hope. The sun *will* shine again when the stormy and rainy clouds lift. Just grab a hold of faith, a life vest and hold onto your rocky boat. Grab an umbrella and look to move out of the rain! It will eventually pass. Have faith and hope. After all, like the old Latin saying goes, "There is no storm that lasts a hundred years, nor any man that can withstand it!"

I want you to be uplifted and inspired. We need to abandon the belief that life's purpose is to only make money. There must be a balance and harmony to life. There must be a purpose for making money. To use it for reasonable personal enjoyment is fine, but there must be a bigger purpose and meaning in the world. Make it count.

It is never too late to focus on the things that really matter. Give someone money and they will thank you for a day. However, touch someone's heart through love, and you will forever make a difference in their lives, and they'll thank you for a lifetime. Place proper perspectives on the quest to making money. However, realize that many times in life we can make a difference that doesn't cost us a penny, however, instead requires we invest our total heart in what we do --- like Brenden Foster showed the world.

> *Some of the most beautiful things in life*
> *Cannot be seen or touched,*
> *They are felt by the heart.*
>
> ~ Helen Keller

Carried Home by Angels

Brenden Foster for having been only 11 years old had the capacity to impact the lives of people locally, and by doing so inspire the hearts of thousands globally. His profound example and legacy reflect passion in action. He will be remembered for his love and compassion for others. Even though he was facing an unbeatable enemy in the form of an incurable cancer, his darkest moment in his deep valley of life became his brightest moment and that he used to shine the light of hope to others. This is a story about his passion and how his actions revealed a true heart and soul.

When I was in Seattle in November 2008 visiting my mother-in-law who was herself dying from terminal pancreatic cancer, detected only three months before, I saw his interview on local television. Brenden was dying from leukemia. Despite that he managed to take up the cause of the homeless. With light brown wavy hair and eyes of steel that reflected resolve yet warmth and love, Brenden described how that cause came about. He stated, "They're probably starving, so give them a chance...."

His example became a cause célèbre that touched the hearts of many worldwide. He said he was not afraid of death and that he "just wanted to make a difference."

Brenden further explained, "I was getting back from one of my appointments and I saw this big thing full of homeless people, and then I thought I should just get them something." His love and wisdom exceeded his age for sure.

In a moment of deep inspiration he revealed when asked how he felt about "purpose in life" and our "dreams" for life he answered, "I feel sad when someone just gives up." His advice was, "Follow your dreams. Don't let anything stop you." Asked what he thought the best things in life were, he said, "Just having one." Asked his opinion on death he replied, "It happens. It's natural...I had a great time. And until my time comes, I'm going to keep having a great time."

On November 21, 2008, the heavens parted, angels came and carried young Brenden home in their loving arms to his Creator. The world will be grateful for his example of self-less love and concern for others. His living left an imprint of love and hope, and a legacy that many multi-millionaires wished they could leave with their money, but many do not, because it's not about that, it's about love...

It is possible to take the lemons handed to us by life, and instead of complaining and whining, turn them into great tasting lemonade or a lemon pie. Brenden did just that. He took what would normally be the pain, the anger, hurt and doubts of terrible circumstances, and focused instead on the miseries and suffering of others. There are no excuses. Dump your excuses now, and search for answers and ways to use your lemons.

He chose to inspire and motivate the heart. Brenden inspired many to define passion and purpose. He inspired many to look above and beyond their circumstances and normal complaints about life and do something worthy.

Times are tough now. I have lived through previous tough times in my life. Growing up tough times, financially, emotionally, facing family difficulties and enduring hardships. For all my current success, not everything in my life has come up smelling like roses. Among those roses were the prickly thorns of life that I did not notice or ignored, and I pricked my fingers. I hope you can relate. Add a little love and a lot of faith to your life, and you shall see a better you and life will begin to take shape.

In my life I chose, faith, an attitude of gratitude and to forge ahead past challenges I faced. I have had to wrestle alligators, swim amidst sharks, side-step snakes and avoid piranhas, as best I could, as I navigated the marshlands, oceans and roads of life. But I saw a better day and climbed each mountain with more fervor, more faith and more passion in order to succeed.

The mind,
Once expanded,
Can never return to its original size

~ Oliver Wendell Holmes

Expand your mind and expand your heart. Once you do that they will never return to their original condition. Expand your soul and faith. Expand your horizons so you can focus, find and unleash your passion and your unique dreams. Expand your possibilities. Expand your giving. Expand your service to others. Expand your living. Once you do that, I promise you will never ever want to return to the kind of life you are living now, and you will forever be a changed person.

Accept and implement the "*The Challenge*" in your life. Though you may believe that you are passionate about life, after reading and putting into practice the principles and steps found in *The Passion-Driven® Life*, I assure you that there will be areas of your life in which you had not focused on before in which you need passion and balance.

The Secret to Harnessing Purpose & Passion

You can overcome any adversity or challenge in your life. It requires determination and a desire to no longer be held captive living a life you deem no longer worthy for you. It requires you to identify and draw a line that from this day forward and affirm to yourself that you are going to be new person that will think and act differently. It requires you to focus on those things you must change.

Focus is one of the most important secrets to achieve not only success, but to have a balance and harmony in all you do. Billionaires and multi-millionaires, Olympic and professional athletes, super achievers and highly effective individuals practice and use focus in their lives. Why are you not in yours?

Therefore, focus on your passion, focus on your purpose, and focus on what you will create and expand in your life. Focus on how you will define and implement success in yours. Focus on that and take action towards your success and goals. It requires you to be in tune with your heart, mind, soul and spirit to God's goodness that He has in store for you, address life's challenges, embrace life's opportunities, and change your thinking.

The secret to harnessing purpose and passion in your life is an exercise that requires you to be open to what is possible, what is not working, accepting life less complicated and accepting yourself as who you are as wonderfully made by God and here to accomplish great things.

The Passion and Purpose Exercise

1. Focus on a unique life purpose that moves and drives you.
2. Focus on passions that inspire you, kindle your heart, and lift your spirit.

3. Focus on abundance: in giving, spiritually, in loving yourself and others, financially, and in creating.
4. Focus on touching and impacting the lives of others.
5. Focus on your "dreams" and how to accomplish them.
6. Focus on making the world a better place.
7. Focus on having fun in what you do!

Observation/Reflection: Have you thought all you needed in life was just to win the next mega-lottery prize in order to be "happy" in life. Or to have a million bucks in the bank and you would be all-set.

Money can be great, but it has no value in our life if we do not take the time to enjoy it, create meaningful relationships through it, and to give some away so that others less fortunate can enjoy the benefits of it. Live and give: give love, give money and give precious time to you, your family, and friends. It can destroy us morally if we place our entire self-esteem and self-worth upon it. It can destroy someone's values. Plenty stories exist to prove just that. Think more about making lasting memories and less about making money. You see money can go just as easily as it came.

He Carries Us

God is Always With Us.
He Cares For Us
During The Darkest
Moments in Our Life;
Even though We May
Not Realize It
At The Time.
We Only See the Presence
Of His Love Later.
In the Meantime,
He Carries Us Silently Along…

CHAPTER FOUR

The Power of Transformation: The Next Level Changes Needed

Therefore I live for today...
Certain of finding at sunrise,
Guidance and strength for the way.
Power for each moment of weakness,
Hope for each moment of pain,
Comfort for every sorrow,
Sunshine and Joy
After the rain.

~ Anonymous

I truly believe that inside every soul, there is a beautiful journey waiting to be started and a heart longing for its unfolding. However, are you in the same circumstance of frustration about a dead-end job, your career, or your personal life? Have you lost the drive in what you do day-to-day? Do you, or have you, questioned your purpose in life and how to unleash it with a passion?

Perhaps you overwork yourself and are looking to have an effective impact in your personal and work/business life. We could always use tools on how to be able to manage all areas of our life with harmony and balance.

I understand that entrepreneur, manager, professional or person who is committed to making his or her business/company successful, and toils away long hard hours while sacrificing family life, personal relationships and putting off pursuing life's simple pleasures. We justify our sacrifices by rationalizing: "Not now, later when I have *this or that.*" But that day sometimes never arrives and we toil away. I was that person. Next level transformation is needed.

The Secret to Creating a New You

Be bold. Be creative. Create a *new* you. You don't have to move out of the country. But you do have to move out of your "comfort zone", whatever that happens to be for you, if that's what it takes to get to the next level and unleash passion and purpose.

Design a new plan for your core areas of life. Stick with the implementation of the plan. Passionately work at what you do where you are now. If not quit and go and do something else. Life is too short for you to be miserable at doing a job you don't like. Your employer doesn't need it and neither do you. If that sounds too crazy in a difficult economy, then wake up, smell the roses, get your act together and begin to do a job worthy of being called *excellent*. Otherwise, you are part of the problem and not the solution.

Do what you believe you were created to do. It may involve major changes, but change is a good thing if we embrace it without fear. Do it now, not next month, not six months from, not "later"--- NOW!

How many people have died with dreams unfulfilled? How many ceased to live and merely choose to exist? The years of quality loving, quality giving and passionate living in between the "dashes" of life, as reflected on a gravestone, are what will matter, not the dashes or commas on a bank statement we leave behind. So many business people or entrepreneurs have sacrificed their family and their sanity for the sake of making a company into a success. It doesn't have to be that way --- we can have a life filled with balance *and* still have a successful career or business career.

In the November 2008 edition of Inc. magazine I read a letter submitted by a reader responding to an article on entrepreneur's wives. He wrote, "I shed more than one tear while reading Meg Hirschberg's article. My wife left me over my start-up business in 2006. The business eventually succeeded, and I went back...she said she couldn't do it again. Too much stress and anxiety...I will take responsibility. She couldn't take it anymore (two kids in diapers and always wondering where next month's mortgage was coming from). She gave me an ultimatum...She said 'Me or the business'. I chose the business...." It doesn't have to be this way.

This reader never got it that it is possible to have a healthy balance in family life while seeking to grow a business. Instead he, in essence, chose to throw away his wife and two children aside for the sake of making money and building a business. I am sure that he looks back on that decision with regret, as he "returned" to his wife once he had made it. There's more to life than sacrificing for a money dream. No amount of money can replace family, fulfillment and love.

In the pursuit of our unfulfilled dreams, hopes and aspirations must align with a divine purpose and be blessed by God in order to have balance and harmony. No purpose and passion-driven person would ever justify that an entrepreneur or business executive leave their family in order to go chasing after a dream to build a company! Though plenty have done that, the success once attained is not fulfilling in the end as there is a void left in its wake.

Make every effort
To add to your faith goodness,
To goodness, knowledge,
To knowledge, self-control,
To self-control, perseverance,
To perseverance, godliness
To godliness, kindness,
And to kindness, love.

~ 2 Peter 5:7

The Questions of Abundance & Life

Hundreds of thousands, if not millions, of people are desperate for hope. They have hearts with broken dreams. They have endless fatigue, stress from running and getting nowhere. They are on the perpetual treadmill and see no end in sight to their progress. There are millions who are frozen by economic turbulence. There are those who've lost jobs, a home, a spouse, and hope for living.

The *Questions of Life* are important for us to ask as we move forward creating a new life. I wish our *Inc.* magazine reader had seriously thought about such questions as:

1. Do I have an abundant personal and spiritual life?
2. What kinds of changes or decisions do I desire to make but am afraid to?
3. Do my daily interactions and work bring me contentment?
4. How can I create a life that will bring inspiration to others?
5. How can I teach, help or encourage others?
6. How can I fulfill my dreams?
7. Am I living the type of life I desire?
8. If I were to die tomorrow, what changes would I make in my life?
9. How can I search for my purpose?
10. Am I neglecting those activities which bring me the most joy and fulfillment to do things which rarely bring me any?

We were created to make a difference in our lives. How are we to be a great living example of life, if we have chosen to allow the pressures of life to suppress our passion for living it fully?

Living a passion-driven life means being engaged in all we do: work, family, friendships, church, temple, synagogue, sports or hobbies. To be immersed in the moment as we give 100% effort in what we pursue.

It means having a plan and knowing what we want in life. Knowing where it is we want to go, otherwise we end up lost in a world of confusion, delusion, side-tracked and being like Alice, the fictional character in the book *Alice's Adventures in Wonderland*, unsure where she needs to go or wants to go!

Alice: "Which road do I take?"
The Cheshire Cat: "Where do you want to go?"
Alice: "I don't know."
The Cheshire Cat: "Then it doesn't matter."

~ Lewis Carroll

The Secret to Tapping Into Your Creativity

Here's an idea to tip the scales back in your life if you desire passion, new ideas, a new path, a new life, a purpose or a new business service/product --- out with the Left and in with the Right! This is not political dogma I'm talking about but about using more of our right-side of the brain versus the left-side of the brain.

We think logically, organize, crunch numbers and think numerically with the "left" side of our brain. The left side is crucial and important in daily living and the implementation of our plans and actions. In analyzing the choices and making decisions. However, we can no longer live there exclusively as a society. We need a connection. Living in the "left" side of the brain has given us immeasurable corporate greed and political corruption beyond measure. In addition, outsourcing of jobs that are primarily "left-brain" capacity has left many a professional in developed nations with less work or none at all.

In contrast, the right side of the brain gives us our creativity, our dreams, our faith, our hope, our feelings, empathy, passion, purpose and morals. The "right brain" capacities have been suppressed by our families, our educational system and, to some extent, corporate America. But they can be the basis for our reemergence as leaders in our families, our communities, our educational system, our businesses, our organizations, and our political system. No company or country can outsource the heart of passion found in the right side of our brains: innovation, intuition, and creativity, love, passion, a spirit of possibility, and the desire to succeed.

These are the areas where passion lives, plays and thrives. It is passion with divine purpose that can be the breakthrough for our global economy, and for all our family's future. It is time for us to let these attributes flow again.

Daniel H. Pink, in his ground-breaking best-selling book *A Whole New Mind,* argues that our current society is in a new paradigm shift from the Information Age to the Conceptual Age. His position is that the abundance in the *Information Age* has made us wealthy nations, but it also unleashed a search for meaning amidst that prosperity. We are not satisfied. We are not happy.

Why? I say because we have lost touch with the *reasons* for achieving financial success and for ways in which we can make a difference. Passionate living is about living a life of purpose.

According to Pink something funny happened along the way to us as we were toiling away on the path to 'professional success' and 'personal fulfillment' in high paying and respectable jobs, that Peter F. Drucker termed "knowledge workers": doctors, lawyers, accountants, software engineers, bankers, engineers, financial analysts, radiologists, veterinarians, etc. (all left-brain capacity work), and which our parents instilled in our brains to seek to become. That "funny thing", Pink argues, is that outsourcing hit the economies of developed countries and shifted the manner of the importance of those "knowledge workers."

Thus, little Johnny or little Jane study hard to get good grades and be accepted into a respectable college and they eventually become, let's say, a computer software programmer. They graduate and cannot find a well-paying lucrative job in that field any longer as those jobs have been outsourced to India, China, Philippines, Russia and a host of other countries where an eager and cheaper trove of new "knowledge workers" will do the work. Voila, they are now in stiff competition with the world for their knowledge.

Pink states that due to outsourcing of these once sought after professional jobs, that the future to success no longer belongs to those who can just reason, but instead to a different person with a different capacity and mind-set. To those people who have the capabilities to see the big picture, have empathy, be creative, pursue the transcendent and yet still think. The *Information Age* unleashed a type of prosperity that, according to Pink, now places a premium on right-brain rational abilities such as beauty, creativity, innovation, spirituality and emotion and less exclusively on the reasoning abilities to make it in life.

It sounds to me that we have a changing paradigm shift in the world vis-à-vis value-based living reliant on God, inner faith and strength, passion, desire, and creating meaning and purpose as opposed to being hard charging success machines.

I watch my two-year old twin daughters explore and excel in things with an uncanny ability. They know the capitals of 40 foreign countries from all South American countries, to South Africa and to Syria! As well, they can recite all kinds of details and information they've been taught. They can do so with ease because they operate in their minds without constraints. No "do's" or "do not's" to inhibit them in their quest to attempt something new. There is no one telling them they are failures; no one dictating to them what they should look like or should do. No "inner" voice to hold them back, creating fears or doubts.

When was the last time you tried something totally new? Took a cooking, scrap-booking or photography class to broaden your horizons or interests? When was the last time you volunteered at a place where you believe in the cause? When was the last time you looked into what you really enjoyed?

When was the last time you shut the computer or TV off and went for a walk along a trail, beach, park, or forest without <u>any</u> interruptions? Just you and nature, and enjoyed the experience? When was the last time you sat down to take your dreams from the clouds in your head and onto paper in the form an action plan? When was the last time you measured your progress?

When was the last time you dreamed BIG dreams and did something about them? America became a great country because we dared to dream of a better world and we were unafraid to seek the answers to the, "Why?" and lived and worked in such a way as to be a testament to the rest of the world of, "Why not?" Isn't it time you did that?

This new shift does not mean that those who desire to become or are in the knowledge professions or line of work cease from their pursuit. No, it means that the world requires solution-based as well as empathy based thinking. A certified tax accountant in India can prepare a sophisticated U.S. tax return just as his American counterpart can, however, the American based tax accountant's practice will only grow because of human intangibles such as personal contact and creating relationships, offering sound investment advice, being available to answer questions, giving extraordinary service and value, innovation, being big-picture minded, and crafting right-brain solutions to issues facing clients tax, retirement, and investment needs and desires.

Creativity needs resurgence in the 21st century and one the major vehicles by which left-brained professionals will survive and

thrive in the new global economy. Otherwise, be ready to get a pink slip. It is there where new ideas develop and new technologies are born. It is there that concepts of service and value are understood and implemented to their highest degree. In business and in life, we must foster a wider cooperative effort between reason, logical thinking and automation (left-brain) and our emotion, creativity, passion and purpose (right-brain). We can no longer rely on our left-brain capacities to get by.

<u>Observation/Reflection:</u> Create a new shift in your heart, mind and soul as you explore and define what it is you are intrinsically good at or long to do. Delve more into detail as why we are here for on earth and how to go about doing things with love. "*What's my passion?*" is a question that will be asked many times throughout our journey. Open your heart, soul and spirit and be open to the possibilities and the answers that will flow to you as we continue.

Pink argues that if you want to get ahead today, then you should consider chucking the advice of the parents and do something that can't be outsourced. The "logical" answer would be to search for and zero in on the passion and purpose in your life and go to the next level in living!

<u>Rays of Sunshine</u>

Allow the Rays of Sunshine
To Shine Through and
Fill Your Life,
Give You Comfort,
And Hope,
Despite the Dark Clouds
That Come Along With It…

CHAPTER FIVE

The Power of Choice: Getting Over Breakdowns, Creating Breakthroughs & Balance

---

> *You see things as they are and ask, "Why?"*
> *I see things as they never were and ask, "Why not?"*
>
> ~ George Bernard Shaw

The Secrets to "Who Am I & What Do I Want?" This question helps us define where you are in life and help you go from where you are to where you dream of going. What are your likes and dislikes? What do you value most? What do you want to do with life? If you had a million dollars would you change or would you essentially be the same person?

You and I need to get back to the basics of simple life. To what made our country great: family values, ethics, balanced living, productive work, entrepreneurship, and a spiritual connection to the creator of the world.

The world is waiting for your passion to be unleashed.

We need to have goals and dreams that make a difference to us, to our family and to the world. Yes, the world needs your passion to be unleashed.

We need to pray for wisdom and insight. If you think you can rough it without that, then you're going to be alone during the storms of your life. Storms and challenges always come into our world. That's just how life is. They can be economic storms, such as we are experiencing now, personal relationship storms, family storms, or other forms of uncontrollable storms beating down upon us.

A breakthrough in the world is needed.

How we react and live through these storms is what defines us as individuals. You can either choose a real life filled with purpose and passion or choose a dreary existence without meaning, direction or hope. After years of pleasuring every need, you may discover little satisfaction or meaning exist in them. The clothes, the cars, the jewelry, the "stuff" gets old and, for some, the partying just loses its luster and lure.

I have been by the side of many people who were like the rich old man in our story. The lesson I learned from such people is simple: Live your life in such a way your life will count. Live your life in such a way that you live without regrets today, tomorrow, and when you are about to die. Live your life in such a way that it matters to God and to you, and leaves footprints that others will want to follow.

Commit to live, love, and laugh today, tomorrow, and until your last breath with an unfettered passion for what you desire to do. Commit to live what you hope of doing. Commit to go where you dream of going along the journey of life that we have been gifted by God. There is a possibility for us to live life fully. To live a life that is not filled with "stuff", just alive and fulfilling with the things that matter in life. Appreciate what you have, who you are; and as long as you are fulfilled and your heart is at peace, then you don't have to buy anymore boats.

Just Buy More Boats!

This is the story of a successful Wall Street financier who finally takes vacation from his dizzyingly hectic work schedule. He goes to a quant and peaceful seaside town far from any bustle and hustle of a large city to rest and goes fishing. He chartered a boat for the occasion. He forgoes any form of communication with the "outside" world: no cell, no computer, and no phone calls. Just relaxation, good food and fishing; it's just him and the owner of the fishing boat.

The boat owner is a most gracious, caring and hospitable host. Daily he has cold drinks, food and snacks for his guest. He takes pride

---

in knowing all the best locations for both fishing and sightseeing. Daily the boat owner and the financier catch fish and eat delicious meals prepared by the boat owner's wife at their comfortable home. After awhile the financier begins to bond with him and asks him what his usual day is like, when he's not taking vacationers fishing.

The boat owner replies, "Well, I get up around 4:00am and go fishing; most of the time I stop fishing by 7:30 am. I come to the port and sell my fish to the local fish distributor. I then go home by 1:00 or 1:30 pm and eat something. I then take a nap for an hour or two. When I wake I play with my children who are home from school. Then before dinner, I lie down in my hammock, visit friends or watch the sun go down. If I have any business affairs to take care of I do them before dinner. After dinner I relax some more or read."

The financier then explained why he asked the intrusive question, "Well, during the past few days I noticed that your boat is the nicest one here in the village. None of the other boat owners go to the extremes to make every guest's experience a special one, like you do from the food, to the fishing, and even to personally picking me up from my hotel daily. Have you thought about buying another boat?"

The fisherman answers, "No, what for?"

The financier patiently answers what he thinks is a very odd question, "So you can be book more fishing tour guests per week! Look, I took a little time to run some figures and came to the conclusion that at the current pace if you bought yourself another boat you could pay it off within two to three years, then you could buy another one. You would then have a total of three boats. When the boats are not being chartered for fishing trips, you increase the amount of fish you catch and sell at the port. In addition, you would partner with a larger international travel agency and offer your fishing tour services worldwide. Heck, within five years you could easily own a fleet of 7 boats for charters and fishing.

Then as the amount of fishing yield increases you could buy or open your own fish processing plant and distribution network. You would not have to sell the fish to the local distributor anymore. You would be the one source for fishing and fish distribution in this region."

The fishermen plainly asks, "Why would I want to do all that work?"

The financier proudly answers, "So you could grow your company and sell it within 7-10 years!"

The fishermen then concludes, "And then what?"

The financier, feeling a bit agitated at the fishermen's lack of vision, answers: "Well, then my friend, you then could have whatever you life in life, spend time with your children, travel, not have to work so hard anymore, or just relax."

The fishermen looks back at the financier and bluntly answers, "I do that already!"

In life and in business we sometimes lose track of the purpose of it all. We get lost in the chase for "more", rather than to be satisfied with what we have. The story of the financier and the fisherman serves to highlight what's important in life after all. Though not pertinent to every single person, in general a person who has little financial worth dreams of being a millionaire, the millionaire wants to be a multi-millionaire, the multi-millionaire aspires to be a deca-millionaire, the deca-millionaire aspires to be worth over $100 million, the person worth $100 million thinks he's not that well off financially speaking compared to the billionaire, so he aspires to be a billionaire.

A friend of mine was once present at a fundraiser where a man whose net worth was over $100 million expressed to those around him that he felt depressed because he was in the presence of a couple of billionaires, and thus he felt less of a "success in life." If I were there I probably would have gone ape on him and told him to get a life. With all the suffering in the world and this myopic and self-absorbed person thinks nothing more than about dollars makes no sense!

We seem that we cannot be happy where we are and with what we have. We always want more. The bumper sticker: "He who dies with the most toys wins!" is a bold lie. Instead live a life that "wow's" the world with love and deep inspiration. Be the fisherman and enjoy life now with no excuses, not later.

> *It's the possibility of having a dream come true,*
> *That makes life interesting.*
>
> ~ Paulo Coelho

I am honored to have been granted the privilege of sharing the following profile of a true story that is tear-jerking and reflects a father's dedication, love, sacrifice and the inspiration he and his son bring to the world.

I Can, Yes I Can!

The father strains with a look of sheer determination. Sometimes he is in pain as he struggles onward, under the added weight, in rigorous triathlons and marathons he runs. The son also participates in each of the 998 races they have competed in so far.

Neither father nor son have ever come close to officially winning any race, nor are they expected to anytime soon. Yet they still train and strain onward. They still endure. They wait to compete for the next one with great anticipation. They still have the passion. They have something to prove. They have a purpose.

Why endure the pain and the sacrifice? The answer is simple: love, inspiration, motivation and dedication to one another, and to be shining examples of what *is* possible when you set your mind and heart to it.

They live by the motto: "Yes You Can." They are "Team Hoyt" (Dick and Rick Hoyt). Maybe you've seen them on national outdoor billboard campaigns about hope. They demonstrate what commitment and self-less love truly is. It is a father and son team. The father runs so his physically disabled and immobile son can experience the joy of competition and the meaning of what it is to be a winner in life. To view their tearfully inspiring video log onto: www.teamhoyt.com.

Rick, who is 47, was born with cerebral palsy. Dick, the father is 68. When Rick was born he and his wife were told by doctors that Rick would be a vegetable the rest of his life, and that they should institutionalize him. The parents refused to do so. Instead, they raised him like one of their other boys. Eventually, the parents convinced engineers at Tufts University to create a device they called the "Hope Machine" so Rick could communicate with them. Rick's first words were, "Go Bruins", the Boston pro hockey team.

Running began one day when Rick asked his father that he wanted to participate in a race for a severely injured hockey player. Dick Hoyt entered his first 5 mile race with him pushing his son. Later, they began to compete in triathlons, and Rick was tethered to the bike and swam with a life raft that contained Rick. Both pieces of equipment chafed Dick as he competed, yet he continued onward for his son.

Dick states, "Rick lives a happy life, perhaps more than 95% of the people." Rick further adds, "When I'm running my disability disappears." So in each race Rick cheers his dad onward with a fist in the air, with an expression that goes beyond words: of pure triumph, pure joy, pure fulfillment and pure passion.

As a testament to their commitment and a fitting reminder to all of us that anything *is* possible in 2008 Team Hoyt received the Omar N. Bradley "Spirit of Independence Award" and was inducted into the Tri-Athlete Hall of Fame.

The world is waiting for change.

The Secret to Dreams That Are Alive!

Living a life alive and *with* meaning is possible. It just requires a different perspective. We must experience and see life with our hearts, not with our eyes. What we sometimes "see" can be a mirage, a false thing we have pursued or sought to have, later to learn that it was "meaningless." We must open our soul to the moments where we can create meaning in our life as we unleash our purpose. We must connect to God and then connect to those in our lives.

It is possible to live a worthy life on this earth. It is possible. Dreams are alive and real. Your dream is alive! It is possible to dream of the things in your life that once unleashed will allow you to be:

- Alive with hope.
- Alive with love.
- Alive with vision.
- Alive with dreaming.
- Alive with joy.
- Alive with meaning.
- Alive with purpose.
- Alive with passion!

Rick Warren, in his ground-breaking book *The Purpose-Driven® Life*, was right when he stated that life is "not all about you." I agree wholeheartedly. There is more to it than looking to please oneself, seeking the next "need" and satisfying our next desire or want. There is a higher purpose for individuals, companies or organizations than to simply exist, to create more capital or a job for people, without making a meaningful impact upon the world. There is a spiritual void that exists in the world. Many people see the world with their eyes rather than hearts and souls.

A disconnection from God and from a purpose has led to the greed, hate, selfishness and hedonism which we see so much in our world. We must work towards leaving future generations the same principles of faith, love, collaboration, hard work, dedication and sacrifice that our forefathers left us, and which made America great. We can be change-agents amidst all the economic worry and calamity we hear about.

You can be that breakthrough as you unleash your divine purpose and passion in life.

I am working on my purpose.

We tend to cater to the egos of celebrities or the rich and famous as if they were truly something special. In reality some are *more* neurotic, insecure, troubled, lack integrity, a healthy self-worth, and have more doubt and negativity than the average person. The false messages we so often get from them as to what is purpose and meaning in life can be extremely persuasive in their allure and they insipidly weave themselves into our hearts and minds, into the very fabric of our culture and way of living: "pursue all you can get, look out for #1 [you], and "grab as much as you can" as a means to being happy.

The sole pursuit of making money without a divine passion or purpose can lead, as it has for many, to emptiness, feeling emotional broken, without spirit, and seeking a meaning where it cannot be found.

A breakthrough in me is needed.

I believe that we desperately need a breakthrough and shift in our mental mindset in order to live and effectuate meaningful change in our world. We need a path on which we can transform lives and organizations in such a way that make a difference felt for generations to come.

Reaching Out Through the Heart.

This is a journey into how we can inspire and transform our mindset, attitudes, beliefs, hearts, and spirits in order to make the changes necessary for us to live a life with purpose and hope. How we can live our dreams out loud, and in the process warm the hearts of those we touch.

It is possible to own or work at a company that is profit driven, yet it can operate in such a way that a difference in society is made beyond spreadsheets, net margins, yields, ROI, and P/E ratios. It is possible to build a business or be an employee/team member where we deliver first-class service and world-class quality products are the goal. It is possible to make lives better and still make money.

My life is waiting for my passion to be unleashed.

America and the world are facing difficult times. We are reaping the consequences of massive greed on Wall Street, bad politics, and a lack of proper governmental oversight. The entrenched corporate mentality of "just make money" at any cost has given rise to greed exemplified by Enron, Goldman Sachs, Countrywide, and Bernard Madoff's and R. Allen Stanford's, among others, multi-billion investment scams.

Capitalism is a good thing. It surpasses any system ever created. The implosion in the late 1980's of socialist and communist countries was good. It freed millions of people whose lives and spirits had been crushed by evil governments.

Yet, the current all-greed capitalism needs to have a breakthrough. We need a *value-based capitalism*. The accumulation of wealth needs to be for a real altruistic end, rather than just accumulation of money for the sake of accumulating money. We need to stop holding onto to it and release more of it to the world. As you'll later see, many passion-driven entrepreneurs have done so.

Believe: The world is waiting for my purpose to be unleashed.

Amidst these concerning times, many seek deeper meaning and ask questions such as, "Which is the correct path for me to follow?" This is part of the path of exploration for you. To determine and define what inspires and motivates you, where you dream of going, what it is you do well, what you like, what your passions in life are, and how you can get to the next level in your own life.

It is in the search, through prayer, reflection, and meditation, that we find ourselves and the purpose for living. Through that process and search we find our passion and what the French call the "raison d'être" --- the reason for our being. Find yours. Dump your excuses not to.

Once we do that we can truly lead a life of abundance and contribution. We then can collaborate rather than always compete. Our life matters only if we believe that it matters, and live it so it does matter. Just like the life of "George Bailey" the fictional movie character.

All our dreams come true,
If we have the courage to pursue them.

~ Walt Disney

The Gift of Life

Each Christmas season one of the popular re-run movies, and one of my all-time favorites, is Frank Capra's "*It's a Wonderful Life.*" It is the story of George Bailey, a starry eyed dreamer whose dreams appear mostly to be shattered. George's bad breaks in life begin at an early age in an accident and continue on until his later years, and culminate in a "run" on his family savings and loan.

In a crucial moment in the film, George is depressed and despondent about his evaporated dreams, his apparent bad luck, his failing family savings and loan, possible prison time, and he sees no hope. He wants to end his life by jumping off a bridge to a torridly cold river below. He wishes he was never born.

He repeats that phrase several times. Clarence, his "angel in training", grants him his wish and George gets to view the lives of the townspeople of Bedford Falls as if he had *never lived*. Once that, occurs George realizes his influence, actions and presence while he was alive was indeed meaningful. He sees his actions and encouragement made a difference in people's lives.

The life lesson learned from George Bailey's life is that we are all blessed to be alive, and that the life we are given by God must be productively lived in the service of others. More importantly, as human beings we must measure our "worth" not in dollars and cents, but in the love we extend to our family, friends and how we express it in self-less service.

George Bailey made a difference in his fictional movie world. We can do the same in our real world if we choose to do so. We can touch one person deeply, and a ripple begins from there, they touch the lives of many more, and so on it continues outward. Pursue your dreams with courage. Pursue your dreams with passion. Pursue your dreams and live life as it *truly* matters.

We are given the gift of life by God. Therefore, use the gift of life to its fullest extent. That is the transformation and breakthrough that must occur more often in our world. We must reflect compassion for others, extend sharing, feel the hurts of those hurting, bolster and support creativity, release our motivation, release our enthusiasm, collaborate more often, open our minds and hearts to reach out and teach others, exhibit empathy and, above all, love deeply. It is time to seek these breakthroughs!

Realize: The world is looking for hope.

We need a breakthrough in living, thinking, acting, and moreover a shift in how we search for our meaning and in how we live. We need a shift in the manner in how we pursue our purpose in life so that we do not drown out other areas of life. The aim is to live in harmony and balance between each of *The 9 Key Areas of Life*.

The Secret to a Life That Matters

Living a life of purpose and passion, aligned with divine guidance, leaves a legacy like no other. As we shall see leading a Passion-Driven® Life is not about recklessly going about doing things only for our pleasure or being driven in success in just one area. Instead, it is living in such a way that we can say with assurance, "So far my life has made a difference to others, has pleased God. I have embraced and learned from each moment of hope, each moment of struggle, and each moment of triumph."

The world is waiting for your passion to be unleashed.

Living a life of purpose and passion leaves a mark like no other. It leaves a trail that can be followed by others. It is a road-less traveled indeed. It is a life worth living, and it can be summed by believing with all your heart, spirit and soul:

If there is a goal, then seek it.
If there is a dream, then believe in it.
If there is desire, then harness it.
If there is an opportunity, then seize it.
If there is hope, then let it spring forth.
If there is possibility, then imagine it.
If there is an obstacle, then overcome it.
If it is worth doing, then pursue it.
If it is love, then give it completely.
If it leaves a legacy, then accomplish it.
If it does the world good, then choose it.
If it is a purpose, then do it.
If it is a passion, then unleash it.
If it is life, then live it fully.

<u>Observation/Reflection</u>: As we continue the journey: enjoy the ride, enjoy the experience in searching for passions you dream to manifest. Open up your hearts and soul to all that can be in your life, all that has been, all that should be, all that you have offered, all that you will offer to yourself, all that you will offer the world, and all the best that is yet to come as you live it fully.

Just know that the world belongs and rewards those who first have and live by total love, total passion and total purpose. Then will you have you have a life of total prosperity.

Your Life Road

Create Your Own Harmony
And Balance in Life.
Travel Your Life Road
In Search of
Your Dreams
Destiny,
Plans,
and
Purpose...

PART III

THE INITIAL STEPS TOWARDS THE SECRETS

Out of abundance he took abundance,
And abundance still remained

~ Hindu proverb

---

www.ThePassionDrivenLife.com

CHAPTER SIX

The Power of the Universal Law of Love and Abundance

In moods of discouragement or despair,
Never forget
That the sunshine will ultimately come back,
That its absence never is permanent.
Hang onto your faith,
Knowing that soon you will
Rise into the sunshine again.

~Dr. Norman Vincent Peale

The **Secret to Sharing, Loving & Thriving Abundantly.** The quality of your questions in life will determine the quality of your answers. What is it that you've been asking yourself about your life? From what frame of mind have you been asking the questions of life? Have you been asking from a view that there is a limit to blessings and abundance, or from a belief that there is enough for all in the world to share abundance, love, blessings and dreams? Passion and purpose require that at the end of the day, we embrace and live by the universal law of love and abundance, rather than from scarcity. It is an ancient principle taught and reinforced over 2,000 years ago by Jesus.

Believe and ask through faith with a heart and mind of abundance and possibility in the world. Do you ask from a frame of mind that only scarcity exists, and therefore you have to desperately figure out how you can, "Get a 'slice of the pie' before it's all gone?" That is limited thinking in an expansive, loving and abundant world God has created.

If that is the place from where you come from, then it may be no wonder why you lack. Because you live constrained in a world where you believe there are limited resources; your giving, love and abundance is limited. Once you unlock the secrets you can free yourself from that world. You can be able to receive *and* give the abundance that God has created for all of us.

I have come that they may have life, And have it more abundantly.

~ John 10:10

God does not operate in a limited world. He is the source of abundance and created a world flowing with it. We do not live in an "either/or" world, we live in a world of abundant living *and* abundant giving. How is it that we got off course?

If you desire to go the next level, start out with abundant living, abundant giving and abundant thinking. You'll see the difference immediately. How can we redefine our dreams? How can we search for greater passion? How is it possible for us to live a meaningful life? Where do we begin?

To unlock the secrets of going to the next level we must embrace universal abundance and love. It is also necessary to embrace and accept that you are in transition from where you currently are to where you dream of going. Remember that you are searching for the path you believe is your destiny, and which will allow you to fall in love with your life once you begin. It begins with the process of reassessing, reevaluation, risking and being open to all possibilities.

You must be the change you want to see in the world.

~ Mahatma Ghandi

The Questions of Life

Asking the *Questions* from Chapter Four and going through *The Passion-Driven® Life* may, for some of you, be a tough assignment.

In fact, it may be downright uncomfortable. The questions are designed to challenge your heart, your thinking and your beliefs regarding what you value most, your priorities, your dreams, your hopes, the relationships you desire to create and, and how you define success in life.

It is possible that initially some answers to these questions will be, "I don't know", or "I'm not sure anymore." There may be some uneasiness in being confronted with these kinds of questions or perhaps an uncertainty about them.

Not knowing an immediate answer to such questions in our media-driven world may be a sign of weakness. We are supposed to be in "control" and know exactly what we want 100% of the time, and be hard-charging towards those goals. In fact, no "reality TV" contestant whose is uncertain about what she or he wants ever wins. They are generally ruthless, lying, cheating, back-stabbing and without compassion for others. In this type of scenario there is no room for passion and purpose, amid all the cacophony of being success-driven.

We have been ingrained to think that going to college and getting a degree was the key to happiness and success. In some instances, it was even better if we went to a prestigious university. That would ensure that we were set for life. So now we have college graduates from top private universities with $100,000 plus in debt in their "dream" jobs miserable because they are sacrificing above and beyond what they expected. They are guaranteed 65 to 75 hours of work. After twenty years or so they are worn-out miserable people just trying to get over this week, and the next, and this year, and just looking one day to retire!

The world by default has us placed our innermost dreams, passions, and purpose on "hold." We get busy chasing success and lose track of the meaning of life. We sacrifice personal life, family life and life in general to achieve a financial milestone of making "xxx" amount of dollars per year. Once there we realize that in hindsight that is not really enough, so again we make more sacrifices to make more. It's never enough. Chasing, catching, then chasing some more, catching, and wanting more.

Serenity is not peace after the storm,
It is peace in the very midst of it.

~ Anonymous

For the past several years in surveys conducted about the "happiest places in the world", most of the rich and developed countries are nowhere to be found in the top ten. That is very surprising to many people. What does that tell us about a life of seeking only making money? It's not the answer to true happiness or living a purpose filled life.

We give up on "enjoying" life and the money we slave to make, and cannot enjoy it that much because we're either too tired or working too much! Is that a "Catch-22" or what? We convince ourselves on the "goal" of working real hard so one day we can retire and really get away from it all and do things we really want to do.

When that day arrives, if it ever does, then we're worn out or too sick from the stress, over work and the sleepless nights we managed to create for ourselves. In other sad cases, life just side-swipes many with a terminal illness or a fatal accident, and it's over. You placed living life "on hold" --- all for nothing!

Hello? Where did we miss the boat? Is that a life with purpose? Where's the passion in living that way? But don't despair. Life can be fun, fulfilling and fantastic, if only we evaluate what is important and what matters most. Life is fabulous if we embrace success in life as a journey and not a destination. Not on accounting "balance sheets" --- but in balanced living.

Remember that when you leave this earth,
You can take with you nothing that you have received,
Only what you have given:
A full heart, enriched by honest service,

~ Saint Francis of Assisi

Passion and purpose is a search for what _you_ define as being true for you. It is a search you undertake in unison with God's help. Search for the passion and the purpose which will revitalize and energize your soul and your life. It may be buried deep in your heart, so you will need to get busy digging to get it out after all these years. It's a treasure waiting to be discovered and appreciated.

I am here to tell you that you can have a life with more joy, more love, more caring, more impact, more meaning, more success and, in some cases, more money if you choose to discover and unleash greater passion.

Passion in life never dies by itself. It dies because we don't water it constantly and nurture it with care. Passion and purpose are like a garden of flowers flowing with bright colors. It is a peaceful and beautiful flower garden where we can relax and enjoy its creator, its beauty, and the comfort it brings to our soul. We marvel at its splendor and feel its power.

The garden, just like our passion in life, however, needs attention daily (through prayer, reflection, affirmation, and meditation), weekly pruning (the removal of bad habits and action plans), the removal of choking weeds (by removing ourselves from toxic situations or toxic people) and, most of all, by care and love --- for ourselves, God, and others.

Otherwise, the garden becomes a dry wasteland, the flowers wither, and unsightly weeds invade and choke out all living beauty. It can no longer then be called a garden of beauty. It is not inviting, no one wishes to be there. It is lifeless.

What "weeds" in your life are choking your passion and your meaningful purpose? Passion and purpose die because we no longer tend to them or don't know how to replenish ourselves. They die because of a weary and hectic life. They die because we become disconnected from their beauty, joy, exhilaration, meaning and impact. Because we become alright with looking out through the hazy window of our life and seeing the "weeds" there, we still do nothing about them. Passion and purpose: replenish them, replant and cultivate them so they'll sprout once again.

Ask yourself: How will I regain my passion for life? How can I regain my passion for relationships? How can I regain my enthusiasm and passion and time for my hobbies? How can I regain my passion at my workplace or for my business so that I make a difference? How will I create a balance?

Answer the 7 Questions that follow with brutal honesty. Begin the process of reconnecting to your heart and soul, to your divine purpose and to your passion. The changes and choices required to do that will enliven, create a new you and a new environment!

People spend entire lifetimes working to build successful companies just to accumulate money, rather than to use their fortune for a greater good and greater purpose. They toil away just to "provide" for a family rather than raise a family. They stay "in touch" rather than create deep relationships that inspire and create breathless moments of memories. They work at a job rather than create an environment and experience of deep commitment and satisfaction.

At the end of their lives they end up unfulfilled and frustrated. That is no way to live. Towards the end in the movie *The Shawshank Redemption*, the main character Andy Dufresne sums up his simple and to-the-point life philosophy when he says, "You either get busy living or get busy dying." To that line I would just add, "And it's your *choice*."

Observation/Reflection: I cannot stress enough that we must connect to our purpose and passion for life. What is it exactly that you were placed here on earth to do? Just eat, sleep, work, and occupy space? Once you realize complete potential and you are clear on a life purpose that you'll implement with passion. All else will fall into place.

The Door

Dream of…
Where You'll Be
Dream of…
What You Can Become
Dream of…
A Better Tomorrow
Dream of …
The Better Person You'll Be
Dream Indeed
Now Get Up,
Open the Door of Opportunity
And
Realize Those Dreams…

CHAPTER SEVEN

The Power of Change: Launching Your Visions & Life Dreams

Where there is no vision,
The people perish.

~ Proverbs 29:18

The Secret to Birthing Visions & Dreams. You can empower your dreams, empower your life, empower your future, empower your hope, empower your purpose, empower others, and empower your passions. You must decide from this day forward to no longer be held captive by life's circumstances. Instead you will grab the wheel of life and move one. Place wheels on your dreams.

There are many people who at one time early on in their life were clear on their goals, and now because of circumstances and financial worries have given up, have no plan or vision to guide them. There are millions question the purpose in their life. Who ask themselves, "Where is my enthusiasm for life?", and "What really matters and how can I make a difference?"

Don't defer your dreams, your aspirations, your passion or your purpose in life. Millions worldwide have delayed living life with gusto in the "here and now", and have placed their dreams on hold. They've left them on a shelf where they do nothing but collect dust and are forgotten. Their dreams slowly die with them.

Many individuals, business executives, workers, entrepreneurs and leaders are scared. Yes, these are challenging times. However, in times of challenge it is when opportunity exists for those who are willing and bold enough to look for them. Reflect what is needed to change the course in your life. I did.

No one can get rich without enriching the lives of others.

~ Andrew Carnegie

Have you lost your passion for life? Have you abandoned the dreams of yesteryear and settled into a rut you call life? Have you wondered what really is your purpose in life or have you somehow lost your purpose already? Is that you? Do you feel lost? Have you been afraid to take action? Are you living without hope, purpose or passion? Launch your visions and dreams. Wait no more.

Life does not have to be an "either/or" choice. You can live your life in an *and* world where you have destiny *and* dreams fulfilled, Godly purpose *and* service, balance *and* harmony, abundance *and* prosperity in finances, health *and* love, passion in all you choose to do, *and* make a difference in the process.

Yes, these are challenging and difficult times. It is all the more reason to pay attention to what matters in life. I want to excite your dreams and imagination so that you can the life of your dreams. However, you must define it for your life.

Are you now realizing after all these years that you are caught "in the grind" you call life? Wondering if it is possible in today's climate for your business or your conglomerate to make a difference, serve a greater purpose *and* deliver extraordinary value and service while still turning a profit? It is possible to operate in that type of world. My company did just that and it was one of the keys to the tremendous growth it experienced.

There is a way to believe and live life in which each day is a cherished treasure gifted to us by God. There is a way to structure a business in which passion, service, value and purpose are the core values that distinguish it from competitors and have profits pouring in as the well earned reward. It does not have to be an *either/or* world. It can be a world of *and*.

Meaning, passion and purpose can be redefined, redirected, and unleashed with greater power in a world that is now seeking more value, more hope, more purpose and more connectedness. It's not all about fortune, fame, and being fabulous. Though money can be great tool to live a better lifestyle, ultimately getting hung up on making more and more can have no end in sight.

Dream dreams that once fulfilled make a difference in the world. I want to challenge you so that you connect to the purpose for your life. I want to challenge you so that you connect with being passionate about life. I want to challenge you that making money *and* making a difference can co-exist together.

Even during personal or economic storms in your life, sit down and ponder the blessings you have. You have more than likely a place to call home, food and things you take for granted that 95% of the world consider luxuries. Stretch your dreams to include the dreams and hopes of others. I want to challenge you give to charities that allow those dreams to come alive for others in the world.

Hope deferred makes a heart sick,
But a longing fulfilled is a tree of life.

~ Proverbs 13:12

I want to challenge so that you *and* your company give money to causes, tithe, serve, embrace empathy, and render value in all personal *and* business dealings. God will take care of the rest. The universe will bring infinite good *and* an abundance of great things to you if you are willing to place others ahead of yourself. I want to challenge to live a life worthy in the "here and now" *and* for you to make a difference while leaving a rich legacy.

In your search to lasso and unleash your dreams, make it a habit to give in life, rather than just to take. When you give, the universe and God will open up the floodgates and extraordinary blessings will come pouring into your life. That is a divine promise. So hitch your wagon to that promise and you shall see the marvelous shift that will occur in your life. If you are open to the possibility of this universal law of abundance, every good thing in life can appear to us during the bad, difficult or challenging times.

If you are dealing with personal, emotional, relationship, or financial challenges, you don't have to stay stuck there. However, tough they happen to be there is a light at the end of the tunnel. Continue to have faith, face the crisis and the reality of the situation, work to prevail past it, believe. And then resolve and continue to dig like mad to get out from under it!

The Secrets to Lassoing & Hauling In Your Dreams:

(1) **Stop the endless limiting "head-chatter" you have about yourself. Stop questioning your self-esteem, your talents, or your decisions. What happened to you in the past is history, and it's now time to not let it hold you back anymore.**

(2) **Embrace the fact that action is required. You must grab a rope and haul your unique dreams down from the clouds to the ground.**

(3) **Learn from your mistakes. Don't repeat them.**

(4) **Accept that you are responsible for where you are in life.**

(5) **Connect to your Spiritual Life. Pray and refocus on what is possible and on your divine destiny.**

(6) **Redirect energy and thoughts into a new destiny.**

(7) **Unleash them with a passion that creates a brilliant spark about you and your purpose.**

I didn't just read about these secrets in a book and think they were great concepts. No, I found them and implemented them in my life during the times of raging and roaring storms. They are what allowed me to turn my spiritual, personal, and business life around.

Live a life worthy of making a difference, however small it may be you believe it is at the time. One small act of kindness can have implications for generations to come. One moral act of character can impact the world.

> *In our every deliberation,*
> *We must consider*
> *The impact*
> *Upon the next seven generations.*
>
> ~ Iroquois Nation Confederacy Great Law

Howard Hughes was the world's first billionaire who despite all the money in the world died a lonely, broken, demented, angry and pathetic man. He was the consummate playboy who acquired whatever his heart desired. Hughes' life was generally about acquiring money, seeking self-gratification and pleasure. His only memorable legacy was that in the 1960s he gifted his Hughes Aircraft stock to a medical foundation. Other than that he lived a quintessentially extravagant and hedonistic existence. So out of tune was he that he even failed to leave a trust or a will for his multi-billion dollar fortune.

Contrast that to the late philanthropist and actor Paul Newman whose non-profit foundation has so far donated well over $265 million to charitable causes. He set it up the company, Newman's Own, with "the end in mind" --- to give away 100% of the net profits. Instead of holding tightly to money or seeking to sell the company for huge gains, he let it go and let it flow to others. What a striking difference to the billionaire Hughes who died desperately holding on to his money. What kind of purpose is that? Where's the passion to make a difference?

What are you doing to make a difference? A difference made through relationships in which you invest time, your soul and love without expecting anything in return. The difference made when we seek to serve the interests of others before those of our own. The difference made when we fulfill our dreams, and live them with passion and purpose. The difference made when we willingly sacrifice and give for the well-being of our family, our community, our company, our country, and our world at large.

The difference made when we live in such a way that everyone "wins." The difference made in the connection to life we have when we live it with unimaginable expression, unfathomable openness, a willingness to be wrong, and where we seek and do live our Divine purpose, find our "calling" and live life with a searing passion.

Rather than search intensely for the passion and purpose millions simply begin slowly to give up. Existence becomes the norm. Asked how they're doing typically reply, "Just hanging in there." Why? They think it is not possible to find their passion, their dreams, their purpose or their calling. Instead they develop a predictable routine called "life", without exploring new frontiers, changing beliefs, disconnected from God and hopeless in finding a solution.

It becomes easier to sit in front of a TV or be on the internet for hours on end, and slowly several hours slip into one week, and weeks slip into a month, and months into another year, and they are no closer to unleashing passion or fulfilling dreams. Sound familiar?

It doesn't have to be that way at all. There is a way to live life that is connected to joy, peace, harmony, meaning, purpose and greater passion. There is a way to live a life that matters; a life where we can sing the "songs in our heart" *and* be totally exhilarated. There is a way to live a life that "wows" us, the world *and* we make a difference in the process.

Life is not about always winning at everything you do. Life is not about walking around seeking to prove to the world you know-it-all or have it all. Life is not about turning to every conceivable "opportunity" that you come across in order to "strike it real rich and retire."

We've seen plenty of that in the tabloids and news to prove the point. In whatever endeavor we seek to excel in, if we do have the commitment to love we shall fail. That applies to relationships, hobbies, personal interests, work, sports, or education just the same as it applies to business. Build a company with love and with dedication to serving the needs and interests of others and you will succeed. I know I've done it time and time again.

Go to your place of work and put all your heart in what you do and you shall excel. If for nothing, you work not just to have pride in your abilities and please yourself, but you please God in the process. Build meaningful relationships based on love and being there for one another and it will flourish. Explore new interests with love and you will totally be enthralled and enlivened because you are doing that which you love. And so on. It starts with love and service.

We must *not* think or be stuck in our desperations, our frustrations or our circumstances, but overcome them through faith; through a belief we can accomplish things, by believing we can succeed as we tap into unfulfilled potential, unfulfilled aspirations and unfulfilled dreams.

You have but one life given to live and it is your obligation to do all that is possible to live it with meaningful purpose, to seek happiness, and to better the lives of others. You must refuse to be defined by your past failures, but be changed and made better by them.

Having the courage to examine and ask these kinds of questions is one of the first steps required on the way to find the meaning in our life. Again it boils down to choices that we consciously or unconsciously make for our lives: choose to live or choose to slowly die. It's just as simple as that. No more excuses. No more blaming others or situations from our past. It's up to us to seek divine guidance, move forward and take control of the direction of our life, our community, and our world.

The future belongs ---
To those who believe in the beauty of their dreams.

~ Eleanor Roosevelt

Observation/Reflection: Do you feel as if it's time to get the lasso out, and haul in those dreams of yours floating in the air? Stop the procrastination and the excuses you've been hanging onto instead, and get busy hauling them in!

≈

The Road of Endless Possibility

**Each New Day in Life
Holds and Brings in It
Possibilities, Hope, & Promises from God.
The Possibility of New Beginnings.
It Brings Turning Point Moments;
If We Have the Faith,
The Power to Act and Embrace
The Promises and the Possibilities…**

PART IV

THE KEY QUESTIONS THAT REVEAL THE SECRETS

You are never too old to set another goal,
Or to dream a new dream.

~ *C.S. Lewis*

---

www.ThePassionDrivenLife.com

CHAPTER EIGHT

1st Question: The Power of Hope - What's Died in My Life?

I learned that courage was not the absence of fear,
But the triumph over it.
The brave man is not he who does not feel afraid,
But he who conquers that fear.

~ Nelson Mandela

The Secret to Reviving Stagnant Dreams. Why do most people give up on their dreams and passion? After all, we all have dreams and passion from the time of our birth. God created man with hope in his heart. Man was made by nature to dream, to hope, and to believe in possibility. Ask yourself, "What stops me from living a life of passion?" Fear?

Untapped limitless possibilities lie within each of us, yet not all of us are aligned with our purpose and are alive with passion while unleashing them. Thus, people give up on their dreams in life. Why is that?

The Top 10 Reasons Our Dreams Slowly Die

1. **A Lack of Faith (No Trust in God/Self).**
2. **A Lack of Clarity (No Purpose).**
3. **A Lack of Inspiration (No Passion).**
4. **A Lack of Precise Execution/Strategy (No Plan & No System).**
5. **A Lack of Diligent Work (Procrastination & No "Perspiration").**
6. **A Lack of Support System (No Mentoring/Coaching).**
7. **A Lack of Self-Esteem (No Personal Confidence).**
8. **A Lack of Courage (Fear of Failure/Mental Paralysis).**
9. **A Lack of Fortitude (No Persistence).**
10. **A Lack of a Tracking System (No Progress Evaluation).**

Our purpose, dreams and passion form within us the requisite peak experiences of our lives. God created us to be alive, creative, seeking his favor, yet being self-sufficient, and attaining self-actualization. Only individuals who attain that can be referred to as passion-driven. They are in tune with God, purpose, passion and life dreams.

As such they fulfill their dreams. They bask in the light of their success. They never stay stuck in failures; just choose to learn from them as they continue to move forward and onward toward their goals. They view them differently than the average individual; as temporary setbacks in their quest to achieve dreams and aspirations.

I have not failed.
I've just found 10,000 ways
That don't work.

~ Thomas Edison

How many of us can have the same fortitude and attitude about not achieving success right away as Thomas Edison had? Instead, we try one time, miss the mark and then we shelve the dreams of life and go about the rest of the years complaining, wishing and living out someone else's dreams, if at all.

So, let's get busy living! Get busy with your dreams and come alive with passion and zest. Choose the less traveled of life, if you have need to, but do choose to move onward and upward. Next time you are in a crisis or have encountered an obstacle, remember that even in a crisis, know that you have yet more to live, yet more to learn, yet more to give, yet more wisdom to pass on, yet more living to be done, and yet more passion to deliver to the world. It's never, never over until it's over. You either "get busy living or get busy dying."

David L. Weatherford's poem is both about hope as well as meaning. Let each line sink into your soul and let the message move your spirit.

Slow Dance

Have you ever watched kids on a merry-go-round,
Listened to rain slapping the ground?
Ever followed a butterfly's erratic flight,
Gazed at the sun fading into the night?
You better slow down, don't dance so fast,
Time is short, the music won't last.
Do you run through each day on the fly,
When you ask "How are you?" do you hear the reply?
When the day is done, do you lie in your bed,
With the next hundred chores running through your head?
You better slow down, don't dance so fast,
Time is short, the music won't last.
Ever told your child, we'll do it tomorrow,
And in your haste, not see his sorrow?
Ever lost touch, let a friendship die,
'Cause you never had time to call and say "Hi"?
You better slow down, don't dance so fast,
Time is short, the music won't last.
When you run so fast to get somewhere,
You miss half the fun of getting there.
When you worry and hurry through your day,
It's like an unopened gift thrown away.
Life isn't a race, so take it slower,
Hear the music before your song is over.

~ David L. Weatherford

Observation/Reflection: **One of the definitions of crisis is, *"a crucial or decisive point or situation, a turning point."*** How are you going to turn the corner in your life now? To some extent crisis is a good thing because it forces us to evaluate our course, our direction, our values, and whether or not we are off course from our intended point, purpose and passion. *What is your turning point in life going to be?*

What fears must you conquer are holding you back from a life you dream of having? Remember that to he who ventures little, little is ever gained.

<u>Storm Warning</u>

**The Storms of Life
Always Come.
We're Either Moving Out of Them,
In Them, or
Moving Towards Them.
It's That Simple.
In the Meantime,
Hold On With Faith,
Embrace the Opportunity, and
The Lessons and Character Building
They Bring Us...**

CHAPTER NINE

2nd Question: The Power of Focus - Am I Spinning My Wheels?

Yesterday is but a dream;
Tomorrow is only a vision.
But Today, well lived,
Makes every Yesterday,
A dream of happiness,
And every Tomorrow,
A vision of hope.

~ Anonymous

The Secret to Finding What Holds You Back. Ask yourself, "What stops me from living a life of passion or purpose?" There are millions globally who are feeling and living disconnected from life. Monday through Friday they grudgingly are awakened by an alarm clock, smash it off, lounge a little longer in bed, and mentally assess what type of day is in store for them. Then reality hits and they let out an audible or a mental groan. The pain of the upcoming day or week unleashes itself in their brain. They finally get up and go through the motions of getting ready. They leave in a hurry to go to work, to school, or just to their live every existence. Then they show up at the doorstep of a company or organization, and proceed *not* to have great days or weeks, even months. Can you relate? Perhaps, you know such a person, or have come across such a person, or *are* such a person.

Maybe you are someone who has gone through extraordinary difficult times. You have been beat down. Your sail has been torn down by the winds of obstacles, by the storms of disappointments, and the waves of bad news: a lay-off, a divorce, serious illness, a financial crisis, strained relationships or death of loved ones. You have given up, or feel like it, on your life journey. You lay drifting along the bobbing sea of disappointment and going nowhere.

I can relate when it comes to hard times, disappointment and storms of all kinds! Never lose hope, faith, and focus on your dreams for life.

I can relate when it comes to tough times and mighty storms. My extended family has been through suicide, cancers, fatal accidents, and more ups and downs than I can count. I've made and lost a fortune, been arrested and indicted, been audited, been in prison, sued for millions, had cars repossessed, homes and properties foreclosed, had business closures, been jobless, and had no money in the bank.

Crushed but always hopeful, I kept the faith and I never gave up. I kept moving. So what stops you from living a life of passion and purpose? What keeps you from being disconnected from your passion and purpose?

A cheerful heart is good medicine,
But a crushed spirit dries up the bones.

~ Proverbs 17:22

An Inward Focus

Maybe you have been thinking and asking the following questions or making the following statements for quite some time:

- I feel discouraged.
- I know I am sidetracked.
- I know I am lacking a zeal for life.
- I desire a new path for my life.
- I realize my dreams are not on target.
- I no longer dream BIG dreams.
- I cannot grasp or define my purpose in life.
- I have a purpose, yet lack the passion to unleash it.
- I am a workaholic and spend little time with family.
- How can I harness my passion into powerful action?
- How do I find my purpose?

- How do I put my purpose into action?
- What am I passionate about?

This is a simple exercise to get your attention focused on the fact that perhaps you do not possess the passion for living that you once had. You realize that, as you have lived longer, the desire to define and place into action a meaningful passion and purpose for your life is twirling in your head, tugging at your heart, and you need a push!

What greater thing is there for human souls
Than to feel joined for life?
To be with each other
In silent unspeakable memories.

~ George Eliot

You have finally focused on what holds you back and are aware know that you need to get back on track with the real business of life, otherwise it will continue out of control. You know that you need to connect with the human souls in your life, to live, to create the memories that last, memories that matter, and a life that makes the suffering and difficult times worth it.

Perhaps, you do have a passion for life, however, know you are not fully engaged in the expression, creation and implementation of it in all areas your personal life, family life, relationships, activities, and professional life. I know I was. Well, then you are at least on the journey of rediscovery.

In the Bible story of Joshua, God assures him and the Israelites, as they wait at the edge of the Jordan River to cross into the Promised Land, by affirming to them, "Be strong and courageous. Do not be terrified; do not be discouraged, for the Lord your God will be with you wherever you go." Afterwards Joshua orders the officers of the people to "take possession of the land the Lord your God is giving you for your own" (Joshua 1:9-10).

We too must do the same with our dreams. We must boldly focus and "cross over", through or around the rivers of our storms, disappointments, heartaches, anguish and setbacks of life, and boldly take possession and claim the dreams as a gift from God!

Observation/Reflection: Which of the statement or questions stand out the most for you? Briefly answer them honestly so that you can gauge what it is you desire to give to life and, in return, receive from it. What is the heart of the matter for you in your Family, Personal, Work/Business, or Spiritual Life? Take possession of your dreams that are on the other side of the raging river of life.

<u>The Storms of Life</u>
During the Storms of Life,
There is Faith to Be Strengthened,
There is Hope to Believe In,
Soul & Mind-Power Changes,
There is Beauty to Behold,
There are Challenges to Overcome.
Choose to See the Storms In That Way…

CHAPTER TEN

3rd Question: The Power of Harmony -
What Matters Most in The 9 Areas of Life?

Human beings may be divided into three categories:
Those who are worked to death,
Those who are worried to death, and
Those who are bored to death.

~ Winston Churchill

The Secret to Successfully Living in *The 9 Key Areas of Life*. In order for you to lead a life of passion, you must live in balance and harmony. It's just that plain and simple. You may be passionate in one area of your life, let's say your Work/Business Life, but you are sacrificing others such as Personal Life, Family Life or your Spiritual Life. One cannot have a passion in one area and neglect the others.

We will look at the major areas of living a passion-driven existence and how it is that we implement and unleash passion in each of these areas. There are nine principle areas of life in which purpose and passion must be implemented into in order for us to live a Passion-Driven® Life.

Sometimes, we do not live a life of passion in all areas of our life. Even though we may not realize it until it is perhaps almost too late. I have witnessed that many times in the lives of the elderly I spoke to and met over ten years of visiting convalescent homes while visiting my dad and later my sister. I want you to avoid that. Implementing or living with passion and purpose in just one or two core areas of your life is not enough.

If you do, there will be an imbalance and you are not living a live with divine purpose. For example, an entrepreneur can be passionate about his company (Business Life) and his financial success (Financial Life). He works extremely long hours, including weekends, because he justifies to himself: "I am enlivened when I am pursuing growing my business that I love so much." Yet there is a sacrifice that he is making while in the pursuit of that passion, his Personal Life and his Family Life, among others. That is not living a harmonious and balanced life. *Balance* is a key component in each area.

To be effective at living a life of passion, you must identify, prioritize, and implement what you love to do or aspire to accomplish in each of these areas of life. If in the course of doing that review you find that in some core areas of life you come up with nothing that is okay for now. You have discovered or now realize that there is an imbalance in how you have been living life, as I did awhile back.

Then my mission is that by the end of this book, you would have a written plan of action for each of these core areas of life that embodies your desires, aspirations, hopes, dreams, and that they would reflect your love (i.e. your passion) for each of the core areas that comprise your life.

Perhaps you have not gone where you intended to go when you first set out in your life journey. But where does it say that you can't start again? Focus on where you now desire and intend to go, then pack your supplies and then set off on the journey. You don't gain anything by doing nothing. You can't advance your future by moping about what happened to you in the past, nor by continuing to sit idle and being angry at life in the present. You tap into the power of life when you tap into passion and purpose.

We live in a world where suicide and murder has increased among our youth. Why? Well, it's no secret that all the negative influences that bombard their souls and minds has become never ending and easier to access than it was 25 or 30+ years: video games, TV programs, internet sites, movies and music. The messages they deliver are to be common and "go with the flow". To party like there's no tomorrow. All matter of self-worth, harmony, love and respect for others is unimportant. Most youth have no concept about a purpose for life; passion is meaningless and what's important is to replicate or mirror the foul-mouthed and the bad***** types they see on reality shows or movies and hear in music.

We as a society do not impose limits and boundaries on children, then we wonder why they turn out the way they do? We must love them unconditionally and model respect for them and others. Then, will we have a generation of people who indeed will respect themselves and the world. We must teach them values and success, balance and fulfillment in all key areas of living, and that life's not just about them!

Thus, our passion in life will be a reflection of what value we give to each of these areas of our life. Some may not have a strong desire to accumulate a large amount of wealth (Financial Life) and that is alright. Yet they have the most passion in their Spiritual Life, Community Life, and Family Life. They nonetheless live passion-driven. Typical of this type of individual would be those that decide to join the Peace Corps, military service, and work for non-profit organizations or be involved in missionary work. Their worth and passion is linked to service --- like the service and devotion of a mother.

How many thousands of heroines there must be now
Of whom we shall never know
But they are there
They sow in secret the seeds of which we pluck the flower,
And eat the fruit,
One form of heroism --- the most common,
And yet the least remembered of all --- namely,
The heroism of the average mother.
When I think of that fact,
I gather hope again for poor humanity;
And this dark world looks bright...
Because whatever else it is not full,
It is at least full of mothers.

~ Charles Kingsley

Observation/Reflection: Whatever it is we value and desire to do, it must be balanced in relation to succeeding or scoring high in almost all of the major areas of our life, so that we can have a wide and deep experience in living. If you want to have a high score look at how a mother's love shines and how they go about living their life and impacting those around them.

The Search

Seek ---
God's Guidance
Seek ---
Life Answers
Through Prayer,
Faith,
Introspection
Seek ---
To Unleash The
Power of Living in the Now,
Not the Yesterday's…

CHAPTER ELEVEN

4th Question: The Power of Reflection –
How Do I Define Purpose & Passion?

He who has no passion,
Has no principal,
Or motive to act in life.

~ Claude A. Helvetius

There is a standard dictionary definition of passion, which we will get to later. Aside from the initial association with passionate love and sex, the word has expressive and deep meaning if we live life in such a way that we display its characteristics in our actions, words, thoughts, plans, and in our business.

Look at what is the meaning of passion in your life. If you were to place examples or meaning that would describe the "passions" you have for life, what would they be? What words or feelings would you use to describe them? Would you say to yourself?

Passion is ... **loving and seeking God's plan for life.**

Passion is ... **service and devotion to a cause.**

Passion is ... **commitment to my vision.**

Passion is ... **a profound love for what I do.**

Passion is ... **pursuing things bigger than me.**

Passion is ... **a willingness to sacrifice, with a balance.**

Passion is ... **making a difference in the world.**

Passion is ... **living each day as if it were my last.**

Passion is ... **no regrets in life.**

Passion is ... **unconditional love.**

Passion is ... **unconditional forgiveness.**

Passion is ... **caring for others.**

Passion is ... **enthusiasm.**

Passion is ... **love given and received.**

Love is patient. Love is kind.
It does not envy, it does not boast.
It is not rude. It is not self-seeking. It is not easily angered.
Love does not delight in evil, but rejoices with the truth.
It always perseveres, always trusts,
Always hopes, and always perseveres.
Love never fails.

~ 1 Corinthians 13:4-8

The Secret of Passion in Life

There are few words in the English language more fervently used than "passion" in relation to attempting to express or define success in personal life, business life, financial success or living life well. Merriam-Webster's dictionary defines passion as "a strong liking, desire or devotion to something or activity." The synonyms are fervor, ardor and zeal.

We use the word "passion" to describe those things which we enjoy, those things which we wish we were doing, those things which are easy for us to do with joy, to describe our past-times or hobbies, or to describe how we feel in relation others, aside from a sexual note, such as family, spouse, or children.

To me there is no better definition than to just summarize it as *love.* Passion is love. Love for God, love for yourself, a love for family, a love for others, love for what you do, a love for how you do things, love for what you say, a love for the search of how you can make a difference in the world, and a love in being in the service to others.

It is our passion that keeps us moving ahead when the storm clouds arrive. It is our passion and purpose that push us forward during the stormy days and nights of difficulty, doubt, and past the obstacles, criticism, or failures.

The Secret of Purpose in Life

Miriam-Webster's dictionary defines purpose as "to intend, propose; something set up as an object or end to be attained; intention, resolution, determination or intentional."

We are all given a divine purpose to live; one that is honoring to God as well as to us. A purpose to be in the service to others; to think of others before ourselves; to educate ourselves, through traditional means as well as non-traditional means, so that we may lift ourselves up from our economic situation and better the condition of our lives.

Yes, we all have a purpose in life. It is just that some choose to ignore it and go out on a tangent in the pursuit of pleasure, personal gain, or greed, or a combination of these. For example, we desire money so we go to college to learn and get a great job. We desire a good job so that we can make more money, but we rarely think about giving back, making a contribution in recognition of all the advantages we receive. Sometimes we find work doing something we may not necessarily like but because it pays the best hourly rate, we work and work so that we can buy the "toys" in our life.

True passion and true purpose forge a frontier of hope for us. They build a road of believing and a highway of possibility thinking. Passion and purpose unleashed allow us to live "in love" with life, not only because we do that which we enjoy, but because we benefit a greater good -- our family, our relationships, our spiritual growth, our company, our community, and the world in general. The by-product for us is satisfaction and fulfillment. So it is a win-win for everyone.

As we journey onward, it will become evident that passion is what drives us forward. It is passion that always perseveres, and does not allow us to fail, but moves us onward towards our dreams. It is passion that guides us onward along the trail of hope. When we arrive at the doorstep of our personal success in life we shall first thank God, and then our passion.

> ### *Hope is the word which God Has written on the brow of every man.*
>
> ~ Victor Hugo

Hope is the passion that we have in each of us. If we lose the passion and hope, then we lose the purpose for our life. I believe hope is a passion embodied in love, a dream whose light always flickers in our hearts, and which ultimately gives our purpose the fire. A passion-driven life is lived when we are living a life that acts out of self-less love as we unleash our divine purpose and electrifies us.

The Mandarin/Cantonese and Japanese languages, give us an even deeper understanding of "passion." They embody amazing values and traits that form a Passion-Driven® Life. They are rich with meaning and are:

- o "Ai Xin" – **compassion**, possessing **a loving heart**. A mind full of desire.
- o "Tong Qing" – **caring** and understanding; when someone is troubled even if you don't know them. Wanting to help, even if all you can do is listen.
- o "Ci Bei" – **mercy**, compassion, or clemency; the **act of giving, charity**. The simplest way to express compassion for fellow humans.
- o "Re Qing" – **enthusiasm**, such as the **passion for a cause**. Cheerful, happy, and **full of spirit**. Doing something wholeheartedly and eagerly. Also, sincere and warm in our actions.
- o "Dong Li" – **motivation**. Means **power**, motion, propulsion or force. It can be an internal or external force that keeps us going. (In Japanese, it stands for "kinetic energy").
- o "Jue Xin" – first character means "to determine", second means character of the "heart" or "soul." It is literally, to put your heart into something. It can also, can be translated as **resolve**, resolution, or decision.

The Secret to Harmony in Life

A passion-driven person lives in harmony. He or she has relinquished living a life of blame, a life lacking forgiveness, a life of resentment, anger, despair or hopelessness. They choose to rid themselves of toxic environments and relationships, and concentrate on those relationships, environments and things which foster their time, love, and talents.

The passion-driven empower themselves and others. As a result, they are always growing inwardly, assured of themselves, and assuring others along the journey we call life. Our passions enable us to be a guide to our destiny. The passion-driven know that life is indeed a journey, and along the way they breathe in every meaningful moment of it, and seek to live their life by the *Golden Rule*: "Do unto others, as you would have them do unto you."

Observation/Reflection: Move your heart and soul to passion. Your purpose will be enlivened and your spirit will be kindled when that occurs. When you do that you will see things and possibilities that were there but which you never imagined could be yours.

<u>The Secret Key</u>

Each of Us Must Look For and Find
That Secret Key That Unlocks
The Door to a
World of Purpose,
Passion,
Meaning,
Fulfillment, and
The Beauty of Living…

CHAPTER TWELVE

5th Question: The Power of Possibility - Where's The Key to Unlock The Secrets?

There is one quality that one must possess,
And that is definiteness of purpose,
The knowledge of what one wants,
And a burning desire to possess it.

~ Napoleon Hill

The Secret to Living a Passion-Driven® Life. Living a great and exhilarating life is about doing that what drives you, what you love and in the process winning the hearts and minds of those you know, work with, your family, friends and community.

The bottom-line is that as individuals seeking to go to the next level you must be focused and committed in heart and spirit to whatever you are dreaming to accomplish. You must be open to seeing it through with possibility thinking.

Passion-Driven® individuals are leader's who have vision and wisdom. They do what others will not do, or cannot do, and are able to easily involve others towards action in fulfilling a mission. They create synergy and enthusiasm for a goal and a plan. They inspire because of their unbending commitment to achieve the goals. They motivate others because of the examples they leave for others to follow. In addition to charisma, which many do possess, it is their "definiteness of purpose", laser beam focus, and can-do thinking to accomplish tasks that sets them apart.

Passion-Driven® individuals and leaders are at the forefront of creating and making meaningful change. That is the type of leadership needed now in our families, businesses, and civic, spiritual and political organizations.

Passion is about believing in something bigger than you; in a cause that is larger than you can imagine. It may be a large cause or it may be a simple dream or vision. It may be a desire to be a part of making a difference as a volunteer at the local shelter, women's clinic, at the local food bank, or by donating resources to them.

Whatever it may be for you, passion motivates us, pushes us harder, drives us, and makes us get up every day to strive on and to fight for what we do and believe in. Passion and purpose are the critical elements that make a difference in the world around us. You contribute, you give back because of it, and you live fully and engaged because of it. You are willing to sacrifice for it, even submit to death for it.

Heart and soul are at the center of passion. Once we have defined our purpose, it is passion that molds, shapes and defines how we go about implementing it. The Bible clearly states that we are to love our God with all of our heart and soul. Do the same in each area of your life: Commit all our energy, focus, drive, and being into that one goal and one purpose.

Being a parent is the grandest purpose in life. Love is the ultimate sacrifice for our children. To me, parenting has got to be one of the deepest passions ever. It's the passion of sacrificing single mothers for their children. We place on personal desires last and the emotional needs of our children first. We passionately labor for our children.

Passion living is all around us. Just open up your heart and listen to the gentle whispers to tune in. Learn the lessons from those who have forged a trail and achieved their dreams so that the world could be a better place for us.

<u>*My Soul is Sick – I Need Some Soup*</u>

Passion living is the stuff of legends, such as the story of two starry-eyed authors who had a dream. They had written a book which contained a collection of soul-lifting and inspiring stories of hope, laughter and faith which they had been sharing with audiences for years. The authors were my friend and mentor, Mark Victor Hansen and his partner, Jack Canfield. They were rejected by over 140 publishers for their book.

They nonetheless continued onward. Their passion and purpose told them it would make a difference in the lives of people struggling with difficulties, heartache, or tough times. Told to give up, they did not; nor did they compromise the message. They saw possibility and promise where most see giving up as the best option.

They finally found a publisher who, according to Mark, "Couldn't keep a dry eye" as his entire heart and soul captured their message, vision and dream. Thus *Chicken Soup for The Soul* series was born and it has so far touched and enhanced the lives of millions worldwide. Over 145 million books have been sold with their "20/20 perfect vision" is to sell 1 billion books by 2020. It launched hope, love, and inspiration. I know it did for me. That's passion, purpose and integrity in action!

One of the truest tests of integrity,
Is its blunt refusal to be compromised.

~ Chinua Achebe

Living Life Without an Agenda

In the summer of 2008 my family went to a county fair. It was a first for my twin daughters. It was a terribly hot summer day and I had reservations about going in the first place but it was the last week and because of them we went. At the fair I came across a grandfather and his grandson who were enjoying exhibit. It would have been a typical sight to see, however, this was no typical grandson. He caught my attention because he was exceedingly loud and highly excited to see people and things.

Several times I saw him go up to his grandfather hug him and scream out loud: "Did you see that, did you see that?" after he saw something he liked. Some people did not quite capture this moment of pure innocence and glee. They avoided being around him. They did so, I observed, not so much because he was being loud but because Michael had Down syndrome. I perceived it made them uncomfortable. I felt the pain of rejection Michael did not as I had a sister who was born mentally handicapped. When I went out with her adults and children alike would sometimes just stare at her constantly. I knew it use to make her uncomfortable and I would do my best to reassure her.

So I came close to Michael and stood looking at an exhibit, then turned to him and in a highly excited voice, "Did you see that?" He looked at me and immediately lunged forward and gave me the biggest bear hug you can imagine. His grandfather literally could not pull us apart. He nervously explained to me that Michael loves giving people hugs but that most strangers don't like it. He said that Michael was expressing his appreciation to me for acknowledging him. I gave Michael another big hug and let him know God and I loved him.

I apparently made his day and he turned to his grandfather and yelled once again: "Did you see that?" It made Michael's day, I think, a little brighter. More importantly it embedded a memory in my heart of the rewards and blessings possible when I risk and reach out to everyone in our life --- even if they are not at all like us.

We win the hearts of others by our passion. If we are open to believing in possibility and our purpose is divinely aligned, passion and providence will open up the doors. Actions often mean more to us than words. Demonstrate passion, caring, empathy, commitment, excellence, purpose and never compromise.

Observation/Reflection: Life is about being sensitive to moments of innocence as what took place with Michael. Of being inspired by and inspiring others who live without an agenda. They spread love just because that's what they do. No hidden agenda, just love. Michael did that and I was blessed by being open to receiving it. As well, I acknowledged it and returned it to its sender.

You want passion and purpose in life? Easy, first open your heart and soul, and then unleash it in your life without having a personal hidden agenda. Do you give back love to those you do not know but are transmitting it? Are you so passionate about your *cause* or your dream, whatever it is, that you are willing to be rejected over and over until the right opportunity opens up?

≈

<u>Leap of Faith</u>

**We Think and Hope
Our Lives Will Change
With a Single Leap of Faith
It Can.
Mostly, We Change and
Accomplish Things
Through Small Leaps of Faith.
Take a Leap of Faith,
Even if Unsure of the Outcome ---
That's What Being Passion-Driven®
Is As All About,
As You Move Forward
And Accomplish Your Dreams...**

CHAPTER THIRTEEN

6th Question: The Power of Massive Action - How Do I Use the Key?

Whatever you dream or dream you can do,
Begin it.
Boldness has genius, power, and magic in it.

~ Johann Wolfgang von Goethe

The Secret Ingredient Required. One of the key elements for success in life and often forgotten elements by many is massive action. Dreaming is great, but you've got to do something about them. If you want to go on the journey of life you dream of, then it requires you to act. As an illustration, it requires you leave your home, get into the car, put the key into ignition, start the engine, turn the wheel and drive out of your drive-way, your "comfort zone" and venture onto the roadway of life!

Before we can implement to *The 40 Days of Passion-Driven® Life Action Plans,* I need to review the importance of action and its relation to quantum physics. That lesson will reinforce the point that *measureable* and massive *action* is absolutely crucial as a turning point in your life or situation. After that, we will review whether or not the thinking behind *The Law of Attraction* is a bad philosophy or not.

Newton's laws of physics described the relationship between force, and mass, among other things. His *First Law of Motion* stated that in order for the motion of an object to change, a force must act upon it, a concept known as inertia in physics.

In the case of a living a *Passion-Driven® Life*, the "force" is *you* acting through your passions upon your dreams. *Nothing* in your life will ever change if measureable and massive action does not begin. An initial push or inertia is required. That means getting off your duffle and doing the things that will propel you towards your goals and plans, rather than complaining about how bad things are in your life. It means deciding to be a change agent in your life, in which you take control and assume responsibility for. You decide its course rather than being the one who is bounced around like the stainless steel roller-ball inside a pin-ball machine.

Newton's *Second Law of Motion* defined the relationship between acceleration, force, and mass. For us it means that once we decide to act and place wheels on our dreams, the process accelerates and creates results in our lives.

Imagine it being like a small snow-ball at the top of a mountain and it rolls forward. As it picks up speed and momentum it becomes larger and larger. Success and passion are the same way. They may manifest themselves initially in your life as small action steps, and that is alright. Then you define and unleash your passion even more. You gain more momentum, until you become unstoppable in your quest.

Newton's *Third Law of Motion* states that any time a force acts from one object to another there is equal force acting back on the original object. That is, if you pull on a rope, the rope is pulling back on you as well.

The Third Law of Physics as defined by Newton is, I believe, the *original* "Law of Attraction." Summed up, if you extend out to the world action, love, giving, a positive spirit, superior service, excellent products, and complete commitment, God and the world, in turn, will respond to your blessings and bring to existence your desire or dream. By your actions, you attract success, increase passion, fulfill purpose, attract people, and your dreams become a reality.

For most of us it is a lack of implementation that is missing. What's the solution? Take immediate and massive action now! Not tomorrow or next week, next month, or "when the kids get older or move out." Action and planning are what will get you the results in your personal life, business or organization. Merely believing that all you need to succeed in life is to believe in your dream and be positive about is rubbish. The world will not come rushing to your door to bring you things. All you will attract are flies to your dreams!

De-Bunking the Law of Attraction

The concepts behind the *Law of Attraction* are really "no secret." The notion of having a positive mind-set, thinking positive thoughts and moving away from negative energy is centuries old. The main idea is that we are like a "magnet" and we create our own reality in our world. Therefore, we "attract" things that we want into our life and we also attract things we don't want. The law is summarized by the belief that you are a magnet attracting all things, via the signals being emitted through your thoughts and feelings. Thus, you attract money, you attract relationships and you attract health.

The law of attraction postulates that *if* our thoughts and beliefs are limited, we in turn will attract limited wealth and compromise our emotional and physical health in the process. The law of attraction is summed up by believing anything is possible and that no limits exist. If you focus on lack, you will have lack in your life. However, if you focus on money and happiness, then they will materialize and "attract" themselves to you.

The three main areas of the Law of Attraction, made popular in the movie *The Secret* are:

1. Asking: You must know with precision what it is you want the universe to deliver to you through your thoughts and feelings.
2. Believing: You must firmly believe that which you want and ask for will be yours, and the universe is prepared to give it to you.
3. Receiving: You must be ready to receive that which the universe is prepared to give to you. After you have asked and believe it to be yours.

The Real Secret behind 'The Secret'

I certainly agree and practice these steps in my life: asking, believing and receiving. In Luke 11:9-10, Jesus told his followers, "Ask and it will be given to you; seek and you will find; knock and the door will be opened to you. For everyone who asks receives; he who seeks finds; and to him who knocks, the door will be opened."

We must nonetheless weigh the motives for our asking in our hearts. We must possess a heart that seeks things for the good not just a genie-in-a lamp that brings into our lives wealth, health and relationships. A positive mind-set and possibility thinking is one of the most critical elements to have in our life. But this world also needs a connection to God and faith. The Law of Attraction is devoid of any reliance on God for wisdom, insight, abundance, blessings or direction. The *Law* has you believing and thinking: if you want it bad enough, all you must do is prepare in your mind and heart to ask, believe and receive!

In addition, there is more to it than that. I believe the philosophy of the Law of Attraction, while being a great concept if implemented with other proven principles, is a bad philosophy by which to operate your life, because it makes you somewhat lazy by believing that all you need to do is think, believe or envision in your mind into existence those "things" (love, relationships, money, health, material possessions, etc.) you desire to have in your life. The Law of Attraction has you believing that you will draw those desires into your life like a magnet if all you do is believe you can attract them.

The concepts of the Law of Attraction can be implemented as part of the plans required while unleashing purpose and passion. However, we must ask God for wisdom and guidance; and ask the motive(s) behind the asking, plan, test, assess if what we are "asking" will be also for the greater good or merely for personal reasons. We need to seek mentors, have physical vision boards, "journal" what works and what does not, and take action now --- massively and immediately.

We need to define our passion and purpose; then unleash them into the world in order for our hopes to become dreams, the dreams to become goals, the goals to become plans, and the plans to become accomplishments!

Great doors of opportunity and possibility will open to us <u>after</u> we unleash the power of our prayer, the power of our purpose, the power of our passion, the power of our preparation, the power of our action plans, the power of our belief, the power of our asking and the power of our possibility; *in unison* with the power our thoughts and the power of our desires.

I've said it before, being happy is not about money in the bank. Too many people are now focusing on "attracting money" into their lives after reading or seeing the Law of Attraction discussed. They now feel they are somehow entitled to "get their share." I've read comments posted on web sites of people clamoring about how they will implement it in their lives so they can get rich and live life well. It's backward thinking. Give first.

Look instead to leave a worthwhile legacy. Look to have great health. Look to develop healthy relationships. Look to give first before receiving. Look to contribute to the lives of others. Look to improve the lives of others. Consider these before deciding on ancient laws that satisfy mainly your personal wants and monetary desires for life.

Passion for Numbers & Passion for Love

On November 10, 2008, my sister, of whom I was legal guardian, passed away. Estella was born mentally handicapped. She had the mental capacity of a six year old. However, she loved creating relationships and engaging in conversation. Estella gave more than she ever got back. She lived a passion-driven life by being her loving, inquisitive, and joyful self.

Despite a mental "incapacitation", Estella tapped into a God-given talent and passion by creating world-class art. During a span of over ten years, "The Numbers Artist" as she was known in her art gallery due to her unique use of numbers one to ten in everything, she created, painted, sculpted, and sketched over 300 pieces of art. Some of it was sold internationally.

She refused to be constrained by her physical and mental limitations; instead she chose to live her life with a passion and be uncommon. As often happens with many people in our lives, when they are gone we yearn for their reappearance back into our lives because the void causes pain. For my sister it was no different.

Yet, in her manner of living and in her special way she left us a daily legacy and reminder of herself through her art. It's as if when looking into the artwork she is reaching out to touch our hearts and soul saying, "I'm still here with you."

I cry sometimes when I look at the art, not only for her loss at an early age, but because of the beauty of what she left behind for so many in the world to remember her by and enjoy. I cry because it amazes me that so much talent lay hidden for years unexplored and unbeknown to us for a long time. During the period of her as an artist she lived freely and fully, and I suppose it is also that which brings me to tears. That is, indeed, a legacy of passion to behold.

<u>Observation/Reflection</u>: As Goethe said, "…Begin it…." What have you envisioned or thought about in your life, in which you have done nothing to implement, so far? It's time to end "it" (the procrastination) and begin "it" (the action). Resolve to leave hurts behind, pour your heart you're your current relationships, and look forward to new ones you are destined to create.

Be open to the idea that those individuals that are "different" from us can perhaps teach us a thing or two about simple living that makes an impact in the hearts and souls of ordinary men and women.

I have nothing against anyone using the concepts of the Law of Attraction to draw and unleash purpose and passion. However, do not rely on them exclusively as the only tool to manifest your passion, dreams, and goals. They are not the Holy Grail or Aladdin's lamp. You also need to take major action steps.

Benjamin Franklin said, "Never confuse *motion* for action." So just because you are doing "something", it may not equate to what you need to be doing as part of your P.L.A.N.S. that will move you closer to dreams being fulfilled. Are you in *motion* or *in action?*

The Mountaintop

Persistence and
Prayer Off!
Move Past Your Obstacles
Flourish Amidst Your Crises
Look Up, Never Down
No Person Ever
Accomplished Anything
While Looking Down.
Look Heavenward and Inward
At the Core of Your Soul ---
Through Enlightenment
Keep Pressing Onward
Until You Get to The Mountaintop…

CHAPTER FOURTEEN

7th Question: The Power of Commitments - Am I On Fire About My Life Purpose & Passion?

Dance as though no is watching,
Love as though you have never been loved before,
Sing as though no one can hear you,
Live as though heaven is on earth.

~ Anonymous

The Secret to Unleashing Passion. Passion is defined as "an intense, driving feeling or conviction; a strong liking or desire." The driving force we call passion then is implemented through *commitment*. Passion is, for the passion-driven, that voice that continually tugs on their inner thoughts throughout the day. It's a Godly calling going to the very core of your soul. It creates a contagious energy that infuses our lives with meaning, joy, excitement, invigoration, intensity, hope, and satisfaction. It is where we create meaning in all we do.

Some individuals have so many passions they seemingly cannot get to all of them. Others have passions and place them on *hold* onto them and call them "Dreams on Hold." While for others, one passion fills a lifetime. Live your passion and be in tune with the happiness that lifts your spirit, energizes your soul and totally fulfills you.

Are you living your passion? Passion empowers us. It takes you from being the victim of circumstances to being in charge and changing the circumstances in our lives. We take responsibility for the direction of our life. Through it we empower our vision, our soul, our heart, and we push onward. We are at the controls of life rather than being passengers along for the ride.

The passion-driven individual is not into the blame game, blaming others for his/her failures, mistakes, or lack of zeal. The passion-driven choose *not* to live life through the "rear-view mirror", looking back at what was, what happened or who did "it" to them. Instead, he or she focuses on the road *ahead*, not what's behind them anymore. They commit to creating change and then seek how to go about implementing it.

The Power of Our Commitments

Are you committed to the change and transformation in your life that you desire and to the goals you want to accomplish? Are you truly seeking to live your divinely appointed purpose here on earth? In order for transformation in life to take place we must be committed to be that positive change which we seek in our life. It must go beyond dreaming and take action in the physical realm. We cannot fool ourselves that if we dream, desire, and ask, that it will occur. God loves an involved and committed individual.

The Power Commitments Needed For the Next Level

1. The Commitment to Make Meaningful Changes.
2. The Commitment to Take Measurable Action.
3. The Commitment to Learn and Grow.
4. The Commitment to Pursue Excellence.
5. The Commitment to Make a Difference.
6. The Commitment to Let Go What Doesn't Work.
7. The Commitment to Love.

Passion is not a gut feeling, impulsive actions, or emotions. It shapes, defines and clarifies our commitment to our God given purpose. One is not separate from the other. Commitment without passion is just plain boring and lifeless.

In our love relationships, it is a commitment, respect, a bond and unconditional love forged by passion that allows us to go beyond temporary set-backs. We look past the small things as passion lights the way to the commitment made between individuals.

Don't let the flame or embers of passion for your relationships be dowsed by the tsunamis of life. Passion keeps the fire burning and the beacon lit until the storms subside, and the rays of sunshine come back into our lives.

Passion is a burning desire that cannot be put out. It is a small ember in your soul that just needs oxygen so it can fully engulf our entire being. It is that intangible which in the face of difficulties and obstacles propels us forward. Give oxygen to your passion and purpose. Rekindle the flame of passion. Don't hold it in. Don't let life smother it out with all its stresses, preoccupations, and sometimes useless running around for the sake of running around. Passion is a precursor to making commitments in life. However, once that takes place make a commitment to live your life with purpose.

Passion and commitment is about getting up every day and thanking God for the gift of a new day, then doing whatever we can to make a positive difference in the lives of people around us. Are you living your passion in your personal relationships? Are you living your passion and purpose in life? Are you living in such a way that it makes the lives of people better? Are you striving to leave a legacy or instead living a life of tattered hopes? Examine the life of a woman who despite being an immigrant and poorly educated left a legacy for future generations to remember her by.

The Passion-Driven® Matriarch

She had a flame of faith and passion. She spoke little English, yet had many English-speaking friends whose lives were impacted as she lived and shared her love for God. To many in her community she was the little old lady that liked to walk a lot and always had a kind word of encouragement to everyone who would listen. Her name was Josefina Bermeo. She lived to the age of eighty-eight; a long life, but more important, is how she lived it --- her passion for life.

Josefina was a matriarch of a large family from Ecuador. To her there was nothing more important to her than God and family. A woman who had a difficult and painful upbringing as a child, and despite that chose not to dwell on her misfortunes and pain.

She lived a life of dedicated service to God, family and others. Unable to leave only a few possessions to her family, she left instead the priceless gift of a lasting legacy of love, and wonderful moments of memories in the hearts and souls of those who were a part of her life.

Josefina endeared herself to strangers quite easily by the manner in which she reflected the passion for life. She lived content and happy with the small things in life. To her everything that was important was small and simple. She walked 3 miles daily and tended to her garden, two passions she did until the very end of her life.

There are lessons to be learned from someone who accepted the role of being a matriarch in a new country with new customs and social pressures. She had a favorite saying when things got real difficult in life which she imparted to others the sage wisdom of having lived through many trials herself: "Be Firm, Strong and March On!"

During our intimate moments of deep conversation she reinforced the fact that people should not measure their value as humans based on the material possessions we give or leave behind, but by the one thing we can all give to everyone that has no price: "unconditional love to our family, Godly hope, and assurance of a better tomorrow, without regard to our present sufferings." After our last moments together she gave me a kiss and a hug and told me it would be alright. One month later she passed and went on to glory "to see her Lord."

Observation/Reflection: Find the activity or desire that pulls on the strings of your heart? That is where, most likely, your purpose and passion dwell. If you believe you are living that passion and purpose, then continue onward with unleashing it. If you are not living life that way, what are you waiting for?

≈

PART V

THE SECRETS TO THE NEXT LEVEL IN LOVE, LIFE & BUSINESS

Trust in the Lord with all you heart and
Lean not on your own understanding.
In all ways, acknowledge Him, and
He will direct your paths.

~ Proverbs 3: 5-6

---

www.ThePassionDrivenLife.com

<u>Refreshment for The Soul</u>

**Passion and Purpose…
Are About Living Exhilarated With Life;
Bringing Forth Your Best,
Not Holding Back.
About Making a Difference in the Hearts,
Minds and Souls of People,
Inspiring Yourself & Others,
While in the Process
Creating a Better You
Bringing Peace, Hope and Refreshment
To Your Soul …**

CHAPTER FIFTEEN

The 1st Secret: The Power of Creating Crystal Clear Clarity

The secret of man's being is not only to live,
But to have something to live for.

~ Fyodor M. Dostoyevsky

The Secret to Digging for Your Passion & Purpose. Passion is where the rubber meets the road as far as dreams are concerned. We all have innate passion. God has placed it each and every one of us. It's in our soul and in our being. When we're real young we were full of dreams and hopes. There were no apparent barriers in our minds big enough that we could not overcome.

No dream was audacious enough when we were children. For example, we dreamed of being doctors, firemen, astronauts, feeding the hungry, saving the planet, helping animals, working with the poor, or making a lot of money to help our mom or family out.

When we were children we were alive with inspiration. We were alive with hope. We were alive with passion. The simple things in life captured our attention and we lived and gave to those around us. We made friends easily and doled out words of encouragement freely. What happened? We became young adults and the world's pessimism, negativity, harsh realities, and even envy slowly began to clip the wings of our hopes, our dreams and our passion for life. Little by little we spread our wings less and less, until we no longer soar in search of a new frontier. We no longer dream big dreams. We are told to "get real" about our expectations or wishes in life.

As we grow older, few of us ever take the time, the energy, to draw out and implement our dreams and passion. We settle into a routine that becomes monotonous. We live our dreams and hopes vicariously through countless TV "reality" or entertainment shows of one kind or another to placate us somewhat. Why?

Go in search of your passion. Dig for your passion. Realize that same passion for living and the zest for doing what you love and desire can be yours. You hold the key to transforming your future and destiny into one in which you can one day say," I came into the world, found my purpose, unleashed it, loved it and lived it." Passion is about investing your sweat, your attention, your focus, and being in the creation, execution, and development of your purpose, vision and goals.

Your living is determined not so much by what life brings to you,
As by the attitude you bring to life;
Not so much as by what happens to you,
As by the way your mind looks at what happens.

~ John Homer Miller

The Secrets to Discovering Your Passion in Life

Step # 1: Ask Yourself Open & Honest Questions.
1. What makes me burst with excitement and/or happy?
2. What am I constantly thinking about that brings joy to me?
3. What do I want to do with the rest of my life?
4. What do I enjoy doing the most?
5. What do I envision as my legacy?
6. If you I was told that I had only one year to live, what would I do?
7. What is my definition of success?
8. What do I love to do as hobbies or past times?
9. If you I had to "do it over again", what would I do differently?
10. Am I willing to take measured risk(s) to pursue my dreams?
11. Is making money or making a difference more important?
12. Is it possible that I can do both?
13. What would I need to do to have that manifested in my life?
14. Am I happy with my life?
15. What motivates me to act?
16. What talents do I possess?

17. What type of work or activity would I truly enjoy?
18. What changes in my life do I need to implement?
19. Am I comfortable with change in my life?
20. Am I willing to sacrifice, within reason, to reach my dream(s)?
21. Whom will I need to hold me accountable for action in my life?
22. How will I measure my progress along the way?
23. Do I have relationships that need mending?
24. What "baggage" do I have that holds me back?
25. When will I start?

Step # 2: Answer the Questions Truthfully.

I know that these are a lot of questions, but they are designed to confront your thinking about true passion and purpose in life. If they make you uncomfortable, then perhaps you are missing out on life.

Go sit alone in a quiet place and take a good amount of time to reflect, meditate, pray and think about these questions. Ponder and entertain those questions that stand out for you. Look into your strengths or weaknesses in those areas that seem to motivate you.

Write down all your possible answers to the above questions. Write down everything, no matter how obvious, silly or trivial it may be. Write down all your goals, dreams, visions, desires and those things that excite and believe you enjoy the most. Don't change anything just let your mind and heart speak to you and write them --- no corrections, deletions or editing! You are searching your heart and sub-conscious mind for answers.

Step # 3: Clarify Them.

When that's done, go back and circle <u>five to ten answers</u> pertaining to interests, hobbies, or things you enjoy the most. Then evaluate and choose with your heart, not your mind, the ONE thing worthy to spend all your time and resources on to bring to fruition, and that will bring out the best in you. Later, you can add more to your list, but only if you've achieved or are on your journey to achieving the ONE thing.

The object lesson is not multi-tasking your way by choosing three multiple things from your list, and begin to do them all at once. That's going back to stress and overwork. A simple life and to simplify it is the object here, not to create more stuff for you to do.

When I enacted changes in life, it was based on seeking simplicity, passion, and more family/personal time. I chose the one thing I felt expressed my dreams and desires and concentrated on that. I later added a few more, while keeping in mind that my goal was to earn more money *and* also spend more time with my family!!

Step # 4: Capture the Possibilities.
Remember you only get one turn at life. There are no replays. There are "do-overs", as exist in the social game of golf where a player gets a chance to repeat a certain shot. You may not do it smoothly right away, but just go ahead anyway and go about creating a wonderful life. Too many lives have been lived in quiet desperation and unfulfilled with excuses such as, "until I have our/my nest egg saved up" or "not until the children are out of school/out of the house" or "someday when I retire."

They usually die and that someday never arrives. They get a terminal diagnosis and then can only focus on survival, let alone living life with passion. It's sad but true. I've seen it time and time again.

Step # 5: Plan & Unleash Passion!
Don't go to sleep one more night without reflecting and deciding on *what you really want in life*. Write down the various ideas, thoughts or visions that come into your heart and how you can begin to unleash them right away into your daily, weekly, monthly routine and life.

Set up measurable time-time tables of one, two, and six month intervals to evaluate and check-off what you have done so far. Then do the same for your one, two, three, and five-year Passion Living Action Needed Steps™ (P.L.A.N.S.).

Step # 6: Test Them Out ("Assembly Required").
You buy something and it comes in a big box. If you are like me you abhor having to labor over the instruction manual written in small print with diagrams that require an engineering degree to figure out. Yet, we bought it and want it, so we go about putting the darn thing together.

The same way is with your goals and dreams. You want them, yet sometimes don't feel like doing the "assembly work" required. Just get to it. Spend a few days evaluating how to make change possible

and make your dreams a reality. **Begin living every day or every week as if they were the last you had. Leave nothing on the side. Cease procrastinating. It needs to be done now, not next week, or next year. There will always be bills, things will always break down or need replacing; there may be storms and everyday situations, but there will only be one life for you to live. It can no longer be placed on "hold"!**

Seek out divine wisdom and the support of a trusted person or mentors. Ask them to hold you accountable for the new direction in your life. Also, seek a mentor or coach who will guide you as you test out the passions which you have identified, and who can also hold you accountable and measure your actions and results.

Step # 7: Take Action! ("Batteries Required").

After you have assembled your dreams and goals into plans, it's now time to place the batteries on them. It's time to get to it. Just like Ron Carlson loved to say: "Ain't nothing to it, but to do it."

- o Don't blame your mother, your father or your country because you did not end doing what you had envisioned a long time ago. Get busy living.
- o It's never too late! You're not in a pine box yet, so what are you waiting for to engage life head-on? Get busy living.
- o Get off the couch and get on with living life.
- o Implement the 40-Days of Passion-Driven® Life Action Plan!

Step # 8: Conclude Effectively.

The most important thing to remember is to follow your passion, your purpose and *use your heart*. Others may disagree with you, but you should be firm with integrity in what you want. Others may offer comments or advice, but the final decision is always yours to make. You should concentrate on what you want, not what others tell you.

Inspiration, motivation and passion come to us when we open ourselves to meditation, prayer and when we seek wisdom and guidance. Therefore, if you feel trapped by past decisions or desperation sets in that you are not living your passion and purpose, don't fret. Remember and realize it's never too late to find it or release it.

Nothing great will ever be achieved without great men,
And men are great only if they are determined to be so.

~ Charles De Gaulle

The Secret Strategy for Goal Setting & Plan Execution.

I realize that for many it can be a daunting task to start goal planning without much direction. **The most often asked question I hear is, "How and where do I start?"**

Therefore, I created a template to get you started. Just write the goals or plans that you desire to accomplish. Fill in what works for you, then later you can expand as needed or whatever fits your style. My personal goals/plans have been consolidated into 7 categories, as a template for you to follow:

The Passion-Driven® Goals/Plans for the Year

1. **Spiritual Life**

   - Attend church weekly.

   - Read an inspirational book on a weekly basis.
     YOU: _____

   - Have quite time and daily Bible reading in the mornings.
     YOU: _____

   - Give (tithe) 10% of income to non-profits, church, and charities.
     YOU: _____

   - Pray for our troops, the poor, charities, leaders, country, and/or our world.
     YOU: _____

   - Read the Bible to the twins.
     YOU: _____

- Be an example of spiritual leadership.
YOU: _____

2. Personal Life

➤ Wake up and thank God daily for another day!
YOU: _____

➤ Pray, meditate, and read uplifting literature 20 minutes a day.
YOU: _____

➤ Smile and laugh at least 10 times a day.
YOU: _____

➤ Participate in "fun" inexpensive activities at least once per week. A nice leisurely walk or hike along the beach, lake, park.
YOU: _____

➤ A free outdoor concert.
YOU: _____

➤ Take nature photography.
YOU: _____

➤ A visit to a museum.
YOU: _____

➤ A picnic with family at beach, park, or mountains.
YOU: _____

➤ Reading non-stop for 1.5 hours.
YOU: _____

➤ Write poetry, a love letter, or thank you card by hand.
YOU: _____

➤ Write in journal.
YOU: _____

➤ Watching a sunrise or sunset (or both).
YOU: _____

3. Love Life

❖ Go out to dinner or lunch weekly with my wife <u>without</u> the twins.
YOU: _____

❖ Say I "love you" to my wife without reason.
YOU: _____

❖ Focus on the small things in our relationship.
YOU: _____

❖ Look for activities in which I may continue to support my wife.
    *   Help out with twins.
    *   Give her daily quite time in morning/evenings.
YOU: _____

4. Family Life

✓ Take out the twins to park at least once per week.
YOU: _____

✓ Continue family BBQ's, birthday celebrations & reunions.
YOU: _____

✓ Read to twins a minimum of 5 times a week at bedtime.
YOU: _____

✓ Begin to audio record the Bible for the twins.
YOU: _____

✓ Become connected with a local parent - twins support group.
YOU: _____

5. Friends/Social/Community Life

o   Stay connected to friends weekly by phone or in person.
YOU: _____

o   Expand local network of friends.

YOU: _____

o   Create Facebook, MySpace and/or Twitter profiles.

YOU: _____

o   Volunteer or lecture at a school for free about business/ personal development.

YOU: _____

o   Lecture at USC about business & personal development.

YOU: _____

o   Become a local panel member of Junior Achievement.

YOU: _____

o   Sponsor 1,000 poor/hungry children through The ComPASSION Project.

YOU: _____

6. Business Life

- Hire two personal assistants.

- Create a program to teach people the secrets of how to make, save and invest money.

YOU: _____

- Book only 30 business speaking engagements.

- Create partnership with financial authority to teach value-based prosperity.

YOU: _____

- Do two radio or TV interviews per week through year-end.

- Touch the lives of at least 1,000,000 through *The Passion-Driven® Life*.

YOU: _____

- Focusing on the bigger picture while keeping in mind the small ones.
  YOU: _____

- Delegate more.
  YOU: _____

- Become a New York Times best-selling author.

- Create a blog.

7. Financial Life

- ◆ Purchase two commercial investment properties by year-end.
  YOU: _____

- ◆ Place funds in higher yielding rates, tax-liens and tax advantaged certificates.
  YOU: _____

- ◆ Create additional $25,000 monthly cash flow.

- ◆ Save at least $200,000 by year-end.
  YOU: _____

- ◆ Save additional money in the following categories:

- ◆ Car insurance, life and/or health insurance.
  YOU: _____

- ◆ Business service fees.

- ◆ No "extended warranties" on products.
  YOU: _____

- ◆ Competitive service packages.
  YOU: _____

Remember, there are no right or wrong goals or plans for life. Do not necessarily follow my goals or plans. This example is not created to stress you out about your own plans or goals, but to have you begin to plan and then thereby implement.

What is important is to create clarity and focus on a new direction. You may have less grandiose Financial Life or Business Life plans than me, and that is okay. But you must have some sort of goals and plans in order to get your dreams out of the clouds and into action.

THE NEXT CHALLENGE: You need to put wheels on your dreams and move forward. After identifying what will motivate, inspire, and move your heart, you must take the necessary action steps to bring them into full and complete existence. Otherwise, you will continue on being a mere dreamer whose ship will never arrive.

This is one of those chapters that needs to be dog-eared because it is where you'll realize where your passions are and how to go about zeroing in on them. Work, work, and work on finding, refining and placing them into action.

Observation/Reflection: Whatever it is you do, passion and a purpose is what you value and think about the most; just as long it is a greater good that is being accomplished. It could be in your Family Life, Spiritual Life, Business Life, or Personal Life. It is about doing those things you love with all your heart, with purpose and harmonic balance.

It's not about seeking to "balance" multiple plates at the same time and saying to yourself or others: "it's okay, I'm doing fine." Then going back to the insanity of keeping the plates spinning so they don't come crashing down on you!

≈

<u>Celebrate</u>

Life Success Grows from
Each Small Triumph,
Each Small Milestone,
Each Small Wind of Change,
Each Decision to Move Forward ---
Each Storm ---
If You are Patient,
Positive,
Diligent, and
Productive,
Your Success and Achievements
Shall Blossom Before You
So You Can Celebrate Them...

CHAPTER SIXTEEN

The 2nd Secret: The Power of Self-Worth, Acceptance & Embracing Achievements

---

It is difficult to make a man miserable
While he feels worthy of himself,
And he claims a closeness
To the great God who made him.

~ Abraham Lincoln

The Secret to Embracing Your Greatness. Believe you are special and embrace it! Don't let anyone tell you otherwise. Don't let that *inner voice*, which we all have, attempt to convince you otherwise. You may think to yourself, "But I do not feel I have done anything worthy in my life so far."

You may have had a terrible upbringing and had parents, family, friends, acquaintances, and teachers who instead of cheering you on with your dreams and aspirations put you down every chance they could. Told you to "get real"; it's not your fault that happened, after all they put you down because they themselves were dream-killers rather dream catchers. They killed off their aspirations and dreams and saw to it as their appointed mission in life to spread the misery and discontentment as long as they could and as far as possible.

So, if that is you, I feel have empathy for your feelings of inadequacy and low self-worth as I had some people in my life as I grew up that fit that mold. However, you can become a better person and unleash a new you.

Now is the time, now is the place and NOW is the moment to stop all that *inner chatter* and move on to a new phase and a new you. You have greatness within your soul waiting to be tapped into as you dig for the gold hidden in your soul. Let it flow and let it go.

➔   **Believe it:** <u>You</u> **have already achieved great things in your life.**

Perhaps you have not achieved everything you set out to accomplish in your life. So what... Keep at it. I doubt very few of us are those alleged "super-achievers" who go around believing and bragging that they have fully accomplished everything they set out to do.

I seriously question that. I am sure if we sit down with them there will be an area or two in their life they feel is void of some form of accomplishment. However, at least I give them credit for having a positive attitude. They believe and operate as if they have indeed accomplished great things in their life. Apply that lesson to your life.

➔ <u>You</u> **have accomplished worthy things.**

What about those who perhaps have not achieved everything they set out to accomplish initially and who encountered setbacks along the path of life, and feel as if nothing at all was accomplished?

Continue to dream, gain clarity, learn, grow and choose divine destiny and forge ahead with passion on your own life journey. Keep at it. Be committed to your success, committed to happiness in your life, committed to making the best out of the worst possible situations. Or what about an individual whose life has gone in a different direction?

When a weary and beaten Britain faced apparent defeat by Nazi Germany during World War II, it was Winston Churchill who rallied the country to face down the enemy. He inspired a country with these famous words, "Never, never, never, never give up!" Let that mantra be yours for your dreams and aspirations.

Take some time to reflect, embrace and appreciate things you have done. Celebrate the small accomplishments and victories in life so far. There are many, if you stop to think about them.

Sit down and think about it yourself and take in all the unnoticed deeds of service, kind acts of humility, encouragements given, the love given someone unconditionally, and the obstacles you have faced and overcome in your life. Some of them may, perhaps, not seem like large or obvious accomplishments to you at first, but when you think about it them, you'll see that they are. Perhaps you have:

- Lived a life of simple living, simple loving and simple caring.
- Continued on life's journey towards fulfilling each goal and dream you have.

- Expanded your personal and educational horizons by reading.
- Made it a point to bring a smile to someone's face as often as you can.
- Impacted people in a positive way through encouraging words, support, and love.

You have without a doubt achieved great things, so embrace them as accomplishments. So take the time to write each and every major one down in the *Passion Life Journal*™ and celebrate each and every one of them. Treasure them.

➜ You **have achieved great things.**

Every time you have shared a kind word, smiled at a stranger, assisted someone in need, or gave to the needy of your time, and every time you overcame some sort of adversity or roadblock along the path of life, you have accomplished great things. Every time you felt as if sometimes you were that little mouse on a wheel going round and round without arriving anywhere or having no direction at all, but never gave up and stepped off the wheel in search of something better, you have accomplished great things.

Each day, each week, each month, each year, and each decade has been a gift from God, and an opportunity to create joy around you. Know that your actions have impacted the lives of those around you and the world is a better place because of your participation in each of the lives you have touched during the life you have lived so far.

➜ You **have achieved great things.**

Have you had moments where you were felt less than brilliant? Of course you did. We all have been there. We are all human and face adversity and moments of stress and indecision. The difference is that those who accomplish more things in life deal with them appropriately and move on. We learn from our experiences, grow as individuals and do our best with the life given us. That's all that can be expected of anyone.

The 3rd Challenge. What will you do with the next few weeks, few months and year that will make a difference in your life, as well as the lives around you and our world? It is up to us to make the best of our remaining time so that our impact is felt.

How will you impact those around you? How will you make your world a better place? What actions will you take to create legions of small victories that add up to major accomplishments?

My second challenge for you is to have you "get outside of your head." Stop all the negativity that resides there. What happened in the past, happened, okay? Move on. No amount of going over it is going to change anything or the outcome. It's done. Look ahead, not behind! Just believe you are a person possible of making a difference.

➔ You have achieved great things.

Therefore, reflect on the fact that you have accomplished great things in life. Just like George Bailey in the movie *It's A Wonderful Life,* your own life has had an influence on many people so far. Your worth in life is measured in the moments of imagination, inspiration, motivation, and dedication and impact to others around you. Embrace the idea that you stand ready, willing and able to accomplish far more ahead of you as you create a life driven by passion and purpose.

Gladly appreciate the moments of accomplishment. Yearn to create even more abundant living in your life. For starters, learn to be appreciative of the moments in which you did make a difference.

The Passion-Driven® Life allows us to define our lives not by the amount of breaths we draw in, but by those moments in which we deeply breathe each breath as if it were our last, and appreciate them; and by those moments of life we create while passionately living, that taken together will indeed take our collective breath away.

➔ You have achieved great things!

Embrace the power and strength that comes from feeling good about you. After all no one else is going to do it better than you! By increasing your personal strength, you become more aware of the great power to transform your life that lies within you. God has placed it there and it's time to release it. When Job, the biblical character, lost his entire wealth and his entire family he could have easily lost all his faith in God and thrown the world's largest pity party. Yet, we see by his example that he kept his faith in God. We need to do grow stronger spiritually when pain and hard times invade our life. To grow spiritually is to actually become more aware of who you really are and be in a much better position to get what you want and go where you want to go.

How to Unleash the Power of Self-Worth & Tap into Your Greatness

1. Appreciate who you are, your positive strengths, talents, aspirations for life and what you already have.
2. Weekly, if not daily, make it a point to learn something new about your work/profession/industry (business/work life), the personal improvement arena/your hobbies (personal life), relationships life, spiritual life, politics, etc. Knowledge is not only important to planning and action for your dreams but is a key component of overall confidence. Remember, "A mind is a terrible thing to waste."
3. Each day write down three things you did well in whatever key area of life.
4. Each day work on two small or large things you can do to build your confidence and boost your self-esteem in a key area of life you feel lacking or requiring some work.
5. Don't be afraid to take calculated risks. It not only is part of action, but allows us to be confident about our decision-making process.
6. Pray, seek wise counsel, and repeat positive affirmations every day, when you wake up and before you go to sleep.
7. Accept that you will make mistakes along the way. No one is perfect, so let go of "I need to do it right from the beginning." If you stay with that mind-set all you will accomplish is to remain stuck where you are. Remember, "Move On!"

Observation/Reflection: Accept my challenge and resolve that you are a person that has climbed many obstacles. Realize that so far you have achieved successes, whether small or major, in your life. Therefore, value them and value yourself in the process, after that keep on moving.

≈

<u>Soar</u>

The Eagle has Amazing Ability to Soar
They Were Created That Way.
No Self-Imposed Limits.
Imitate the Eagle and Soar
With Your Dreams, Plans,
Purpose and Passion in Life,
You Were Designed by God to Do That…

CHAPTER SEVENTEEN

The 3rd Secret: The Power of Abundant Life Success

But those who hope in the Lord
Will renew their strength.
They will soar on wings like eagles;
They will run and not grow weary,
They will walk and not be faint.

~ Isaiah 40: 28-31

The Secret to the Golden Key of Life. I've had occasions when there just seemed to be no gas in the tank. Not too many, but I've had them, where my purpose was clear as a bell but getting up and out of bed and staying focused seemed hazy. Where you find your dreams and your passion, you will find your purpose.

The equation for life success is simple: dreams + passion = purpose. Passion for me is the E=mc2 for living life. So my question is, "What drives you?" A passion for what we do and want to become is central in executing our purpose in life. It is where a perfect harmony exists and things are accomplished. It is where purpose unites with passion in the mission to go from having an okay life to a wonderful life, and to the next level!

That is why purpose can sometimes devoid and dull. Passion fires me back up. I look at what moves me, what defines me and what can I can do that makes my time fly by? The passion that we bring to our purpose in life is the perfect combo. The jet fuel for the plane!

Passion is the source and power of abundant life success and is what calls things into existence in our life; passion places in motion the things you must do to fulfill and live life with purpose. Passion when united with our purpose, allows us to believe in our cause and in our potential.

Passion is a fusion of our purpose, our values and ethics, and our dreams and goals that meet in the middle. The following will visually illustrate this:

Desires and Goals

Passion-driven individuals are empowered in their thinking, planning and action towards their goals. They act from a place and a mind-set of abundance in the universe, not scarcity. They act and believe in the abundance of love, an abundance of wealth, and abundance in sharing it all.

Passion-driven individuals are aware of their desires and goals and make no excuses about their passion to achieve them. They live in harmony with God's laws, happy in what they do and fulfilled in *The 9 Key Areas of Life*™.

They are not complacent, though fulfilled, continuously moving forward towards accomplishing more dreams (small and big), and creating new goals, and being of service. Be in action as well as motion.

In short, the passion-driven individual does not think in terms of "lack", rather from a perspective of accepting what they have and looking to make it better. They think from a perspective of values and seeking ways in which to fulfill a purpose, and loving every moment.

The passion-driven are aligned in the implementation of their purpose with a value system. The values are intrinsically moral values --- such as goodness, being of service, being productive, being empowered, sharing in love, and having empathy. There is an embodiment of integrity in what they do. They value themselves and lives of others. They combine passion with a values based purpose and unleash it upon the world with such a force and impact that it will leave a trail of accomplishments. How can I do that? Follow the path of the cycles of life.

> *We are living at a time when creeds*
> *And ideologies vary and clash.*
> *But the gospel of human sympathy is*
> *Universal and eternal.*
>
> ~ Samuel Hopkins Adams

The Cycles of a Passion-Driven® Life

There is a universal cycle of how passion can take hold in your world: *Love* gently plants and sows the small seeds of *Hope* in our lives. *Hope* lovingly waters the seeds of our *Passion*. In turn, it blossoms into a *Purpose*. Then purpose blooms forth with much more vigor, direction and strength. It is passion that sprouts the eternal hope in us, an abundant meaning and a fulfillment. Passion spreads across the canvass of our life and plants more seeds of love. The cycle goes onward.

Love is an original creation from God that is entrusted for us to plant, cultivate, and spread. If we fall short in that mission, we have failed at life. The missing ingredient in the cycle of life, for most, is love (i.e. passion). For those that doubt constantly, have destructive thoughts, pessimistic and self-defeating attitudes, there is no doubt a lack of love and a lack of passion. Love then is a key to attaining acceptance and achieving self-esteem. To love others, we must first love ourselves. A lack of that inner love and acceptance is a major basis for a lack of purpose. We must first possess love, hope and passion in our lives before we can delve into what our purpose is. Unless that occurs, we can never set the cycle in motion.

As you unite your dreams and passion and create a purpose, and move towards spiritual and life abundance it is important to measure your progress along the way. Here are some questions that will allow you to do that:

1. What results or dreams have you accomplished thus far?
2. What habits or tasks do you need to change to obtain better results?

3. Are you now healthier, wiser, and more spiritually grounded than before?
4. Are you now wealthier than before?
5. Are you winning at life, losing or barely holding your head above water?
6. What results are you committed to achieving by year's end?
7. How have you grown in heart, mind and spirit throughout the process?
8. What pending issues need to be addressed in your life for you to continue?
9. Are you pursuing what's most important on a daily basis?
10. What holds you back from massive action or keeps your performance levels low?
11. Do you now have a keen sense and feeling of purpose?
12. Are you now passionate about your plans or dreams?
13. Do you embrace the pulse of life with passion in your soul?

Observation/Reflection: Therefore, first love God and then love yourself. That will allow the manifestation of forgiveness in yourself and a love for others. Then respect, self-esteem and self-worth can emerge. Only when that happens, can the cycle of a passion-driven life begin for you and you can fully experience abundance.

In a Hurry

Do Not Look To Do Everything
In Life in a Flash.
You'll Miss Half the Fun of the Journey.
Relax, Breathe In, and Appreciate the
The Serenity, and
The Miracles,
That Surround You.
Live Life *Not* at the Speed of Light ---
In a Constant and Stressful Whirl of Motion,
But at the Pace and Slow Speed of Passion ---
Embracing Each Moment, Each Action
And Making Them Memorable Occasions…

CHAPTER EIGHTEEN

The 4th Secret: The Power of Imagine-neering Your Life Plan

Within your power lies every step you ever dreamed of stepping,
And within you power lies every joy you ever dreamed of seeing
Within yourself lies everything you dreamed of being
Become everything that God wants you to be
It is within your reach
Dare to grow into your dreams,
And claim this as your motto: Let it be me

~ Mary Kay Ash

The **Secret to a Life of Success.** Later I will address vision, planning and tapping into power of the conscious and sub-conscious mind in order to turbo-charge your dreams, purpose and passion. For now I will cover the powerful concept of mind-mapping for success in life and goal achievement. It is a principle and technique that has been in use since the 12th century.

It will require for you to sit down with a pad of paper and a pen. A computer is not as effective because creativity is blocked somewhat. Ideas flow more rapidly when we just write what comes immediately into our minds.

Mind-mapping opens up the floodgates of our imagination and taps into our most hopeful of dreams, desires and plans. It allows us to freely express them in a tangible manner. We "imagine-neer" our dreams, desires and plans onto paper and through that process begin the initial stages of designing them and manifesting them in the physical realm. Through that process we unleash the power of imagine-eering a game plan for action and for life.

Mind-mapping is using a diagrams to represent words, ideas, goals, or plans, arranged around a central key word, idea or dream. Mind maps have been used to generate, visualize, structure, and classify ideas, and as an aid in study, organization, problem solving, decision making, and writing. Mind-mapping allows you to come up with ways to manifest goals, plans or dreams in a connected "linear" manner and in a "brainstorming" approach to the planning and implementing of goals and dreams.

So write down the top five goals, dreams and action plans you want to accomplish. What are they? Then in the middle of the page write down a word or mental vision of what that is or what it represents. Then brainstorm from there in a circular fashion the steps you need to take to move towards the accomplishment of the goal or dream. That is mind-mapping in action. Practicing this technique along with answering the *40-Days of Passion Plans* will allow you to define and refine the dreams and passion for your life.

> ***Love life and life will love you back.***
> ***Love people and they will love you back.***
>
> ~ Arthur Rubinstein

Implementing Passion-Driven® Mind-Mapping

Some of us have no clear cut goals or visions. We have hazy dreams of what we want, but no tangible manner in which to attain them. Too many of us are stuck in the mud spinning our wheels. We labor all day at something we don't really like, work at a place we don't feel moved by, and work alongside people we don't have a connection to, or in some cases, don't really like at all. Yet, we tolerate it. We rationalize the reason or reasons why we are where we are, and not where we want to be.

How sad to live disengaged from the power of passion and disconnected from our purpose for life. We breathe just to exist, we despair at what our lives have become, yet do nothing to change the circumstances. We talk of our "dreams", yet lack the drive and dedication to place them into existence.

Now that you have mind-mapped some areas of your passion, or at least for now know how to start the process, you can begin to take the cow-webs off those "dreams." The next thing to do is to jump-start them.

A 10 Minute Quick Start to Dreams for Life

To break out from under this situation, you need to be clear about your dreams, ambitions, desires or goals. You need to analyze and inventory what motivates you, what inspires you, and what you love in life. You need to take the *40-Days of Passion Action Plan* and the Passion-Driven® Life I.Q. test ("I.Q." stands for *Inspiration Quotient*), which we will cover later, as a start to a new life.

I know that finding a passion and purpose, and unleashing it can be a tough assignment for many. Especially if you are struggling with life's daily or weekly challenges, and your main task seems to be to merely maintain your head above water. But you must begin on the path towards the process of discovery, definition and expression of your purpose and passion in life. Otherwise, you are destined to continue to lead a dreary and perhaps hopeless existence.

Some simple and initial steps you can take are:

1. Set a specific time and date to get started along your journey.
2. Get a partner or mentor to hold you accountable.
3. Seek your partners or mentor's wisdom and encouragement.
4. Ask for words of encouragement from them to build you up.
5. Believe in hope and trust in faith.
6. Manage your task:
   a. Break your dreams into small pieces and achievable goals.
   b. Decide what to tackle first that makes sense (start small).
   c. Identify one or two small steps you need in order to place the goal into action and, eventually, into its completion.
7. Share your small step successes with your partner/mentor.
8. Continue onward with other smaller goals.
   a. Soon enough this practice will become a part of your being and you will automatically and sub-consciously be able to complete most of your bigger dreams.
9. Be steady and not so swift to accomplish all at once. Learn from the morale of the story of the tortoise and the hare. The race does not necessarily go to the swift, but to the one who steadily stays the course, without being side-tracked, and keeps his eye on the finish line.

10. Take 10-15 minutes a day to evaluate your steps along the road. Are you moving closer daily towards achievement of your goals, small or big? Makes these 10-15 minutes a day dream review a "practice" in your life, just as you do prayer and meditation.

The 10 Minute Passion Quiz

1. **Are your vision and dreams in line with action?**
2. **Do you have the tenacity to pursue your dreams?**
3. **Are you willing to face massive rejection to pursue your passion?**
4. **What will you need to do to place your dreams into action?**
5. **What are your three, six, and 12-month Passion-Living Action Needed Steps (P.L.A.N.S.™) to get there?**

The Chinese believe in the balance brought to life by the "ying" and the "yang", a balanced harmony in living life. Therefore, as you move forward, have a balanced life. Do not forsake other areas of your life just to follow one single passion. You may alienate your family, sever relationships or stress your body into health problems.

You can get a free sample of how to mind-map your dreams, goals, visions and plans and a recommendation for easy-to-use mind-mapping software on the web-site: www.ThePassionDrivenLife. com. **It's a great step towards re-wiring your brain and subconscious mind for ultimate life success.**

You will find your life's vocation
Where the world' needs,
And your talents meet.

~ Aristotle

Question/Reflection: Reflect and ask what yourself, "What am I doing to make a difference in the lives of others?" In the course of mind-mapping your passion(s) and purpose be aware of the action steps needed (P.L.A.N.S. ™). Planning is critical, however, implementation is one of the most essential elements for success.

When mind-mapping be bold, be creative and without restrictions. Let your imagine flow and see what is possible and ignore what the world will usually call "impossible." That is where real genius and inspiration reside if you move forward.

The Light

When in The Process of Defining
Our Dreams and
Charting Our Course for Life,
They Could Appear Foggy;
Still Persist Forward ---
God Has a Path Lit For You.
The Haze Will Clear,
The Bright Sun Shall Emerge.
And Then You'll See
With Crystal Clarity
Your Dreams and Future…

CHAPTER NINETEEN

The 5th Secret: The Power of Digging Deep in Your Heart, Soul & Mind

---

Try not to become a man of success, but trather,
Try to become a man of value.

~ Albert Einstein

The Secret to a Life of Meaning. Living a life of passion and purpose sounds as if we simply order it and it is delivered to us. The Passion-Driven® Life requires commitment, it requires work, it requires change, it requires planning and action, and it requires that we lay down a solid foundation from the start in order for us to be effective at what it is we are here on earth to accomplish.

It requires us to roll up our sleeves and metaphorically get a shovel and dig deep in our heart, soul and mind. It is there we find our loves, our desires, our courage, our faith, the values we hold to dearly in life, and also our fears, what holds us back, our limiting beliefs, and ultimately the power to dismantle them, and place our dreams and passions on wheels and into action.

One of the most powerful nouns and action-laden words which captures the thoughts, feelings and aspirations of souls world-wide is the word: *hope.* The varying definitions for hope, according to Merriam-Webster's dictionary are: *"trust, reliance; desire accompanied by expectation of fulfilment; something longed for; gives promise for the future; confidence, certainty."* Yes, one of the most powerful thoughts and feelings to embrace in life is indeed hope. It is hope that allows passion at first to breathe and then fully explode forth with burning desire to accomplish things in our life.

I came across the following cute story from John Hampton in the devotional book *Romancing Royalty*. It puts a unique spotlight on having a positive attitude and the flame of unending hope burning in our hearts.

The Hit List

An elderly but spry lady lived in a retirement home. She spotted an older and distinguished gentleman who was a new resident seated in the dining hall. She promptly sat down in from of him and attempted to get his attention with warm smiles.

Growing uncomfortable, he asked, "May I help you?"

She replied, "You look just like my third husband; the wave of your hair, your warm smile, the look of your hands."

Now, feeling very uncomfortable he said, "And how many times have you been married, Madam?"

She smiled and said, "Twice."

Hope embraced and fully expressed in our life allows:

- Us to never quit in life despite the harsh storms that come.
- Transformation in our personal life.
- Unending faith in God's provision & protection, no matter what.
- Our dreams to be kept alive.
- Us to transfer our fears into power.
- To live life with amazing passion.
- An abundance mind-set.
- Strength to go past our brokenness and difficult times.
- Us to embrace opportunity and get busy living.
- For us to make a difference in the world.
- Seize opportunities.
- Appreciate each day as a gift from God.
- Keeps you going and going and going and going....

Values and Passion

Our core values are the manner by which we define success. They are the things which our passions align with. Therefore, having proper values determines what it is we pursue.   Values are the deepest beliefs we subscribe to and believe in. They are invariably the things that matter to us the most and a guide which allow us to make choices. They are intangible spiritual belief systems, ideas, philosophy and character traits we tend, for the most part, to live our lives by --- they form our personal core as humans. We have learned them from the Bible, the Torah, our parents, spiritual leaders, teachers, mentors and friends.

Every personal and business success story is based on internal beliefs and core spiritual values. Possessing values is not sufficient; we must possess values based on doing what is morally correct.

A further basic foundation for an effective passion life requires us to identify and prioritize the core values which we possess, and by which we live our life. Not the worth or values the media or current phase in our culture wants us to adopt, but values that call forth our best and increase personal self-esteem, self-worth and make a difference. These internal values are what give us our true value as human beings. They reside deeply within our subconscious, and are wholly integrated into our view of every day existence and woven into the fabric of our being. They shape how we interact with society.

Pursuing the incorrect value system in our personal lives can cause us to sacrifice many things around us. The unfettered drive to accumulate money is not as fulfilling as accumulating wealth while, at the same time, giving 10% to charity. Scripture teaches that us that it is the love of money, as a value, that is cause of evil; not necessarily money but *our attachment* to it. Values help guide our behaviors and decisions. Values allow us to place meaning on those things we hold dear in our hearts.

In general, the media and the world constantly bombard us with "values" that we should seek with reckless abandon: (1) Pleasure, Possessions and Power. That pretty much describes what we see daily on television, magazines, and hear on the radio or conversations, as worthy values. Anything that is scandalous or is sexually appealing creates a stampede by media outlets and internet sites. What happened to integrity, ethical and moral behaviour, and family values? Then we wonder in amazement as crazed gunmen commit atrocious crimes against other human beings.

If our lives are guided by these values as the sole and ultimate pursuit, the result is that we can end up superficial, baseless, frustrated, faithless, depressed, and broken. Take a look at the supermarket tabloids that give us a small peak into the tattered lives of so many of the rich and famous, and that proves the point. These warped "values" by themselves have no level of satisfaction. They only satisfy temporarily. There will always be someone with more money, a bigger house, more fancy cars, more cool "toys," better looks, better connections, more pretty people around him or her, and presumably more time to pursue the pleasures in life. Measure your real worth not by your wallet but by your heart.

> *We live in deeds, not years;*
> *In thoughts, not breaths;*
> *In feelings, not figures on a dial;*
> *We should count time by heart beats....*
>
> ~ Aristotle

It was Solomon, the wealthiest man of all-time, who finally came to the conclusion that to seek pursue pleasure, possession and power as ends unto themselves was meaningless. His advice and conclusion after doing just that was, "Fear God and keep his commandments" (Ecclesiastes 12:13). That is indeed the best wisdom and values to follow.

For the passion-driven, the values they hold dear are spiritual growth, family life, relationships, contributing to society via time, talents and treasures (money), and striving for a balanced life filled with laughter, love, the pursuit of hobbies, parental success in rearing educated and morally responsible children, and to interact in their daily lives so that they empower the lives of others.

Hope and Passion

Wonder where it all begins for the passion-driven? Where do they gain an initial push? Where does it come from, so that they have the audacity to dream, the audacity to imagine, the audacity to think we can actually make a difference in the world, the audacity to

think there is a better way and a better life? The audacity to believe that there is a better tomorrow in store for me? It all begins with the unyielding burning hope and passion in our hearts and souls. So *dig* deep there.

It is hope and passion that allows us to think in ways that the impossible does become the "possible." Hope is there alongside the passion in our lives. It is embedded into our DNA. It is hope and passion that open up the doors to our imagination. It is hope and passion that birth our dreams and, in turn, lovingly kindles the embers of our inspiration. It is hope and passion that never allow the flames of life to die out. It is hope and passion that fill our hearts with a glimpse of a better tomorrow. It is hope and passion that never fades. If they do, then call it quits because life would then have no purpose.

Passion takes over and turns embers of hope into a fire in our hearts. It creates a vision, a plan, and produces action in our divine purpose. There is no doubt that God placed that hope and passion universally in the hearts of each and everyone one of us, but it is up to each of us to birth the hope into the physical realm that eventually becomes our life's passion and purpose.

The difference, however, with the passion-driven individual is that he or she has tapped into their hope and is actively pursuing their purpose in life. They are in tune with their hope, imagination, inspiration, vision and plan for life. Harness your dreams to your hope and passion.

Hope is the thing with feathers that perches in our soul,
And sings the tunes without the words,
And never stops at all.

~ Emily Dickinson

Habits

Real transformation in life goes beyond habits. To have real transformation in our lives we must embrace the change we want to accomplish. We must believe in the change which we want to achieve. We must emotionally invest and believe in the dreams or goals that we have.

They do not entirely do that by themselves. Habits are repetitious and robotic things we attempt or force ourselves to do. <u>If</u> we do not bring passion to them they can become highly structured and boring routines. We must have a love for what the end goal we seek to accomplish in order to cease from being robotic.

Habits, otherwise, are mechanical motions devoid of emotion. That is why "working out" can be such a chore and tough habit to follow for so many of us, unless we develop a passion for our health and embrace the good things exercise can bring to our lives. Then and only then do we look forward to pushing our bodies week after week.

A Measuring Stick for Progress & Passions

Get "Crystal Clear Clarity" and measure your passions by answering the questions in Chapter Fifteen. That will enable you to identify what your dreams are, where you desire to be, what makes you tick, what you love, what you desire to do, and will allow you to draw out the passion in line with your vales.

Passion in life is all about achieving an appropriate *balance* between our careers, professions, goals, business, dreams and our personal lives, family lives, spiritual life, and our community.

We do not have to sacrifice our mental state of mind, physical health, or family and personal relationships while seeking success in life. I did that and believe me it's no fun. Bible scripture clearly reminds us, "What does it profit a man to gain the whole world, but lose his soul?" We must always remind ourselves in our pursuit of success in life that we must stop to smell the roses along the way.

Live life at the pace and speed of passion, where we embrace the vigor of life, not at the speed of light where we live in a constant flash from one thing to the next, appreciating very little in between.

A divine purpose as our ultimate guide and passion alongside it to propel it allows us to embrace the meaning and pleasure of life, work, relaxation, family and hobbies. We need time to enjoy the fruits of hard labor. Too many people in our modern world have pushed themselves to a brink of slavery to work and technology.

We live in unprecedented times of technological advances which have been both a blessing and a curse to our personal "down-time." We now have the capability of a 24/7 link to work and the world via the internet and our Blackberries, iPhones, laptop computers, and other cellular gadgets. They give us instant access to the internet, e-mail and social network sites that can hook us into constant interaction. Admit it, even when we are on "personal time" we have this urge to answer each and every e-mail, text message, check Twitter, Facebook, MySpace, or whatever social page you are attached to.

We are hooked on the way to the movie-theater, while at a show, on the drive to or from home, it goes on and on. That is being a slave to technology and it is eating away at our fabric of connection to family, friends and our community. Therefore, measure the level of your passion in the key areas that are important to you, your family and your overall well-being. When you have an appropriate balance and harmony among them, you will indeed be leading a personally impacting life.

Observation/Reflection: Passion and purpose are *not* "habits" by which we mold our life, but they are the values that mold our life and define how we live and act it out day in and day out. They are what move us to fulfill our dreams and aspirations.

≈

The Shores of Hope

**In Your Present Storms,
You May See Things
As Dark or Impossible.
However, the Key
That Reveals the Secrets
To a World of Possibilities
Indeed Exists for You.
Never Quit,
Never Cease to Believe You Can Find It
Have Faith That You Will Be Guided
Out of the Storms and to the Shores
Of Opportunity & Hope...**

CHAPTER TWENTY

The 6th Secret: The Power of Vision-neering a Life of Fulfillment

---

A vision without action is a daydream,
Action without vision is a nightmare.

~ Japanese proverb

The Secret to Making a Difference. Abundance, or total prosperity, is a subjective term with different meanings to different individuals. Almost automatically we think in terms of financial prosperity or riches.

But remember, financial success does not equal happiness, harmony or abundant living. Success, first of all, is a journey not a destination. To the enlightened person, abundance is doing that which they do with love and true commitment.

They feel it a privilege or a calling, to be doing that which they love -- raising a family, being in the service to others, a profession, or perhaps a hobby. They feel alive and engaged in their true potential when they are pursuing their dreams.

The blessing of the Lord brings wealth,
And he adds no trouble to it.

~ Proverbs 10:22

Their spiritual soul is filled with abundance with the blessings received from being inspired, acting out of love, and knowing they are making a difference. As for monetary abundance, it can be a by-product of the way they lead their lives, if they have chosen a line of work or business by which it can become possible. The passion-driven, however, do not define themselves by what they possess. They are not possessed by their stuff; they own and enjoy their stuff, yes. But possessed and their self-esteem or self-worth as human beings based on a car, a house, money in the bank, country club membership? Not likely.

For the passion-driven, abundant love, abundant caring, and abundant living comes from the heart and soul. For them the truly blessed and prosperous person is one who gives out of the abundance of the heart. So, they give, give, give and give some more.

That is how one moves from passion to abundance. By giving more and expecting less. You flourish when you give. You are most alive when we do so. Give of your knowledge, time, money, love, and above all, give from our heart. In the act of giving of love, life continues and the passion-driven individuals thrive in abundance.

Create a vision of where you want to go and be in life. What activities you envision yourself performing in various areas of life. See yourself being a productive and empowered team member or owner of a business or company that not only makes great profits, but does something worthwhile with the money as well. A vision will empower and allow you the ability to unleash more passion into your life. Create the vision of the legacy you desire to leave behind and the kind of life you want to live in the meantime.

We may affirm absolutely
That nothing great in the world
Has ever been accomplished
Without passion.

~ Georg W.F. Hegel

Passion & Purpose in Action

Passion is the catalyst for succeeding once we have our purpose in focus. Passion for a lot of us, has been lost, displaced, set aside, or placed on hold while we maneuver through the throng and chaos of living. Where is our zeal that we had when we were growing up, without measure or boundaries to inhibit us? The passion we had for sports, laughing, hobbies, and simple things? Passion is what feeds our soul and kindles our spirits.

Get the passion back in your life. Unleash a passion that will move your heart and kindle your soul. Turn off the TV and live again. Let's see what passion looks and doesn't look like when vision-eering takes place in people's lives:

Family Life Passion

Passion in family life is all about achieving a balance between our careers, goals, companies, dreams and our personal lives. You do not have to sacrifice your family or personal life.

I saw an interview of Carl Icahn, the multi-billionaire investor, who is an admitted workaholic. Icahn says he owns homes across the country that he has no time to go enjoy and a yacht he rarely uses, all because of the same reason: work and more work. His daily life is *consumed* with his multiple business ventures, mergers, acquisitions and next corporate decision or take-over candidate. What kind of true joyful living is this? It's not all about just the money. There has to be something more. Simple things such as having quality time with family and friends, and quite relaxation. Many hugely successful businessmen are now coming to grips that chasing money has a cost some wish they had not paid so deeply. Let's look at the comments of a CEO of a billion-dollar conglomerate on that very subject.

Can't Have a "Mulligan" With Family

Andrew Cherng is co-founder of the $1.2+ billion dollar Panda Restaurant Group. As of January 2009, it had 1,197 Panda Inn and Panda Express restaurant locations in 38 states, Puerto Rico, and Japan, and over 13,000 employees. In an interview given to Los Angeles Business Journal, for all his business success Cherng spoke little about those accomplishments as he did about his deepest regrets.

He stated that he worked exceedingly long hours in the initial start-up phase of the company and all through-out his business career, and he admits that he has *not* always been able to be attentive to his family and family life issues.

> Moreover, he regrets having to sacrifice the business at the expense of not spending more quality time with his daughters as they were growing up. He now realizes that precious time can never ever be re-captured and he regrets having to do that to himself and them.
>
> In his own words Cherng states, "...I put all of my energy into the business and probably cheated my family as a distant second... So if I were to redo it again, I definitely would do it differently."
>
> Unfortunately, life and family memories are not a *mulligan* --- a "do-over" shot taken in informal golf games that does not count against your total score. Life is a one shot deal, especially with family growing up. So do it right from the tee. And if per chance you have not, then tee up again and create impactful family memories this time.

A founder of a $1 billion+ company regrets having to sacrifice for his business and cheat his family because of work and building a company! Wow, heart-breaking for him and his family. Passion combined with purpose allows us to embrace, at the right moments, the pleasure of work, and at the same time enjoy the rewards that hard work can bring us. Work hard and live with no regrets. A workaholic is a person working hard towards a goal that may end up destroying family and relationships. Be careful for what you desire in terms of wealth. You may be sacrificing other important matters in life! Instead look to leaving behind the kinds of things that really matter, above money, and you can leave an amazing legacy.

Top 10 Things to Leave As a Legacy

The middle class, rich and super-rich strive for decades to make money, save and/or build fortunes so they can leave it to their children when they die. Immense energy and money is taken up in that task when we should, first of all, focus on leaving a legacy of love and wonderful memories. As parents what we should give and seek to leave our children, whether we're ultra-rich, middle-class or poor, is the following:

1. Love, Affection & Moral Upbringing.

2. Love God and a Spiritual Guidance.
3. Necessities --- not luxuries.
4. Affirmation, Wisdom and Support.
5. Proper Boundaries and Limitations on Behavior/Attitudes.
6. Guidance and Mentoring.
7. Respect for Others and Themselves.
8. Trust of Themselves and Decisions.
9. Appreciation for Work and Money.
10. Letting Go of Past Wrongs.

If we succeed in doing that and leaving that kind of legacy, then we would have raised mature, spiritually guided and respectful children, and citizens who are self-reliant, assured and empowered to contribute in the world.

Personal Life Passion (Hobbies)

Remember that thing you used to "love" to do? What happened to that? Get back to fulfilling your dreams and explore new frontiers and things. Try cooking classes, snorkeling, fishing, college courses, photography, reading, writing poetry, exercise, walks, scrap-booking, or writing family memories down and creating family albums for generations to share. Life without passion is not living. Get up, wake up and touch someone. Re-energize yourself with your hobbies, if you have none, then explore and create new hobbies.

With soccer practice, choir rehearsal, over-time, cell phones, Blackberries, FaceBook, Twitter, MySpace, blogs, iPods, iPhones, instant messaging, e-mail, television cable, 24-hour news and programming, when in the world do we have time alone just to relax? Take time daily to smell the fragrance of the roses.

Create rules, boundaries and limitations in your other "life" activities to be able to enjoy the fruits of your labor. Otherwise, you may end up like people I have known, or read about: dying fairly young after leading a hard charging life. Their only purpose was to live to work, with very little in between.

Spiritual Life Passion

We need to spend time one-on-one with God. Thanking him deeply from our heart about the goodness and the blessings we have. Thank God for his grace, goodness, protection, provision, and love. It is more than going to church or temple and calling it quits during the rest of the week. It is about living it daily.

Community Life Passion (Service)

This may mean not just opening your wallet. Do that by all means. It could mean volunteering at the local Y, charity organization, church group or company sponsored programs. Give back hope and help to others who are in need. Jesus said that is better to give than to receive. John F. Kennedy famously said, "Ask not what your country can do for you, but what can you do for your country!"

We are in the "Me" Generation --- me first, me second, me third. The music, TV programs and movies have glorified a persona of getting ahead no matter what. Cheat, lie, steal your way to being famous, it's all okay. Our country and world needs a new direction and change.

It is more blessed to give,
Than to receive.

~ Acts 20:35

Health Life Passion

I don't mean to be a health nut either. But take care of what you eat. We are going to die someday, but we must be responsible for ourselves so that we can spend time with family and enjoy simple pleasures. Resolve to take care of your body, what you eat and release the stress by exercise and relaxation.

Business Passion & Culture

Many companies are redefining the manner in which they take care of their employees. They share in the company culture and passion to deliver the best possible service. Happy employees make for productive and passionate ones.

These are just a small sampling of companies that get the concept that it is a good idea to follow passion and create a raving corporate culture --- inside and outside the company. Because of the productivity and synergy of team members/employees their passion invariably impacts and increases revenues, and affects loyalty. Some passion-driven corporate industry leaders are:

→ Zappos (online shoes).

→ Whole Foods Markets (supermarkets).

→ Apple (computers, phones & tech applications).

→ Southwest Airlines (airlines).

→ Ben & Jerry's (ice cream).

→ MonaVie (health supplements).

→ Microsoft (software/media).

→ Starbucks (coffee/franchises).

→ Google (internet search engine/marketing).

→ Amgen (pharmaceuticals).

→ The Virgin Group (airlines/consumer products).

→ Nike (sports apparel)

→ Edward Jones Investments (investments/financial advice).

→ NetApp (software applications).

→ Genentech (pharmaceutical/research).

→ Cisco Systems (software).

→ FedEx (package shipping/office services).

Many a corporate leader would do well to consider the positive impact and company passion culture these companies have implemented in order to be on the cutting-edge. They foster an environment of creativity, cooperation, team-building, incentives, and a passion for what they do. Companies can no longer get by on the old used up question of: "What's your USP? (i.e. "Your Unique Selling Proposition"). These companies instead have implemented the 21st Century USVP – "Unique Service & Value Proposition." I'll cover the new 21st Century paradigm in Chapter 28 in more detail and how at my former advertising agency/sales and marketing training company I fostered that environment, and successfully implemented it for our corporate clients.

The "USP" branding or marketing recipe no longer works. Companies advertise like mad. Yet, many complain that not enough prospects respond to it. And when they do receive responses, via a phone call usually, an employee on the other line more often than not answers with a so-so attitude, lacks enthusiasm and is reluctant to answer questions upfront.

A cat and mouse game ensues in which the caller ["prospect"] wants information and the employee (sales representative) is unwilling to be upfront and wants them to "just come down." The first step of establishing an honest rapport, offering service and value is side-stepped and the sales representative goes straight "for the kill" with high pressure sales tactics, techniques and strategies he learned from his superior or some weekend rah-rah event.

You give but little when you give of your possessions.
It is when you give of yourself that you truly give.

~ Khalil Gibran

That is not value based sales nor having an ethical passion-driven business practice. At the advertising agency I co-founded, I implemented technologies and training that changed that mind-set. We created proper, effective and team-building philosophy and training from the top down. It's about passion. It's all about service. It's about rendering value. It's about up-front integrity. No one minds a business making a profit, so stop the games.

Our clients were the leaders in their industries ranging from healthcare, to insurance, to finance, and consumer products. The results were obtained based on identifying core values, quality products & service being offered, company passion, and purpose, and uniting them with service and value given to the public. Happy and informed prospects make for good customers which, in turn, make for happy and loyal repeat customers. Change the paradigm of business from mere greed to service, passion and value, and we change the end results in profitability.

> *What our age lacks is not reflection,*
> *But passion.*
>
> ~ Soren Kierkegaard

Observation/Reflection: We must be passionate about our own personal lives, our personal relationships and the legacies we leave behind. It cannot be just about how much of an inheritance we leave, but the lasting loving memories imbedded in the hearts of the lives we have touched by our living life. Discover your passion and turn that into abundant living.

In organizations, we must be passionate about results and connecting to the client's needs. A passion for service and value can lead into a profitable company that lives and fosters a values based capitalism where everyone wins.

<u>Seeds</u>

To Produce Results,
We Must Plant
Seeds of Preparation
Prayer, and
Persistence.
Water Them Daily
With Buckets of Faith,
Love, and
Patience.
Those Seeds Will Bloom Into
A Thing of Beauty,
And Reflect a Life Well-Lived…

CHAPTER TWENTY-ONE

The 7th Secret: The Power of Spiritual Abundance - A Mind to Soul Connection

---

All men dream, but not equally.
Those who dream by night,
In the dusty recesses of their minds,
Wake in the day to find that it was vanity;
But the dreamers of the day are dangerous men,
For they may act on their dream
With open eyes to make it possible.

~ T.E. Lawrence

The Secret to Keep You Going Daily. The journey to living an engaged life of passion, hope and purpose requires work. It requires action on our part. It requires ceasing to operate in life as a victim. It requires us to disengage from the negative dialogue we have in our brains.

You must empower your inner spirit. Go to the one place of refuge that is constant and never changing when you are in times of doubt: God. Continue that connection through prayer, meditation and reflection. Also do that by working in your inner self.

I will keep a smile on my face and in my heart,
Even when it hurts today.

~ Og Mandino

Therefore, the best way to measure and prove to yourself that you are capable of success and attaining goals is to create a record of your successes. You need to create a mind-to-soul connection, and that can be done with a *Success & Passion Living Journal.*

Success & Passion Life Journal

1. <u>Write, record or videotape your successes</u>. **In each of those moments when you feel empowered, accomplished, hopeful, happy, in control, successful and passionate in a particular area of life you are celebrating. Remind yourself why you are in that state of thought and feeling.**

2. **Explain what it was that you did in order to accomplish what you did. What you overcame from your past, the obstacle(s) that were initially in your way, and what you did to overcome them to get to arrive at the celebratory stage you are in.**

3. **Enjoy and embrace the feeling of that moment. Remember to give thanks to God and all others that allowed and/or assisted you in your success.**

Place this record of triumph and success in a handy place as you will need it for the future. This is a written or audio journal of you moving towards accomplishment. If you prefer, you can write the same exact feedback in a traditional journal format. The point is to have something to boost you up when you are down.

Now when you have those moments when you feel all is not going well feel dejected, frustrated, depressed or hopeless, get a hold of your journal and read or hit the "PLAY" button. As you read or hear thoughts and feelings you memorialized, sit down and let it all sink into your brain and inner core of your soul. I promise you it will be as if a different person is speaking to you or who wrote those words.

You may not recognize the power and enthusiasm that is coming from you, as your ears hear the positive words or read the lines that bring forth possibility. I promise you that it will put a different perspective on how you will view the down moments. You will see yourself as a doer, a victor, a success, and a person who can do anything you set your heart and mind to. You will see success as a long journey in life but with a few bumps in the road. Once you get that concept, then you can allow the down times to exist, but briefly in your life, as you move ever forward with renewed hope.

Now you will be able to understand that the moment(s) of being down and feelings are only temporary, only if you let them be so. You are a conqueror and victor. You can accomplish all things with God's mighty help. You must realize that you are the key element in you leading the type of life you dream about. Have hope and desire to pursue passion in life and scale those "mountains" of challenges that will come up.

Summits of Life

They call them the "Seven Summits" --- the highest mountain peaks of the seven continents. "Summiting" them, or climbing to the very top, is regarded as the prime mountaineering challenge. They represent well-known names like Mt. Everest, Mt. Kilimanjaro, Mt. McKinley and Mt. Aconcagua, among others.

You may have seen programs on television about the rough training required in order to climb, for example, Mt. Everest; and the sacrifices and pain endured by those that attempted. Whatever it may be, we are all pretty much familiar with some of the Seven Summits. To us, climbing these mountains is an incredible feat and something beyond comprehension. It is the "Iron Man" competition of mountain climbing.

The training is arduous, excruciatingly demanding and lonely. The days are long, cold and cruel when you are at 20,000+ feet. The obstacles are known but impossible to control. Weather can change in a moment's notice and turn a day of well-earned climbing merit into horrific tragedy.

When most people of his age group desire to live a life of comfort and relaxation, and the most strenuous activity they engage in is walking around a mall, there is Werner Berger, a seventy-two years young passion-driven individual, who has climbed *all* seven summits!

Werner's accomplishments are indeed proof that there can be no limitations that we should place on ourselves when we seek to pursue our dreams, and take the action required to have them become a reality.

For Werner life cannot be viewed from the spectrum of impossible, but possible. It is the attitude he has brought to bear in his training for the rigorous and dangerous climbs he has undertaken. His heart fixes on a dream, he harnesses the passion, and it moves the mind to action. His body obeys. Shear will-power, persistence and dedication to achieve the goal. The example and inspiration he gives the rest of us on how to live with passion and live your dreams, at any age, is quite compelling.

At the end of my interview, Werner proudly informed me that he had begun re-training for a second summit attempt of Mount Everest to take place within a few years!

Now that you can see there are very few limits to your dreams, keep that in mind when you journal your successes. You will find that the *Success and Passion Living Journal* exercises are extremely helpful to pick your spirits up and prime you for the next challenge, the next mountain to climb. As you climb higher over each obstacle and summit each moment of life.

Observation/Reflection: What are the "mountains" facing you in life that you need to summit? Are they, at first glance, impossible for you to climb? Rearrange and rid yourself of the self-limiting chatter about being "too hard", being "too old", or "taking too long."

If anything individuals like my sister, Werner Berger and Dick and Rick Hoyt teach us is that life holds endless possibilities to unleash our passion, our talents and our dreams, if we only open our mind and hearts to do so. The point is: it's all possible when you believe it to be so and begin to do something about it.

<u>Embrace</u>

**Passionate Living
Involves Many Things ---
One of Them
Is Embracing, Accepting and
Celebrating Who You Are,
The Blessings Received,
And Your Achievements...**

CHAPTER TWENTY-TWO

The 8th Secret: The Power of Persistence -
Being the Energizer Bunny® of Life

Nothing in the world can take the place of persistence.
Talent will not...Genius will not...Education will not...
Persistence and determination are omnipotent.

~ Calvin Coolidge

The Secret Alchemy for Life Success. Persistence is one of the crucial elements of success. You must adapt the capability, mind-set and heart-set to keep on going past your difficulties without ceasing. You must persist! Education is and can be important in life; however, truthfully by itself it is no automatic indicator of success. In my business career I've found out that **I.Q tests ("intelligence quotient") generally do not equal success** *at all.*

There are indeed many who do not possess a college degree. They possess, however, that certain tenacity, drive and will-power to be creative, search and to find the answers to challenges that confronted them. An inspiration that bubbles up from a spring of passion and hope; they in turn lead others by inspiration, persistence and dedication.

All dreamers, accomplished and highly successful people have one thing in common: a high passion and "Inspiration Quotient." They are not necessarily the most educated, talented or gifted, but they have the capability to attract success to their lives.

Passion-driven people see life differently. Where the world sees pessimism, hopelessness, and failure, they see opportunity, hope, and dreams. Their imaginations are not limited by physical or financial constraints they may have.

Genius is 1% inspiration,
And 99% perspiration.

~ Thomas Edison

They live big dreams and empower even bigger ones. They cherish every day. They understand their purpose and put their heart into achieving their goals with sweat and perseverance. They just keep on going like that Energizer Bunny® commercial where "it just keeps on going, and going, and going...." Do the same in your personal and business life. Have it be said of your life that you never gave up nor lived with life full of excuses --- no matter what came your way. The passion-driven are inspired and inspiring by what they do and not as much as what they say.

Their inspiration quotient moves them toward their life dreams and making a difference. The quotient is made up of their inner essence --- it is what drives them. They are passionate about God, poverty, hunger, education, justice, the environment, politics, family, their community, their church, or their business life. They are driven to contribute and to a balance in their own personal life.

You can make a difference in life --- yours and the world around you. It all starts small, like a ripple in the center of the lake that finally reaches the edge. Decide beginning today to stop the excuses, and live with passion and hope.

Seek inspiration. Seek to inspire others with your dreams. Seek change. Seek to implement that which you desire in life and organization. Seek to fulfill your dreams. Dream BIG impactful dreams, not meek weak wishy-washy-wannabe wishes you think are dreams. After that place them into action and go, and go and go... you persist until you bring them into reality in the physical realm.

Dream to implement something that matters and motivates others. Seek to end the "stories" in your life that have held you back. Just accept that all the bad things happened and they were there to mold you. As carbon becomes a diamond only through pressure and external forces, you too were molded into a rare gem, and it's now to embark on a new life.

> *The more I help others to succeed,*
> *The more I succeed.*
>
> ~ Ray Kroc

The essence of success is placing others before you. The essence of success is to build a bridge by which not only you can cross over, but rather so that others may cross before you do and others who will come long after you have crossed yourself. That is legacy building.

The business of living our life with purpose and passion requires undeterred commitment to our principles and a dedication to not letting the "No's" in life ruin our commitments, rain on our dreams or rule our life. Such is the manner in which our next heroine has led her life.

"No" Is Not the Final Answer!

Buffy (the name has been changed to protect her identity) is a vivacious, articulate, pretty, and unabashed young woman who has had ups and downs in her life. After high school she mainly drifted and at one point had drug use issues. She floated around for awhile without any sense of direction or purpose in life. For her *passion* was a meaningless word.

Years ago while in Northern California she had a harrowing experience with drugs and the people who grow them that left an impression on her. She returned home and finally, sick and tired of being sick and tired, decided in her soul that she needed a life transformation. She enrolled in junior college in search of what she might like to do. She did quite well as she tapped into her inner power and God's blessings flowed. Later she transferred to a 4-year university and earned her college degree in sociology. She dreamed of becoming a teacher.

Almost two years later and after many challenges, she applied to a local university's teaching credential program. As part of the selection process she was interviewed in person. All went well and she was confident that acceptance into the competitive program was a certainty given her excellent grades, bi-lingual capabilities, some teaching experience, and her interview skills.

A little while later she received an envelope from the university. Excitedly she opened it and read the first paragraph in which they thanked her for applying and kept reading until that one line that struck the core of her heart and soul, "We are sorry….", and she dropped the letter in tears. She had been denied admission.

While most people would give up or sit around and mope, this little bunny of persistence kept on going and going. She began a campaign of contacting the university admissions officers, the administrators and anyone else she could get hold of on the phone. She made a trek to the school and continued the pressure for answers.

Buffy persisted to know the exact reasons why she had been denied admission. At first no one gave her any straight answers. She kept the pressure as she needed to know the "Why?" so that in the future she could be more prepared to re-apply there or to a different university program the following school year.

Based on her "take 'No' for an answer" demeanor the university admissions staff re-opened the application file. Inquiries and calls were made, more questions were asked.

One week before classes were scheduled to start Buffy got a telephone call from the admissions representative informing her to report to the university for fall classes the following Monday as her application had been re-evaluated and she had been admitted into the teaching credentials program!

The passion-driven live is a life of inspiration, of compassion, of hope, and of unabashed persistence --- of not letting go of your dreams in spite of the set-backs and the negative responses that will come.

Live life with purpose and passion so at the end of it you can say, "I lived life fully, accomplished more than I failed, and I made a difference in my life and in the lives of persons I came across." That is how the passion-driven measure their true effectiveness while implementing their "I.Q." in life. Be like the bunny and just keep going and going … no matter what!

Observation/Reflection: Have you been sabotaging your own success or the unleashing of your dreams because you thought you were not smart enough? Stop the pity-party! Stop the blame game! Stop the excuses! Be persistent and just keep on going! Begin the journey of discovering your purpose and craft a new life-style, a new opportunity for yourself and your family.

The Gift

**God's Gift to Us Is
Granting Life, Hope,
Love, Faith, Grace, and
Second Chances.
He's the One That Can Bring
Calm to Your World, and
Sunshine and Peace
During and After the Storms…**

CHAPTER TWENTY-THREE

The 9th Secret: The Power of Passion-Driven® Planning & Goal Implementation

---

The journey of a thousand miles, Begins with the first step.

~ Lao Tzu

The Secret to Implementing Passion. It happens to so many people. They become disenchanted with life. No purpose for living, a life without passion. They do not know how to turn it around. It feels like such a huge wall or mountain to climb. Many, sadly, choose to remain living such a life and instead toil in despair. However, you can live passionately and without regrets!

Success in life requires a willingness to stay with a plan of action. Thus, the creation and implementation of the *40 Days of Passion P.L.A.N.S.* ™ ("Passion Living Action Needed Steps") which are designed to encourage, affirm, coach and support you along to a new way of living, thinking, and believing in your life.

Here are the major components of just how you can do that in your areas of life:

- Make a list of things or hobbies that you enjoy the most.

- Make a list of things or hobbies you enjoy.

- Ask: "How you can I spend more time doing these things?"

- Make a list of daily things or activities that prevent you from doing those hobbies you truly enjoy (TV, excessive work, the internet, friends, too much sports, the phone, sleeping too much, etc.).

- Make a list of the things you can implement now, and measure within 40-days, to make your family relationships better.

- Make a list of things you can implement now, and measure within 40-days, to make your work environment a better place.

- Make a list of things you can do now, and measure within 40-days, to make your community a better place.

- Make a list of the ways in which you can serve others.

- Notice in which of *The 9 Key Areas of Life* you are most passionate about.

- Make a list of people you care for and how you can help them.

- Make a list of at least 25 goals (spiritual, love, family, health, work/business, personal, financial, social/relationships, travel, and community) you would like to accomplish in the next five years. Whether small or Big goals.

- **Make a list of at least 25 dreams (spiritual, love, family, health, work/business, personal, financial, social/relationships, travel, and community dreams) you would like to accomplish in your lifetime. Whether small or big dreams.**

- Make a list all of the places you would like to visit in your lifetime.

- Make a list of what you would have in order to do accomplish Items # 11 and Item #12?

- Make a list of what you would need, beginning today, in order to be able to accomplish your Goals and Dreams? Examples can be (you fill in what works for you):

  - Make more money by _____.

  - Save per _____ (week, bi-monthly).

- Spend less on money on items, such as jewelry, clothing, flat-screen TV's, or _____.

- Join the local _____.

- Call _____ and ask how _____ I can _____.

- Take a _____ class.

- Take up the hobby of _____.

- Learn from _____ how to _____.

- Teach _____ what I know about _____.

- Ask _____ to be my mentor so I can learn about _____.

- Give more of my _____ to _____.

• Take the things that you enjoy or those which concern you, and figure out how you can incorporate these into your daily life. Now ask yourself, if it applies to your area of life, could I possibly build a career or work out of any particular one item?

• Work from the list of things that you can do to make a difference.

• From the list of those you care about:
   a. Do something nice or encouraging for one person each day. A visit, a phone call, a letter, a card, or a very nicely thought out e-mail.
   b. Do something nice or encouraging for one person on your list each week.

• Fulfill the list of things you'd like to do in your life-time. You don't want to leave this world with the weight of regrets. Start small and locally. Then go small, then Big, Bigger, and Biggest.

Of the places you'd like to go, start regionally (in your state) and go from there. Build up measurable success regionally in your dream travels, and then expand from there to the exotic locations such as Europe, Greece, Machu Pichu, Australia, etc.

Dream no small dreams,
For they have no power
To move the hearts of men.

~ Johann Wolfgang von Goethe

The next step is, after you answer these questions, to create 40-day action plans to incorporate changes in your daily life that will begin to get you closer to doing more of those things you enjoy the most. Answer the questions over a 20-day period, and then begin to implement them over the next 20-days.

After the end of the first 40-days P.L.A.N.S™. [Passion Living Action Needed Plans], begin another 40-day action plan in which you will work on the things you want to accomplish in the next five years, then move on to the lifetime ones.

Observation/Reflection: Begin with small things or small action steps. For example, you may say, "I want to end global hunger", so take a measureable action step such as, "I will donate my time to the local food bank." Then go on from there as you succeed along the way.

Ask

At Times It May Feel
As If Chaos Runs Your World.
Put Aside Your Worries,
Problems, and
Doubts.
Ask for Divine Help,
Seek Advice,
Seek Mentors.
Lighten the Load.
You're Not Alone.
Ask for Balance, Harmony
And Meaning In Your Life…

CHAPTER TWENTY-FOUR

The 10th Secret: The Power of Creating Life Attitude Adjustments

---

We must not only Act,
But also Dream,
Not only Plan,
But also Believe.

~ Anatole France

The Secret to Shifting Your Thinking & Situation. You must believe in yourself no matter what. If no way or no how are you going to achieve the dreams you have set out to accomplish. Perhaps you believe that you are "limited" in living a passion-driven life because of a lack of education and, therefore, poor job prospects. If you're like most American adults, you've already spent twelve years going to school for a high school or GED degree. Unfortunately, as many are now finding out, employment and earning statistics for high school graduates are not at all inspiring. What to do? Whine, complain and lead a life of daily drudgery, or do something about it?

There are options available that may lead you to a new career path and more financial stability. With two more years of study one can earn an associate arts degree and open new employment prospects, new passion for work and live a new life.

Community colleges, private institutions, and vocational schools offer these degrees and you can pick from hundreds of programs ranging from communications, firefighting, nursing, business administration to paralegal, arts and design. Many institutions offer online programs, a convenient option if you'd like to work while earning your degree. The majority incorporate hands-on training to prepare students for a smooth transition to a new work environment.

Feeling as if life has no passion and the train left you behind? Be bold and take the steps to recreate your life. Create new dreams,

envision the new opportunities available to you, aspire to make or earn more money, advance in your current job, begin a new career or start life as an entrepreneur from home. In life we get back what we spend our energy on. Stop wasting your time and energies on activities that bear no fruit, and direct them to making progress.

There is power when you decide to create positive attitude adjustments. Those translate into passion and purpose being unleashed in your life! So continue to make progress however slow it may seem at first. The journey of a thousand miles does begin with the first step and with the first mental mind-set changes you make.

Never discourage anyone
Who continually makes progress,
No matter how slow.

~ Plato

It is a good start if you have come to the end of the line in terms of earning potential in your existing line of work. It is not easy to re-tool yourself, but it certainly is not impossible to do. At one time in the 1990s after I had legal problems that landed me in federal prison and experienced a financial meltdown, I had to take a job paying $1,200 per month. That did not stop me from being on the look-out for ways to increase my hourly pay or to start a business. You should do the same in your life. Look for opportunities exactly in the place where you find yourself.

The skills or knowledge you gain can translate into a better paying position that you will enjoy. Then you can train yourself into saving and investing for the future, and have a better outlook on your life. Whatever you begin anew, harness it to your hopes, dreams and, above all, your passion so it will get implemented.

Or perhaps the next step is for you to start looking for a new company that has the products, services and philosophy you value. Find out what it takes to be a team-member there and make connections with someone within that organization. It is a lot easier to be "connected" in the current web connected world we live in. There are countless business oriented networking sites that enable you to get connected "to people who know people" so use them to expand your opportunities and network of contacts. Therefore, few excuses suffice for us not living a life we would dare say was passionate.

Observation/Reflection: Figure out what it is you need to "jump start" your passion and your purpose in your personal and work/business life. List them below and then, DO IT! Use the resources found at www.ThePassionDrivenLife.com to help you get started, stay connected, share your story, be motivated, and above all --- be inspired.

≈

Each Obstacle

We All Face Our Obstacles.
Sometimes We're Unable to Respond.
Don't Stop, Move On ---
Believe You Can Do It.
Act with Power, Fortitude,
Resiliency and Resourcefulness.
"Keep on Keeping On"
Past Each Obstacle
In Your Life...

CHAPTER TWENTY-FIVE

The 11th Secret: The Power of Intention - Unleashing Purpose & Passion

---

They can,
Because they think they can.

~ Virgil

The Secret to Accepting God's Gifts for You. God has great things in store you. He wants to bless you and prosper you in all areas of your life. He can only do that if we are willing to first trust Him and then be willing and able to do our part in the process.

Aside from prayer and faith, it is no secret that to be successful in whatever endeavor or project you set out to accomplish you must believe it will succeed. You must master and control your thoughts!

Intention is defined as, "Something that somebody plans to do and the quality or state of mind of having a purpose in mind." To unleash purpose and passion we must bring it forth from within our soul in conjunction with intended thoughts in our mind. Putting the two together is the difference between the doers and the "I'm thinking about" crowd in life. Passion-driven people have the capability to harness the power of their mind that brings forth the action required towards reaching their goals.

Harnessing the Power of the Mind

Napoleon Hill in his ground-breaking work, *Think and Grow Rich,* outlined the critical importance of the sub-conscious mind in shaping how we think. In essence, we are what we think. Hill stated that the power of the sub-conscious mind as a road map to reach financial success was one the most important elements in the process. There are many steps along the way as we have seen in *The Passion-Driven® Life* but the power of the mind is critical.

Your thoughts, whether negative or positive ones, are what you will manifest in the physical realm. Do you think negatively about yourself? Have low-self-esteem? Think from poverty rather than abundance? Rarely think positively about your health? Do you believe you have hurdles you cannot overcome, have excuses, blame others and situations for you not being fulfilled and living with passion?

If that is so, then they will become a self-fulfilling prophecy. Stop the limiting "I can't do it" chatter and remove the "t" from the word, and make it a bold and powerful statement of: "I CAN!" You have two choices --- "Get busy living or get busy dying." Which will it be for you?

The Power of Goal & Plan Setting

Manifesting, setting goals, plans and life dreams, as I noted earlier, does not depend on your education. It is not determined by your environment. It is only the result of how and what you think.

It is impossible to accomplish anything in life without dreaming of it, creating a vision, setting goals, and then planning how they can be implemented and executed to completion. Small or large, we need to harness the power of goal and plan setting. Goal setting is akin to the compass or the GPS for the captain of a ship. They guide and allow us to measure our progress along the way.

Every thing can be taken from a man
But one thing;
The last of human freedoms ---
To choose one's attitue in any
Given set of circumstances,
To choose one's own way.

~ Viktor Frankl

The Power of Your Sub-Conscious Mind

The one constant in our lives is that we can indeed choose how we respond to adversity and obstacles in our life. How we choose to implement passion in life as we pursue our divine purpose. The words of Viktor Frankl are inspiring and he spoke from experience; he was a Nazi concentration camp survivor.

I was, at one point in my life at the lowest of lowest times, yet I looked to the future with promise, hope, prayer and potential. My Godly inspired faith and my sub-conscious mind were more powerful than the circumstances encircling me. I would not tolerate failure, and quitting was never an option. Hardship can change your will or break your willpower. Challenges can mold you into a person of great character, persistence and victory.

We set goals consciously; however, achieving them occurs for the most part as a result of our subconscious mind. Our subconscious minds use 82% of our brain mass. There is incredible power to be tapped there.

Tap into your sub-conscious mind for faith and passion. At the same time, I challenge you to cling to hope and look to God for answers and guidance. There lie possibilities, the power of change, and the promise of better days ahead.

Your subconscious mind is one of the most powerful tools available to you. It uses more power and processes more information than your conscious mind. It can process over 400 billion bits of information simultaneously. Therefore, use it!

The Power of Affirmations

You must *first* believe in yourself. Then you can unleash your purpose and passion in life. One of the best places to affirm your positive intention is right in front of the bathroom mirror every morning. It can and does boost confidence, reinforce your dreams, and allows for the sub-conscious mind to devise a plan of action to fulfill the goals.

The practice of affirmations and prayer will do wonders to unlock and unleash your potential, passion and total prosperity. It can be the turning point in how to reshape and redefine your destiny and life.

The Power of Passionate Affirmations

Create and use powerful, positive and passionate affirmations, prayers or statements which reflect your goals and dreams in life. Whether these affirmations or belief statements are about your Health Life, Financial Life, Relationships Life, Personal Life or Professional Life, they are an essential tool to re-program our unconscious minds and free it from negative thinking.

Too many people go through life with negative statements stuck in their minds. They push the "rewind" button of their life almost daily. Fear of past failures and repeating them, failed relationships, or a lack of self-esteem permeates their conscious minds, and filters into their subconscious minds. However, negative thought patterns can be reversed. Your conscious and subconscious minds can be reprogrammed into believing the positive thoughts that will help you launch a new life. Doing that along with action is the way to make your goals, plans and dreams a reality.

Positive affirmations give us the strength and motivation to focus on our goals. They are only a tool, but not the one at your disposal as we seek to move towards living a Passion-Driven® Life.

By positively affirming our purpose and passions every day, they will create the power necessary to believe in your dreams and pursue them by changing your mental mind-set, attitudes and, eventually, your behavior.

The Power of Effective Affirmations

Simply standing in front of a mirror making statements of intent is not enough to be effective in the implementation process. Here are simple steps to making your affirmations more effective. Ask yourself, *"What do I want to create in my life?"*

Then decide in which *9 Key Areas of Life* you seek to have success, harmony, and balance. Make sure it is something you truly desire and would love to manifest in your present life. Tailor your prayer life, affirmations and believe systems around those areas of life you want to excel and improve in.

There are only two ways to live.
One as though nothing is a miracle.
The other, as if everything is.

~ Albert Einstein

The Power of Creating Context

Positive, passionate, and powerful affirmations work by training your subconscious mind that these beliefs or statements are a reality, even if they are yet not manifested or unleashed into the physical realm. Create them in the "now." If your goal is to be a change-agent for helping end hunger world-wide instead of affirming," I will help end hunger" as that is quite vague and has no action plan; affirm to yourself and take action by stating, "I am going to help end hunger by giving of my time and money to … (pick the cause)." By creating them in the "now" it will force you to begin to enact and bring into existence your plans today.

The Power of Repetition

The subconscious mind is trained and re-programs itself by repetition. For the next 21 days, repeat and believe each affirmation in your mind at least three times per day until they become a part of your thinking process and ingrained in your mind, heart and soul. Say them aloud to yourself in front of the mirror. Verbally making affirmations in this manner brings them into the physical realm and enables you to hear them and programs your sub-conscious mind.

The Power of Focus

Positive and passion affirmations need to be stated with deep conviction and meaning. When you are saying them, focus your energy and passion while saying them. Believe and embrace each and every one of them and make them yours. They are your creation so make them your reality. God brings to us those things which we firmly ask Him with an unbending faith that we will be blessed with their manifestation in our life.

Make positive and passion affirmations as soon as you wake up. Thank God for another day of life. Along with action, they are the most effective technique to achieve goals, plans and dreams. If the first thing you do every morning is pray, then after that setting your mind to positive thinking via positive affirmations, you're giving yourself the correct start required.

Focus on what you are good at, your marvelous talents, your dreams and goals then begin the process of affirming your thoughts about them. Here are some examples of positive affirmations to get you started. You can tailor them to fit your style as you progress along or create additional ones:

- I create passionate abundance in what I do.
- I am financially abundant.
- I am abundantly happy.
- I am abundantly blessed in everything I do.
- I am engaged in all areas of my life.
- I have/will have people around me that will assist me.
- I have/will have connected meaningful relationships in my life.
- I am connected to and thank God for all my blessings.
- I use my abundant health by being in service to others.

The wise man will make more opportunities than he finds.

~ Francis Bacon

The Power of Soul Acceptance & Mind Manifestation

You must mentally create your vision. Learning how to visualize is an equally important step in getting the most in *The 9 Key Areas of Life*. Visualization is an essential concept for you to live passion-driven. It will allow you to create and envision the opportunities you will create.

Then after asking, you must be ready to accept the blessings in your soul that God will allow to flow to you in the areas of your life you are seeking change. They do not all have to revolve around more money.

Look at all the relationships, balance, happiness, joy and fulfillment you can create by transforming your way of living life.

You must harness the visual aspects of your dreams and goals for them to come to reality. Painting or envisioning in your mind a vivid picture means blocking everything else out, no distractions.

Many people think that they can just say or think, "I want that" and expect it to happen. If you don't focus your vision and harness that emotional energy you'll have a hard time getting the things you desire out of life. Think with the end in mind. How successful, for example, will you be? How will your relationship(s) with _____ improve? How will you create a legacy?

Start out by creating a vivid picture in your mind of you *already* having achieved your goals. Many people will make the mistake of not being specific enough. Get detailed with what you visualize and dream. Feel the experiences, the moments of success and the benefits that the dreams fulfilled will mean in your life, and the joy they can bring to others in the process.

Make your visualizations *very* specific, not generic. If your passion is to start your own business, then visualize in your mind the exact name of the company, the business location, the types of services or products marketed or offered, the capital required, how you will obtain it, the product pricing, and gross and net profit margins, the target market, how many employees required, and so on.

You have to focus on visualization and repeat the process at least once a day for a minimum of 10 minutes. As you get more comfortable with the process, you can increase the time you dedicate to this important exercise. The more frequently you use the power of visualization the more the ideas will sink into your mind and manifest into the physical world.

The Power of Physically Creating Your Vision

Jack Canfield, the co-author, along with Mark Victor Hansen, of *Chicken Soup for The Soul®* series states that visualization is the key to our achieving the goals and dreams we have been drawn to accomplish. The easiest way to do that is to create a physical "vision board."

As we have seen, mental visualization is crucial to our success and essential for balanced living. The next step is even more important: A <u>physical</u> <u>creation</u> of your mental visualization. Something that daily you can look at to keep you focused on your goals and dreams.

Peggy McColl, one of my mentors, is a N.Y. Times best-selling author. She imagined she would be on that the New York Times best seller list *before* it occurred. She went online and made a copy of the N.Y. Times logo and placed it on the cover of her book, copied, printed and placed it in a placard next to her bed. It was a daily reminder to her of what would be in the future. I did something similar with *The Passion-Driven® Life.* I envision it becoming a N.Y. Times best-seller and being a catalyst to deeply impact individuals lives worldwide. It's an audacious goal alright. That is how the passion-driven create useful and powerful physical vision boards to propel their goals and dreams.

The best and easiest option is to go online to either Yahoo® or Google® and search under "images" those items you want for your vision board. Create an electronic vision board on your computer or laptop that will physically display the goals and dreams that are your passions. I suggest you start with the following images:

- A picture of yourself! Loving yourself is a key to living harmoniously.
- The exotic places you will visit for pleasure and relaxation.
- The names or types of charities you will donate your time and money.
- A picture that will reflect what type of home you desire to live in.
- A picture of the city where you dream of living in.
- An image of what your dreams signify. For example, travel destinations, spiritual relationship with God, financial stability and abundance, work environment, business, relationships, love life partner, and children.

A vision board must be specific. Think of it as is if you were standing with a bow and arrow and looking straight ahead at a target. You see the middle of the "bulls-eye" target. It guides you and lets you know what to literally aim for. The same is for the vision board.

However, keep in mind that it needs to be balanced. Being passion-driven is not all just about you making money! There is more to life than just aiming for that. To help you get started here are some suggestions to include on your vision board:

- Images of family reunions, laughter, and celebrations (Family Life).
- Images to represent the children/grandchildren you desire (Family Life).
- Image(s) to represent the spouse you have or will have (Love Life).
- The ideal profession/work you will prosper in (Business/Work Life).
- Realistic image to represent your fine-tuned physical body (Health Life).
- Image of place of worship and relationship with God (Spiritual Life).
- Image(s) of the hobbies you will enjoy (Personal Life).
- Images of the charities you will contribute to (Community Life).
- Images representing relationships you will enjoy (Social Life).
- Images of savings, retirement and investment portfolios (Financial Life).

If you wish success in life, make perseverance your bosom friend,
Experience your wise counselor,
Caution your elder brother,
And hope your guardian genius.

~ Joseph Addison

Observation/Reflection: What affirmations in your life do you need to begin to practice and place into usage? What power do you need to manifest in your life that is currently missing so that you can properly and effectively realize your dreams? What is missing in your business that holds it back from being the leader, the innovator and the role model? The only limitations, roadblocks, obstacles or walls are the ones we ourselves put up.

≈

Brilliance

For Every Dream You Have
Its Fulfillment is Awaiting You.
Ask With Good Intentions,
Believe and Accept the Blessings.
Then Divine Power Will Intercede
And Allow You to See Its Manifestation
And the Light at the End of Tunnel
As Brilliance Comes into Your Life...

CHAPTER TWENTY-SIX

The 12th Secret: The Power of Faith & Love - The 7 Laws of Life

---

Lord, grant that I may seek to be a comfort,
Rather than to be comforted,
To understand, rather than to be understood,
To love, rather than to be loved.
For it is in giving that one receives.
It is in forgiving that one is forgiven....

~ St. Francis of Assisi

The Secret to the Universal Laws of Life. The physical realm operates on laws of physics. For example, laws of gravity, laws of motion, laws of speed, etc. These laws are unchangeable. The same concept applies to the Laws of Life. If we obey them, then we can live a more fulfilling, abundant, meaningful and worthy life. We'll be on fire as we go from one victory to another.

The 7 Laws of Life of being passion-driven, which you can implement and practice on a daily basis, are:

1. The Law of LOVE

STEP: Place hands on your heart.
   ... LOVE with all your heart:
      ... First God.
      ... Yourself.
      ... Then, others in the world.

2. The Law of LISTENING

STEP: Place one hand on your heart and one on an ear.
   ... LISTEN intently with all your heart then with your ears:
      ... To God and His wisdom.
      ... To others and their wisdom.
      ... To your heart and your spiritual wisdom.

3. <u>The Law of LEARNING</u>

STEP: Place one hand on your temple.

    … LEARN with your mind and your open heart:

        … From all successes (yours & others).

        … From divine wisdom (God's, mentors and trusted friends).

        … From failures (yours & others).

There is more hunger for love,
And appreciation in this world,
Than for bread.

~ Mother Teresa of Calcutta

---

4. <u>The Law of LETTING GO</u>

STEP: Extend both hands out with palms up.

    …. Release and LET GO:

        … Of your "baggage" (failures, disappointments, hurts).

        … Of your vulnerabilities.

        … Holding on tight to your money.

        … All the love you have. Don't hold back.

5. <u>The Law of LETTING IN</u>

STEP: Take open palms/hands and bring them to your heart.

    … LET IN:

        … The abundant love the world will return.

        … The abundant help the world will give.

        … The acceptance of you as a person.

6. <u>The Law of LEGACY</u>

STEP: Return one hand to your heart and one to your temple.

    …. As you CREATE LOVE and PASSION, Ask:

        … What have I done to contribute today?

        … What am I doing to create better relationships?

        … What am I doing to make the world a better place?

        … Am I making a difference?

7. <u>The Law of LIVING</u>

STEP: Raise both hands up in the air in victory!

Life is a truly journey if lived fully with passion and purpose which will allow us to:

… Love.

… Make a difference.

… Celebrate.

… Enjoy.

… Connect to God.

… Connect to others in our life.

… Create treasured memories.

… Cherish the special moments that move us.

… Cherish the breaths of life.

… Leave a legacy.

… Give back more than we received.

… Learn from our triumphs.

… Learn from our downfalls.

… Pass on these lessons to the next generation.

… And say: "I learned, I loved, I wept, I laughed and, above all, I lived."

Sow a thought, and you reap an act,
Sow an act, and you reap a habit,
Sow a habit, and you reap a character,
Sow a charachter, and you reap a destiny.

-Anonymous

<u>Observation/Reflection</u>: Write out the 7 Laws of Life and place them in a location where you can find them so you can remind yourself to use and implement them on a daily basis. That, along with your P.L.A.N.S. exercise, will move you into the realm of living a passion and purpose driven life.

≈

<u>An Amazing Life</u>

A Passion-Driven® Life ---
Is About Expressing and Demonstrating
Love in All We Do and Those We Know.
A Passion-Driven® Life ---
Is About Being Authentic and Magnetic.
A Life of Purpose ---
Is About Enlightenment,
Spiritual Abundance,
Destiny.
Unite Your Passion and Purpose, and
Make Your Life Amazing…

CHAPTER TWENY-SEVEN

The 13th Secret: The Power of Harmony in Life Success & Financial Success

---

Life is a game.
A serious game.
You do your best.
You take what comes.
And you run with it.

~ Anonymous

The Secret to Life Balance & Harmony. There is no doubt that life in general is best summarized as a journey. We have a start (birth) and we have a finish line (death). After all, each and every one of us will finish the journey. But not all of us will be able to say that we ran the journey of life with passion and having fulfilled our divine purpose. Ah, that is the mission, and the intent and purpose of leading a Passion-Driven® Life.

At the end of our life, we should not have to look back and tearfully ask questions such as: Did I quit constantly along the race in discouragement? (i.e., I lost hope and had no faith). Did I run the race half-heartedly? (i.e., I had no passion). Did I just mope along the journey of life taking different paths and end up getting side-tracked most of the time? (i.e., I had no true purpose).

Unfortunately, not everyone finishes their life journey according to God's advice and happy with the outcome. People get sidetracked or get held up by life's distractions. People get disqualified because of that. Or they start out the race or journey with vigor, strength, and speed thinking they can do it all alone in one fast swoop without advice, guidance, or mentoring. Somewhere in between they stop running it (i.e., they lose the passion). And as result, for one reason, excuse or another, they die with unfulfilled dreams, visions, and with unrealized potential. They die bitter at themselves, at others and at God. They die not having lived a well-lived life. That is a tragedy.

All of us have different talents, different passions, different visions, and different values. We all have our own unique and special journey to travel. We're not supposed to copy the media's version of it. Or follow someone else's version of how to go on about our unique journey.

We're not supposed to run somebody else's race and no one else is supposed to run ours. We are all responsible for how we ultimately run it and finish it. We are responsible for how we train and prepare for the journey, to whom we listen to, or not, for wisdom and mentoring.

Along the journey there will be plenty of distractions from all around us, in front of us and behind us. Some have good intentions and empower us along the race by keeping a pace alongside and offering words of encouragement. It is a journey we embark upon initially alone; however, we cannot successfully complete it by ourselves.

No act of kindness,
No matter how small,
Is ever wasted.

~ Aesop

It is a team effort. Loving, supportive, and caring people in our lives and God are the solid foundations for it. They are a doting mother, an encouraging father, a supportive family, a trusted mentor, a confidant, or a loyal and wise friend. All these are our team members. Treasure these gems, as they will be the ones that will help you along the long and sometimes difficult journey that is life. They will lift us off the ground when we stumble. They will provide both physical and spiritual water to quench our thirst, and they will always cheer us onward and upward until we finish with both arms up in the air in victory knowing we ran the journey with purpose, with all our heart, with complete passion, and made a difference in the process.

Success is not determined
Not so much by the position that one has reached in life,
As by the obstacles which one has overcome
While trying to succeed to get there.

~ Booker T. Washington

The Secret "Rules of the Road" for the Journey of Life

Life is a journey, no question, in which we can travel effectively, with passion and balance. Here are the ways you to do that and the "Rules of the Road" to follow:

Ready yourself for the journey. Just as runners train --- train your mind, your heart, soul, and body.

Rely on God before starting to give you wisdom, fortitude, favour, and daily strength along the long, long miles that lie ahead of you.

Rally support before you begin the journey from those who matter the most to you, and from those who will always give meaningful insights to you.

Reach out to others along the journey. They want to help. Offer yourself to others who appear to be stumbling along the route.

Realize the reason for the journey of life is not to come in first place, but to make a difference your life and in the lives of others. To finish the journey with knowledge that you gave it your all.

Recognize the meaning of the journey is the love and true meaning you bring to others. Remember that there will be detractors and distractions along the way.

Refuse defeats to hold you back or slow you down. Persevere onward no matter how badly it may hurt or how hard it becomes.

Relax and enjoy the scenery along the way. Set your own pace and don't struggle to follow someone else's. It's your journey.

Rejoice at each milestone, each accomplishment or victory along the road, no matter how insignificant they may seem.

Resist short-cuts. They usually end up side-tracking you from your purpose.

Risk. Forget about looking good. Risk in life. Success and true living does not come to the weak. Therefore, leap with faith towards your purpose.

The Ancient Secrets to Abundance & Financial Success

The purpose of this book is to be a guide on how to live a fulfilling and successful life in all aspects. One area in which we strive to have that in our life is financial success. There are ancient secrets that must be learned in order to achieve financial success.

Yes, I have been blessed, worked smart and hard, as a result have experienced financial success in my life. God has shined his countenance and grace upon me, and allowed doors many of opportunity to be open for me. Even in terrible circumstances he allowed me not to lose my focus.

However, it was always up to me to recognize the opened doors as "opportunities", and for me to work at it and go through them on my own is true. You have to do the work yourself. No one else is going to do that for you. Many people ask me, "How did you do it?" Obviously, all the other steps and secrets I have so far covered all come into play when seeking to achieve financial success: attitude, beliefs, focus, vision, planning, etc.

Next, let me be clear about one thing: success and leading a passion-driven life is not defined by the amount of capital or wealth one has acquired. There are plenty of rich miserable people in the world to debunk that belief. That aside, the reason for my success and for being able to come back from financial ruin lay in clear laws and/or keys that I was taught, studied and put into practice. They are never changing and universal in application. I believe it is useful to reveal them so that you can have the keys to life of purpose and passion, above all --- meaning and abundant sharing of it.

The reason? So you can, as I like to call it, "row your own boat" without having to ask for government hand-outs when you retire. So that you can give a tenth of your wealth to charities that serve to help, uplift and give hope to humanity and the world. So you can empower your own destiny. So you can take control of your future. Nothing else can better accomplish that then to be financially successful.

Keep in mind all the principles that I have covered about balance, harmony, priorities and values in life, as one seeks or achieves financial success are a means to having a lifestyle and leaving a lasting legacy --- not to just accumulate money for the sake of accumulation. Keeping that in mind as your guide will allow you to embrace God's abundant blessings and success that He has in store for you.

The 9 Ancient Secrets to Wealth

1. Work Hard & Diligently, but Smart.

Money will flow to you after you understand that it is nothing more than a flow of opportunity and of creating value and service for others. Start with that mind-set rather than your pocket book and you should do well. It is not a function of an hourly wage alone. I was making only $1,200 a month, yet I was diligent and looked for opportunities to make a better mousetrap. I came up with a plan and proved it could work. Stop thinking as an employee and come aboard as a "team player", and a whole new world will open up to you as an opportunity seeker and problem-solver.

Of course, just working hard will not do. You can work at a job for over 25 years and not apply any other secret, strategy or tool and end up begging to receive help from the government (it then becomes the years of "golden tears" not the "golden years") or worrying whether after you retire you'll have to get another job to make ends meet.

Ultimately, realize that unless you are working at a company that has amazing stock employee participation plan and that company's revenue and earnings climbs steadily year after year, the likelihood of you becoming financially successful is much less, than if you were self-employed. Nowadays there are few 'millionaires next door' that are employees, barring they work at Google, Microsoft, Amgen, Genentech or some similar company that offers highly lucrative employee stock option perks or incentives.

Therefore, look for a way to secure your financial future by (a) having a solid 401(k) plan and (b) creating a home based business while you stay at your current place of employment.

Unless you plan for your future by working smart, not necessarily hard, you'll be a slave wage. That is not the secret to financial freedom, but a sure way to "work" yourself into oblivion for twenty-five to thirty years and up with a pittance for your worries, time, sweat, and stress.

2. Save at Least 10% of Income.

I can already hear the groans and cries of, "Oh, but I can't." Yes, you can! It requires some sacrifice somewhere, somehow. But you must. Look to areas where you can reduce or cut expenses altogether. Cut the fat from your lifestyle, your self-indulgent "extravagances", your salon or your Starbucks purchases. You don't need them for now. Learn to live without them. I don't care where you cut, but save. If you want to move on in life you need to save, without excuses. America and the world will prosper when we save more than we spend. Invest in your mind and in training that works.

After you develop the practice of saving 10%, it will be an easy task. You will perhaps wonder why you did not do it before. Later, I prefer if you save between 10 to 25% of your income. Live frugally is my rule. There is no shame in looking for the best possible deal or price for whatever it is you are buying.

The same is true in investments. In investments you essentially "make" your money when you invest. Whether it is a stock, a commercial or residential real estate property or business opportunity the rule is: If you look and negotiate frugally and fairly, then going into it you will already have an upside in built-in equity. You realize the profit when you sell the investment. Be a frugal investor. Buy when others are selling, and sell when others are buying. It's okay to be a contrarian in life and in business!

3. Operate Under a Budget/Live Within Means.

Oops. More excuses. You have to place yourself on a belt-tightening budget. The movies? No, rent them! A car? No, keep what you have. A big-screen? Nope. Travel? Not unless you've got money coming in and are saving 10% minimum already. Clothes? Go find a quality bargain store and stop trying to impress everyone around you about what it costs or where you bought it. Unless you're a multi-millionaire, change the habit. Anyway, you get the point about being on a budget.

It is quite amazing to me how many individuals get sucked up into seeking to appear to be well-off when they are barely making it. "All flash and no cash" is what I call that. Driving around in a new or newer luxury vehicle, wearing expensive and fashionable clothes paid for on credit cards, constant high-rolling it at the "hot clubs" and fine restaurants, and always with the latest and greatest expensive high-tech gadgets, jewels or watch. Wow, they sure look like they're pretty rich or well-off; however, all the while behind the scenes they are scraping to see how they can afford it all at the end of the month. They have no savings and no investments to account for their outward appearances or work.

Living frugally and yet enjoying life is an art. It can be accomplished. You can have a balanced and satisfying lifestyle; it just requires different thinking and different approaches.

4. Invest.

It is quite logical that unless you are saving 10% of your salary, that you cannot be in a position to invest in anything. Right now it is a great time to invest in stocks and real estate. Some of you can because you have diligently saved and are looking for the correct opportunities, others of you cannot because you made the choice not to.

Now I realize that there are many others who are making it pay check to pay check, and what I am saying seems improbable. However, look at options: learning to earn more, performing at an incredible level of work at your present place of employment so that you merit a raise when you ask for one, and creating an additional income stream from a side home-based business or venture.

5. Guard Against Savings/Investment Losses.

This is sometimes easy to say and hard to do. Especially, when we are now in age of so much slick get-rich schemes or you have friends or relatives who shower you with the latest "best opportunity of a lifetime." Invest wisely in real estate (they're not making more of it lately), a business of your own that you understand and can expand, the stock market with careful due diligence. Don't just turn your money over to a smooth sounding talker with nice offices. Have any questions or doubts on that? Go and read about, for example, the Bernard Madoff or R. Allen Stanford news stories to prove the point. Be the advocate in evaluating opportunities. Take them apart from different angles. It's your money and your future. No amount of "Gee, sorry we didn't see that one coming" is ever going to help after the damage has been done to your money.

6. Use the Magic of Compound Interest.

The simple explanation, mathematical formulas aside, for compound interest is the concept of adding back accumulated interest to the principal you began with. This concept is different from simple interest wherein you do not add interest into the original principal. For example, if you begin with $1,000 and compound it at 1% per month you will have at the end of one month $1,010.00. That $1,010 will then "compound" (not $1,000 this time) at 1% again and so on.

The magic of using compound interest lies in investments in which you do not touch the interest, earned equity, capital gains or dividends but roll it over into the original amount invested. For example, you invest in a stock and reinvest the dividends into purchasing more stock or you sell a piece of real estate and do not touch the accumulated equity growth but instead reinvest in another property the total original principal plus the equity return. It is at this junction that money literally is working for you rather than you for your money.

7. Ensure Passive Income.

This is one of the many overlooked concepts of becoming financially independent. There are many who follow Laws 1 through 6 quite diligently. They, in fact, become quite good at it, however, they fail to take their gains and make investments that give them passive income today or in the near future.

Therefore, they become asset rich but cash poor. They own a business, have little debt, and have cash savings in money markets and CD's that yield very little returns. As a result many are almost by default forced to work into their late 60s at their business in order to maintain the same lifestyle they have grown accustomed to.

I learned this first-hand as a bond trader and stockbroker from all of my clients who were investors in income producing property and had passive income investments. They had started, of course, small and later built up their holdings. The monthly income they received was quite large --- and mostly all passive. They did very little work day-in and day-out. Guess what? They devoted a lot of time to family, church/synagogue, community and their hobbies!

From their mentorship, advice and example I learned that one must plan for how and when you will retire, and work towards creating income from having to do much of nothing other than asset management. Remember Rule #1: Work Smart.

8. Learn and Apply Knowledge.

Knowledge is supreme above all else, if placed into action. A child sees a key and thinks it is a toy to play with. He or she does not know that it is an instrument through which it can open up doors.

It is by experience and seeing our parents use a key that we then learn the proper usage for a key. The same is true for us. We must expand our knowledge base of investments and business in general by reading, attending seminars, being coached or trained by experts, reading magazines, books, blogs or newsletters on your industry or area of interest, and by joining relevant networking groups.

Business climates change and yesterday's knowledge will not suffice. I encourage everyone I know to read and stay on top of things in general. Less television will accomplish that very well. In fact, I rarely watch any during the week anymore. Instead I focus on expanding my mind, heart and soul, not relaxing my eyeballs and appearing comatose in front of a tube for five to six hours a day.

9. Stick to What You Know, Love & Like.

There are limitless ways to be financially independent. The best advice is to stay in a business or area of expertise you're comfortable with and understand readily easy. For example, if you are not an expert in currency arbitrage or a finance whiz, then stop and think seriously about investing in a $5,000 course that will teach you how to become an expert in currency trading in less than thirty days. The promises, rewards, and lures sound great; however, it's not that easy. I was an active investor and arbitrager in currencies and precious metals. And while it is true that the financial rewards of trades can be considerable, the downside is quite large. You can lose your shirt and then some. I've seen it happen to countless traders who were highly intelligent.

This principle applies to whatever endeavour or business you are contemplating starting or buying into. There are some exceptions to the rule. There always is. You can partner with someone you trust and is an expert in the field or business arena you look to be involved in. They can be your source of information as you learn the ropes fast.

Yet, you must still be on guard and control the flow of money at all times. Even when you have experts and gurus involved, you still must be familiar with what is being done with your hard-earned money. I recall the Ronald W. Reagan mantra: "Trust, but verify", when it comes to your money. Learn, read, and invest the time to know the business. If you don't, then that is when you set yourself up as an easy target for charlatans. Knowledge is power, but so is being wise and frugal.

At the end of the day, even if you can make a lot of money in a particular position or business, you must like and love what it is you do. Otherwise you won't enjoy it and it will begin to become in your mind a "sacrifice." That is what happened to me with the advertising agency.

Balance & Winning in Life

To me winning in life is fun and worthwhile to pursue. In all of us there is that competitive spirit. However, that is not the ultimate calling for our lives. We cannot expect to win at every single endeavor. Expecting to win 100% of the time is setting you up for stress and certain disappointment.

Remember that winning always is not the purpose in life. Dick Hoyt and his son, Rick Hoyt, compete in rigorous triathlon races not expecting to win, but to prove it is possible for a physically handicapped person to compete nonetheless, as well as contribute meaning and hope to others in the process. Werner Berger scales mountains because of his passion for adventure. In the process he proves to the rest of the world that there are no age or physical limitations when it comes to unleashing passion. What matters to these people is how they compete in life and how they can inspire others through their accomplishments.

Through our passion and hope, we are in harmony with our purpose, enjoy what we are doing, empower who we touch and love life. When it is all said and done that is how we should be remembered: That we left a lasting legacy of giving, sharing, and having lived a life to the fullest extent possible.

The Chief and the Two Wolves

There's a story of an old Cherokee chief who was teaching his grandchildren about life. He said to them, "A battle is raging inside me ... it is a terrible fight between two wolves. One wolf represents fear, anger, envy, sorrow, regret, greed, arrogance, self-pity, guilt, resentment, inferiority, lies, false pride, superiority and ego.

The other wolf stands for joy, peace, love, hope, sharing, serenity, humility, kindness, benevolence, friendship, empathy, generosity, truth, compassion and faith."

The old Chief faced the children with a firm stare and said to them, "This same fight is going on inside you, and inside every other person, as well."

The grandchildren think about it for awhile. Then one of them finally asks his grandfather with anticipation, "Which wolf will win?"

The wise Cherokee chief replies: "The one you feed."

A little faith will bring your soul to heaven,
A lot of faith will bring
Heaven to your soul.

~ Dwight L. Moody

<u>Observation/Reflection</u>: Which "wolf" in your life have you been feeding so far? As you continue onward in your unique race create joy, peace, love, hope, sharing, serenity, kindness, friendship, generosity, compassion and faith your beacons of light to guide you along the dark nights that will come.

≈

The 8 Ball of Life

Life Can Be Like a Game of Billiards/Pool.
You're Playing Well and in the Game,
Avoiding the Dreaded "8" Ball.
Then a Wrong Move and You Lose.
What Next?
Start the Game Over!
The Same is True in Your Life
Remember: Never Quit, Just Start Over…

CHAPTER TWENTY-EIGHT

The 14th Secret: The Power of Purpose, Passion, Service & Value: The Next Level in Business

---

Success is not the key to happiness.
Happiness is the key to success.
If you love what you are doing,
You will be successful.

~ Albert Schweitzer

How purpose, passion, service and value make all the difference. Most people, business owners or entrepreneurs alike rarely take the required time to seriously evaluate or figure out their purpose and role in life. As a result, they rarely exhibit a passion for life and most other things. Oh sure, they have their weekend hobbies here and there, sports on TV, and a few other things, but true committed passion and purpose is not there.

In business, to be successful you must take the necessary time to create a crystal clear purpose for the enterprise, and bring forth and infuse it with your passion. No, the "purpose" of just making money is not a legitimate passion. People see through that in a flash and in today's consumer mind-set it no longer suffices. *Everyone* **goes into business to make a profit, yet not everyone in business is profitable. You need to figure out what drives your company, you, and what makes your service and company uniquely different from all the competitors?**

Turn your business or organization into a cause or purpose that people can grasp onto and attach themselves to you without any problem. People will come aboard and put their money at stake for what they believe in. They'll not only do that but also align their heart, soul and mind behind it. That is how you turn a business or organization into a really amazingly successful and effective one.

In fact, they'll immediately adopt the purpose and be inspired by the passion of the business, and will willingly sacrifice and commit to its success. They will position themselves behind that purpose or "cause" and identify with it --- they will be your loudest and most enthusiastic supporters of your products, service, mission and vision. Why is that?

Because at the end of the day if your company or organization is a passionate business or passionate organization with a clear purpose that benefits everyone inside *and* outside the organization they want to learn from you, be associated with you, do business with you, be influenced by you and your purpose and passion-driven company or organization. When it's all said and done, they get to be a part of a purpose bigger than their own. When you are capable of doing that then you are an influencer and leader much more than a businessperson.

That's why people choose to be a part of non-profit organizations that moves their heart and soul. They work hard and long hours for free because they identify with the cause behind the purpose. Imitate that in business, it's fairly easy.

The same is true of passionate companies. Both team members and clients and users of Google® rave about its technology, products and their can-do service attitude. As a customer or end-user we willingly refer them to others. They revolutionized the search engine industry on the internet. Nowadays no one hardly says, "Oh, log onto the internet and go onto a search engine and look for the information you need." The common used reply is, "Just Google® it." They created a winning business with a purpose in mind and infused it with incredible passion.

Do that and you attract amazing talent to your company or organization --- whether in the corporate arena or the non-profit world; people identity with something bigger than they are.

Next, besides having amazing purpose and passion in your business, you will need to know, accept, and understand your strengths and weaknesses, and utilize them to your advantage. If you stink at writing, then don't fool with it and give it to someone else; if you lack technological skills put aside the "How To" manuals on web sites and programming and hire someone internally or outsource that part of the business.

Too many business people want to be the 24/7 know-it-all "pied piper" of their business and do it all. Sound familiar? It's a sure recipe for disaster in most cases and a guarantee of immense needless work, stress and heartache. Your strategic advantage in business will come from you leveraging your strengths and talents and infusing them with purpose (vision and planning) and passion (execution and leadership). Purpose and passion is the engine that drives success to any enterprise --- large or small. Again, it's that willingness to be uncommon in the face of commonness. Purpose and passion separate you from the pack.

Strategic business success comes about when these critical elements are in place *before* someone ventures out to start or buy a business. Too many times people believe they have a great product or service to offer the world, yet they never have a crystal clear concise purpose and a plan. They have never devised an exit strategy, a proven strategic marketing blueprint, and instead concentrate all their efforts on the "entry" strategy --- that is, the start-up phase of the business. Then they wonder why they do not have profits cascading into their bank accounts.

Anyone can start a business nowadays, but can they make it succeed is a different thing altogether. Businesses fail because they did not properly plan, and they fail because they lack a proper motive and focus beyond cash. If you are able to win the hearts and minds of people, from your staff to customers, you'll not only be successful but you'll make a difference in their lives, and they'll thank you for it and, in turn, become loyal long-term team members and clients/customers.

When a business strategically positions itself in the marketplace via a defined service, value and purpose proposition along with strategic research and marketing, it beats its competition to a pulp. Simply put marketing is not selling; it is positioning your product, business or service in such a way that the market (consumer/ customer) desires your product or service above everyone else's, regardless whether or not it costs more. When they buy into your cause or purpose, they perceive immense value being received from you and your business. That is the true secret of success in business!

The Art of Inspiring and Bringing Forth Others Brilliance. I don't like motivating my employees, management teams, or any key staff members. It's laborious, draining, and a time-consuming process of attempting to "pump them up" on one day or on a weekend bonding trip. I have tried that and I don't encourage it.

Companies and organizations spend billions in bringing in the latest motivational experts to give employees pep talks and get them fired up. In the short-term it may work but then old bad habits creep up and usually employees go back to their routine of slacking off when unseen or not under the microscope.

The problem in motivating lies in the actual task at hand. Merriam-Webster's dictionary defines motivation as, "the act or process of motivating… a motivating force, stimulus or influence."

Motivating employees is an *external force* seeking to work upon their *internal spirit or psyche*. It's looking to see which buttons you can push to get employees excited about their company, vision or sales goals. The act of motivating them is a hard battle to wage.

In professional sports, which require a constant level of maximum performance to compete and to win championships, that concept has sunk in. They know they just can't motivate their professional athletes. It must be something else that comes from within their being in combination with collaboration that is the key to winning.

The Art of Inspiring, not "motivating", employees/team members is where the secret lies to having employees or staff members who internally compel themselves to deliver a higher degree of work quality and performance. That is how we can bring forth brilliance from employee, staff, and management teams.

Why is that? The origin of the word and concept of inspiring or inspiration goes back to the 14th century. The word derives from Latin and French combination and means, among other things, "to breathe."

Celebrate your success and find humor in your failures. Don't take yourself so seriously.

~ Sam Walton

Merriam-Webster's dictionary defines inspiration as, "an animating, enlivening, or exalting influence on; to spur on, to breathe or blow into or upon, and to infuse (as life) by breathing, and to draw forth or bring out."

Inspiration is the ultimate manner of leadership, especially in business. The military operates under concepts and rules of leadership that don't allow for dissension among the ranks. In business, dissension is an everyday occurrence and well-coordinated exercise that employees have crafted into an art form. Give marching orders at a meeting and the "troops" dutifully nod in approval, but thereafter behind your back they march out moaning under their breath about one thing or another.

However, bring forth their passion, infuse and breathe meaning into them and what the company does, inspire them from within and we have a totally different outcome. We empower employees and we create collaboration, a bond, when we work as a team. That is the art that successful small to large businesses put into practice, and one of the reasons why these types of companies or organizations will survive economic upheaval.

Inspiring one another allows for common ground to be reached while going to the next level for a company or organization. It is being inspired by the mission statement, the purpose of the company, its products, its reputation, and benefitting in the end from its success.

The early successes of Ford, General Motors, Toyota, Microsoft, Wal-Mart, IBM, Xerox, and countless multi-nationals and small to medium-sized business had to do with founders and management's ability to inspire, lead, and bring forth the best in people. It was not a matter of calling a meeting or going to a pep rally to motivate employees to make sacrifices or produce better results. No, it was having individuals realize that they were vested in the success of the company. That they were key player's not just pawns paid hourly wages to perform their job.

Tap into inspiration and you tap into creating a sustainable and successful business, as well as a great leadership model. The reason being is that inspiration taps into the dreams and passions of employees. That is how you bring forth brilliance to your company or organization.

In a May 2009 interview in *Fortune Small Business* magazine, Chip Hazard, a partner at a venture capital firm, stated that he views "the entrepreneur as the pied piper of a company." Hazard is of the opinion that when he is evaluating candidate companies to invest in he looks for an entrepreneur who is "…an articulate, passionate CEO who can excite others --- employees, customers, business partners."

Be inspired. Be passionate about your company. Be passionate about the products or services offered. Be inspired about your team employees/management or related vendors. It will become contagious. Inspiration is not phony or hype, it comes from the heart and you "breathe" it out through your pores in your daily interactions with staff, management, customers, suppliers and vendors.

When you genuinely believe that you are capable of delivering the best service, the best product, and the best quality, you then inspire others into believing the same. They see your vision and place into motion the actions necessary to accomplish the tasks at hand to bring that about. That is how you bring forth the brilliance of employees, management, and team members.

The Secret Paradigm Shift for Business

The mistake that I made with the advertising agency was that it was not set up from the very beginning to be automated nor to be run from a remote location. That is bad planning and bad design to build a business around. A big mistake which can be very taxing on your personal and family life, as it was on me. Most likely more than a few business executives and entrepreneurs can relate to that. Instead, you should design the business around a measurable quality of life *and*, at the same, look to reap the financial rewards that owning or being a part of a successful business can bring you.

You go into business to succeed financially, be in control of your life, and hopefully contribute to society by employing dedicated team players, producing and delivering excellent service and world-class products.

You did not go into business with desiring to be a "firefighter." By that I mean having to constantly put out all fires, rather than focus on the core business, making it grow appropriately, and being hands off as much as possible.

Competition has been shown to be useful
Up to a certain point
And no further.
But cooperation,
Which is the thing we strive for today,
Begins where competition leaves off.

~ Franklin D. Roosevelt

Therefore, in your business model structure seek to keep that in mind and goal in focus. What kind of lifestyle are you going to have and how can you plan and design the company around that?

Focus on being *really* productive rather than us really busy with e-mails, phone calls, human resource issues, text messages, faxes, etc. That does not necessarily bring in new business accounts so delegate and supervise that aspect.

If I had to do it again I would focus on what moves the needle in sales and leave the rest of the administrative and financial side to others. Moreover, I would have set massive parameters around my family time with my partner. I did not stand my ground and the business encroached upon quality family time. I later realized it after I was pretty miserable and knee deep in the mud.

So outsource a multitude of services and administrative tasks. Also, if it makes financial sense joint-venture rather than doing everything on your own. Remember, it is possible to have cooperation or collaboration as opposed to constant competition. We could have partnered up with our competition and eased the pain of growth and reduced the stress of massive over-work. Log onto the web and you will find a treasure of individuals that you can utilize to help you with time-consuming administrative tasks and to joint-venture in various areas of business.

This is our purpose: to make as meaningful as possible this life
That has been bestowed upon us;
To live in such a way that we may be proud of ourselves;
To act in such a way that part of us lives on.

~ Oswald Spengler

Whatever you do, set up boundaries from the start in your business and your personal life. It's ridiculous that all of my ex-partner's clients had his cell phone and would call him at all odd ball hours of the day and night, and weekends, simply because he never established the proper boundaries. I got dragged into that and made my life miserable as I wanted to have quality of life but repeatedly could not. Too many daily calls from the office and clients into evenings wore my spirits down about continuing on with the advertising agency and the business model it had been built around.

Again, more is not necessarily better. My company came within $10 million in revenue in a short time; however, our overhead was growing out of control because we decided to do everything "in house." Truth: bad decision and bad planning; my advice is outsource whenever possible to reduce overhead, stress, and thereby bring sanity and bring *balance* back into your business life. Something's got to give if you don't, and that is usually health problems down the line, and eventually a loss in family and relationship connections, at its worst.

Generally, entrepreneurs go into business to feel and be free, but not be a slave to the job or the company. How then does it end up taking place? Burn out rates and health related problems caused by corporate America and in small businesses are at an all-time high because so many of us do not place proper boundaries.

Consider and heed that advice. If you are running on empty, then face the *challenge, choose* appropriate options and make the *changes*! Remember, it's not an *either/or* world, rather it can be a world of *"and."* It is possible that you can make a great living, have a passion for what you do *and* have a great purpose *and* quality of life in all areas of life.

Passion and Business

Now let's see about passion and business. Given the current corporate lay-offs many people have a burning desire to start their own business. They want to be independent and successful business entrepreneurs. They want to own a piece of "The American Dream." Being a business entrepreneur is indeed an adventure, a rewarding experience and liberating, if the correct pieces of the puzzle are in place before you start your business. Otherwise, you trade a job you don't like for another one that consumes you almost 24/7, as the advertising agency did to me.

I have also started various businesses. What has made most of them successful has been a detail to planning, innovative marketing, great sales strategies, business optimization, maximization and strategic execution. I've learned from both my mistakes as well as my successes to figure out what does and doesn't work.

The 21 Laws of Business Success

Of course, there are more principles to business success. However, generally speaking these are the governing laws from which the principles originate from. These laws of Business Success have been gleaned from the wisdom of business sages, wealthy mentors, my business experiences, failures and successes.

The Twenty One Laws of Business Success and Passion are not necessarily in order, but in their entirety they comprise the most important aspects required to succeed with a passion in the business arena from small but profitable venture to a thriving Fortune 500 company.

1. Develop a vision, purpose and passion plan for the business.
2. Solve the problems and pains of people and you have loyal clients.
3. Seek niche markets and become its expert.
4. Identifying a problem in that niche market.
5. Offer the new and exciting products or solutions to the pain in that market.
6. Offer a unique service and value proposition.

7. Establish yourself as the authority by being original, not an imitation of others.
8. Innovation and originality always trumps imitation.
9. Give away more than you receive, then give some more.
10. Never start an interaction by asking for money right away.
11. Establish ahead of time to give a portion of profits to benefit others.
12. Deceitfulness and dishonesty in the long run equals doom and disaster.
13. Truth begets truth, and trustworthiness in return.
14. Use your personal strengths and individuality.
15. Seek authenticity and substantiate any benefits.
16. Don't just say it, prove it.
17. Strategic research and strategic implementation is key.
18. Imparting of your expertise is best when you prove what you say and do.
19. Develop relationships and trust; without relationships no products or services can be sold.
20. All major success, accomplishments and achievements are found when you join efforts and energies with others. Don't expect to be the lone ranger of business.
21. Remember that your business has and serves a purpose --- beyond making money. When you unleash it with passion the world will respond.

Most Important --- Be You.

This is not so easy to do given we are bombarded with celebrity images that reinforce our inner-voice saying to us, "We are not good enough." Don't fall for it! Rise above the noise and allow for the real you to stand out with passion. Choose to be different. Many a highly successful business people have done so.

Resolve to stand up and share the real you, then watch people take notice. Your passion for what you do and how well do it will attract others to you. Passion is the magnet that moves things your way.

Be yourself unapologetically. You have unique talents, unique visions, unique goals, unique gifts and unique abilities to offer the world. If you have a great plan, then the world, in turn, will respond favorably to you and your business. Your business plan or idea, if carefully crafted, will allow you to manifest and unleash the passion and autonomy in the business arena.

Choose to Live Your Passion & Purpose.

I re-identified my passion and purpose, and have now aligned it with The 9 Key Areas of Life™. I knew that I had the ability to write, formulate and communicate ideas that inspired and allowed change to take place for individuals and organizations. **I finally had the answer to the question, "What am I here for?" I knew in my heart that God had a plan and purpose for each and every one of my experiences, trials, and difficulties. The same can be true for you.** Once we are able to identify that purpose He will allow us to be infused with a passion for the pursuit of it. It's just that sometimes we get lost in the translation of the process. We muddle our lives with every day ordinary living and time goes on.

Do I have what it takes to be that person? Will I have the courage to define my business as an extension of that purpose and do what I was born to do? What will people think of me? After a lot of reflection, I decided it was important to do what was best for me and my dreams. Define and consider your life purpose, what you are here to do and then unleash it.

The Challenge: Get it Done and Take Immediate Action.

Remember this point is crucial to your success in business: Implement, implement, implement! Successful corporations and small businesses implement their ideas goals and plans, and unsuccessful businesses do not. We live in a time of "analysis paralysis." I've been guilty of it myself. I've attended seminars or meetings and know how easy it is to fall in love with a plan. You've spent lots of time thinking great thoughts and had the courage to put them on paper. Plans are invaluable as they provide direction and vision. But there comes a time to implement.

There comes a time when you have to put down the paper and do something, and that is simple: Take Action! Implement your P.L.A.N.S. If you choose not to act, you will not have a service, or product to offer and eventually, of course, no customers/clients. Without a customer/client, you will undoubtedly not have a business. No matter how scary it is or how tough it appears, if you have a great plan, product and service to deliver, begin the process of unleashing it.

The difference between success and failure,
Is the ability to takes massive and immediate action.

~ Bill Gates

So take the time to formulate your <u>P</u>assion <u>L</u>iving <u>A</u>ction <u>N</u>eeded <u>S</u>teps (**P.L.A.N.S.** ™) exercise worksheet and begin the process of acting on them without hesitation or procrastination in your personal and work/business life.

You Don't Know It All: Seek Wisdom.

Once your family and friends realize what you're doing, they're going to have ideas about your business. Unless they are your target market, wealthy entrepreneurs, or respected experts, just respectfully ignore them and their advice on how to run things. Love them, but do not let them drive your business plan and business vision. No matter how much they love you, they will not understand, unless they have been in the trenches themselves. For the most part they mean well, but it's hard trying to define passion, business plans or goals to someone who may not have a clue about it. If you have a great thought-out action and business plan, a great product or service coupled with a passion, then go for it!

Seeking guidance and wisdom will allow you to formulate the correct financial, marketing and administrative plans for your business. There are plenty of places where you can get a massive amount of business advice and direction from seasoned and successful entrepreneurs as well as former Fortune 500 corporate titans. See www.ThePassionDrivenLife.com for resources.

These wise sages can guide you along the sometimes treacherous waters lined with, you guessed it, alligators, piranhas, snakes and sharks waiting for any slight smell of blood to pounce on you. Dare I say that I speak from experience after having navigated such waters?

Business can be a very rewarding life. However, if you do not seek proper wisdom and advice, and have all necessary elements in place to protect yourself legally and your assets from potential liability, it can and will be a brutal and expensive learning experience. Given that we are in a litigious environment for decades now, without any signs of lightening up, it is well worth your time to seek out proper and professional advice. Build your team around your core values, core goals and core business dreams. Build your business so that it suits your needs and desires, and so that it does not suffocate you entirely and lose your life balance and harmony.

Be diligent, but also learn how to let go. Delegation is an art that must be learned; otherwise you'll find yourself muddled deep in paperwork or tedious minutia of details into the late hours when you can outsource much of it to ease your burden. Part of seeking wisdom is seeking help. I am a big advocate of, for example, getting a virtual assistant so that your time can be freed up doing that which you love and spending time with those whom you love. After all, we started out in business to give our family more stability not to alienate them with our absence from home. That alone would be a great start even if you have an established business.

Implement Courage and Perseverance.

It can be very tough in the business environment. Today's technology offers both a competitive edge as well as realization that you are not the only company out there producing or offering the "xyz" product or service. So it can be discouraging, only if you let it be so.

Business takes courage and perseverance to go on your own and create something from nothing, not to mention money risked in

doing so. The best thing you can do is to stay in action, seek advice and support from a mentor group that will allow you to make it through the bumpy roads. Some days you'll accomplish a lot, other days not as much, but keep moving in action. If you continue onward with a passion and a perseverance that knows no limits, you will all of a sudden leave trail of accomplishments. Learn and practice both perseverance and patience.

You're Not Perfect --- Accept Mistakes Made.

Leave your presumed perfection at the door. All the legends of business success we read or hear about had their moments of horror and failure. If it was so easy to succeed, then everybody would be doing it. So leave your idea of perfection at the door. It does not exist! It makes for a harder working environment and makes you come across as the ogre task master if you persist in believing that and demanding it from yourself or employees.

Pride yourself, your company and employees on a culture of doing a job well done and move on. You are in business to be producing the best possible product out there or deliver the highest quality service to your clientele. So do just that. Get things to a level of high quality and then just unleash them into the world.

If an idea or product does not work out to your satisfaction, then just test a little more and make changes if necessary. Realize that your mission is to stay in business and not necessarily to give yourself or others around you undue stress. Your business will evolve as you test what works and realize what does not. Your passion and purpose will guide you as you adjust and make mistakes accordingly. You will then be able to know what really works best.

Let Go of Control --- Just Create Purpose and Have Fun.

This is my most sincere advice. Have fun and be creative. Be always searching for ways to be different from the competition and business will flow to you. This is hard to remember when you are mired deep in difficult choices to make, have demanding clients or customers and the alligators are nipping at your heels, the sharks are encircling your business, and the snakes begin to entangle all around you.

There is joy in the process of creation. Enjoy the process of growing your business and unleashing your passion for it. Enjoy your success but do not be consumed by it. Again I speak from my past experience. I must confess this did not come easily to me, at first, after spending many years on as a bond broker and having formed many businesses, but time and wisdom learned from my mistakes taught me that it is vitally important to just enjoy it.

The Passion-Driven® Billionaire

An example of exhibiting massive passion in business and enjoying life in the process would be Sir Richard Branson, the founder of Virgin Group, a billionaire businessman, philanthropist, world-record seeking adventurer, and humanitarian. If ever there would be a great example of "just have fun while you're at it" in business, it would be Branson. He has climbed mountains, repelled off of high rises, and has multiple world-record global balloon flights under his belt. This man is passionate about giving and living, just as he is about business.

He founded Virgin Unite, a non-profit foundation, dedicated to finding solutions to societal ills such as education, hunger and environmental concerns. The driving force behind it is the belief that business can be the driving force for good and that they have the capacity to improve the human condition. His philosophy is that capitalism has solutions to the world *if* it is compassion based.

His example and lessons to corporate titans and entrepreneurs alike, which he sometimes extols on retreats to his personal island (Necker Island), is to just have fun in business, be passionate about what you do, and above all love what you do. Yet keeping in mind that one must have a purpose for doing it all, therefore, give back to society. Branson hopes others in business will catch the vision and follow along.

That is how you inspire and lead people. That is an excellent vision to have in business: focus on profits, people *and* philanthropy at the same time. You should try that some time in your own organization and see the difference it will make on company morale and productivity. Remember, it's about inspiring others towards the greatness you are building. That just might be the missing link to your company's or organization's success.

There are other equally enlightened billionaires who also share Branson's vision and philosophy of giving back of their wealth to society. Individuals who believe in abundant giving and not hording the financial blessings God has allowed be bestowed upon them as a result of their diligent productivity, innovation, and dedication. Individuals such as Warren Buffet, Bill Gates, Peter G. Peterson, Oprah Winfrey, Eli Broad, Michael Bloomberg, Andrew Grove, Larry Ellison, and T. Boone Pickens, to name a few. They all believe that business can serve a greater purpose for humanity.

There is no greatness without a passion to be great,
Whether it's the aspiration of an athlete, an
Artist, a scientist, a parent, or a businessperson.

~ Anthony Robbins

Passion and Creativity within Organizations

It is very important to understand that everyone has creative potential, and within a company or organization it is management's goal, purpose and task to foster an environment in which creativity and passion arises. It benefits the entire company or organization, and the client base they serve.

Passion allows the conditions for creativity to emerge throughout the company or organization, for expression, ideas, free flow of information, great goals, immediate feedback, a lack fear of failure, and collaboration.

The passion-driven leader treats everyone as if they can do great things. They foster an environment of cooperation and creativity among all team members. Creativity is one of the keys for expressing the passion that leads to innovation and has an effect on the bottom-line.

The Secret in Business - The 21ˢᵗ Century "USVP"®

In the 21ˢᵗ century, corporate leaders, small business owners, community leaders, and politicians should be asking themselves the "*21ˢᵗ Century USVP® Question*: **"What is Our Unique Service, Value & Purpose?" If you have these components well in hand you hardly have to go crazy selling yourself silly. Your company's solid reputation, quality and service will speak volumes and you will develop a "following." The USVP® will have to replace the old used up question: "What's Your Unique Selling Proposition?"** (USP).

Every single company is intent and seeking to sell us something. The traditional "USP" no longer sets your organization apart. For consumers it has become "Ya-da, Ya-da, Ya-da" to their ears or eyes. The consumer is sick and tired of just being *sold* things and positioning of products. Everywhere we turn there is a bombardment of TV, radio, print, internet, direct-mail, text, and billboard advertising. I know as I was in the world of branding and positioning company's products and services. People don't mind paying for receiving great value however they expect great service. The last factor is a rare commodity in a lot of companies.

Consumers and clients want world-class service and do not mind paying for it. They want unique concepts and products. Go to the nearest Apple store and you will see all the raving fans lining up to pay top dollar for the latest iPhone or iPod to prove my point.

In my consulting and business maximization series, we look at how to position a client's product and claim a uniqueness that would set them apart from other companies out there. We have achieved an amazing amount of success when clients allow us to focus and deliver a message that combines elements of pricing, quality and, above all, *service and value.*

We have trained entire organizations top to bottom on how to shift the corporate mind-set vis-à-vis its customer base; on how to deliver not only the most extraordinary product or service, but to over-deliver on first class customer service. We've trained and inspired their teams on how to implement follow-up customer-care systems and have effective customer relationships that make a difference.

A culture of passion, purpose and service was established on how to develop raving clients and on how to think and implement ideas, service and product delivery with a passion for success, and setting the company apart. The idea is to bring the entire organization back to the core of their existence in the first place.

I have trained sales and management to stop looking at the "bottom-line" exclusively and concentrate on service and quality as a way to differentiate their business. It's just good leadership, business sense and stewardship of both employees and customers. In the end, you not only increase sales but more importantly you build a loyal base of raving clients, fans or customers.

When the companies I worked with have allowed us to implement these strategies they rocketed to the top of their industry in sales revenue, customer satisfaction, and team member/employee efficiency, loyalty and morale. That's just good business. That is connecting to both your management and team members. It can happen when passion and purpose are united to deliver that type of service. That is how you get to the next level in business.

The measure of a life, after all,
Lies not its duration,
But its donation.

~ Corrie Ten Boom

Companies need to understand that great creative ideas don't just happen all of a sudden. They usually manifest themselves and appear when we encounter an obstacle that challenges us; an obstacle that forces us to reconsider our thought processes.

It is during these times of critical analysis and defining challenges that creativity and passion surge, and we get the answers and discoveries that make an impact. That is the essence of the American business spirit. Countless businesses were started during times of difficulty by individuals who were not buying into any dooms-day mentality, but instead worked on a plan, acted on it and inspired others to come aboard their dream.

Create. Innovate. Explore. Lead. Be Brave. It has given us in the last decade Googles, Nikes, iPods, Facebooks, Twitters, Pixar Animation Studios, Zappos, and so on. Harness the creative energy of the corporate organization because it most likely one day will be the element that will allow the company to survive and thrive.

The competitor to be feared
Is the one who never bothers about you at all,
But goes on making his business better all the time.

~ Henry Ford

Passion-Driven® Corporate Excellence

Passion in business is about defining what inspires you as an executive or business owner, your employees, and your organization in order to achieve the ultimate good, deliver superior service, and achieve success in your field.

Passion in business is about making your own business better and better. About excelling in areas where your competition falls short. Google did it. So did Apple. They figured out what was not working and made their company deliver quality and innovative services or products.

In corporate America, the implementation of a corporate "passion culture" has been relegated to the back burner by many companies as it has been misunderstood or misapplied. Having passion-driven corporate excellence is not about a weekend raw-raw hype event where a company staff attends in order to pump up the morale of the "employees" or a memo touting the new sales/production goals, the bonuses and/or incentives. It's hard to just seek to "motivate" employees. You must instead look at what inspires them, and show them it is possible to live, work and operate at that level.

Passion-Driven® organizations are led by imaginative industry leaders and innovators. They are continuously and actively in touch with the needs of their clients or customer base. Their CEOs, leaders, management and employees/team members all understand and subscribe to a mission statement.

These companies also know that what may have worked in the beginning stages of their success is certainly not guaranteed to work forever. A striking contrast are The Big Three auto makers who for a very long time sat back and lived off their laurels of being the industry leaders, while Japan quietly, efficiently and with unbending passion to produce excellent automobiles, snuck up on them and overtook them in categories of quality, excellence, customer satisfaction and customer loyalty.

As I have already alluded to, a well known-case of business passion culture is the massively successful internet search engine: Google®, Inc. They were founded much later than Yahoo! yet because their founders were in tune with delivering a better-mousetrap they became the market leaders for search engines and advertising pay-per-clicks.

Today Google® now accounts for over 70% of all U.S. searches, while Yahoo!® is a distant second at slightly more than 21%. Yahoo!® projects 2009 revenues between $7.18 billion to $7.38 billion, while Wall Street analyst's projections are for Google® to have revenues in 2009 of $15.7 billion.

One of the major reasons is the passion culture within Google®. They have one of the most dynamic approaches to team member relations around. Their customer service is phenomenal, thus their customer loyalty is astounding. They constantly are making changes to improve their customer reach via effective and measurable advertising, customer service, and leadership training that empowers its employees. Google's mission statement is clear, concise and compelling for its management, employees, users, advertising partners, and even its users.

In summary of their approach, they truly believe and subscribe to the idea that you should promise something good, deliver upon it, and keep making it better with passion and a commitment to be the very best. If more businesses and organizations operated with such vision, we would not only have higher quality service, better products, and a more giving environment.

> *Do not follow where the path may lead.*
> *Go instead where there is no path*
> *And leave a trail.*

~ Ralph Waldo Emerson

Passion, Politics & Leadership

The 2008 presidential elections in which first-term U.S. Senator Barrack Obama was elected to the highest political office in America --- President of United States of America --- is a prime example of a nation clamoring for change and believing that their candidate, though lacking the usual political pedigree and experience, brings a passion for change to the job that will allow him to fulfill his promises.

Passion is what allows true transformation in one's life. Politicians are for the most part egocentric and power hungry. Their next yearning tends to be centered on being re-elected so they can maintain their position, power, and prestige in the halls of government.

They are serving a purpose by serving their constituents, although many seek to retain the position because being in proximity to power and prestige is advantageous. For many politicians, the passion has left and it's about being re-elected. Passion, however, is what transforms a common run-of-the-mill politician into a leader. Politicians are many, but true leaders are few and far between. The vacuum that exists in politics is based not so much on the traits, but on the meaning, purpose and passion that a person brings to what they are doing. It is the reason for all they do and are. A cause is what defines leaders. The passion they have for the cause rather than the position or the power that they seek.

Our political leaders must tap into the passion for service, rather than just a purpose. Then will we have true empowered leadership that is passionate about a cause, a crusade, and about addressing and serving the needs of a people, a nation, and a world.

The true call of politics is a call to serve. To bring change that helps more than just a select elite or corporate donor. Politics is, indeed, a noble pursuit. Unfortunately, many a noble person has been drawn to it because of a passion to serve and have been swallowed up by the "political machine." Our world needs a transformation from that political model and one to passionate service for the good of a greater number of citizens and to one where values and plans of action are morally based.

Observation/Reflection: The global corporate environment needs effective change. True passionate and effective business leaders are molded during times of difficulty. As you move forward in your own business or company, envision the benefits of having an entity that not only makes a profit, but which has a clear purpose for its existence, makes a difference in the world and pursues excellence. It is time for leaders to do just that: lead!

Moments

Life is Never Perfect or Easy ---
Yet, It Holds Moments of
Serenity, Love, and Joy,
That Take Our Breath Away.
Appreciate Every One of Them and
Create Out of Them
Memories To Be Cherished...

PART VI

THE POWER OF LIVING LIFE AT THE PACE OF PASSION...

What lies ahead of you and
What lies behind you,
Is nothing
Compared to what lies within you.

~ Mohandas K. Ghandi

∞

It is not the critic who counts...
The credit belongs to the man in the arena...
Who knows great devotions,
Who spends himself in a worthy cause...
If he fails, at least fails while daring greatly...
His place shall never be with those cold and timid souls
Who have never known victory nor defeat.

~ Theodore Roosevelt

CHAPTER TWENTY-NINE

The 15th Secret: The Power in Asking "What's Next In My Life?"

If you wish success in life,
Make perseverance your bosom friend,
Experience your wise counselor,
Caution your elder brother, and
Hope your guardian genius.

~ Joseph Addison

How to Apply the Secrets towards a Passion-Driven® Life. Applying all the secrets we learned requires faith, action, and work. And it also requires we live life with balance and harmony. We must live and thrive at the "pace of passion": absorbing each moment of life; appreciating the small things and little details about people, and making the best of each day no matter how tough the day has or will become --- it could always be worse. Life is lived and enjoyed at such a pace.

The Passion-Driven® Life requires we live it at the pace of passion --- *not* at the speed of light. At the speed of light, everything swirls around you in chaos and confusion. It is where we embody constant daily stress and where we break down physically and emotionally. A rush of adrenalin is good for us in small doses. We need it to finish an important project or finish that last part of physical exercise. But we cannot stay "hooked" to it.

Life is best lived at the pace of passion where we slow our walk, our rhythm, our pace and embrace life's purpose, life's meaning, and life's beauty. It is there that we learn to let go and trust God, while also trusting and accepting ourselves with all the quirks, believing in our dreams and unleashing an abundant life.

We now live in an age where "speed" is deemed essential in everything in our personal and business lives: fast food and fast at-home meals, fast cars, faster phones, fast overnight service, fast 1 hour developing, faster internet service, fast check-out lines, fast highway lanes, drive-through banking (fast), drive-through pharmacies (fast), drive-through convenience stores (fast), fast 10 minute work-outs, "fast, fast, fast" --- the world's gone and turned up the dial on speed as if it were a thing of beauty. It can be, but taken to extremes we create amazing stress in our lives and slowly kill our passion and ourselves. Faster is *not* better.

In his book, *In Praise of Slowness: Challenging the Cult of Speed*, Carl Honore, a professed "speed-aholic", turns conventional thinking on getting things done in a hurry on its head. Honore advocates the need for slowing down our hectic pace in life as a requirement to a more balanced existence!

He writes, *"In a world where time is money, faster is better, and 'if you snooze you lose', millions of people are doing the unthinkable: they're slowing down. What's more amazing, they're healthier, happier, and excelling at both work and play. Speed can be fun, productive and powerful, and we would be poorer without it. What the world needs is a middle path, a recipe for marrying la dolce vita with the dynamism of the information age. The secret is balance instead of doing everything faster, do everything at the right speed. Sometimes fast. Sometimes slow. Sometimes in between."*

It's no coincidence that in the last thirty plus years the amount of heart attacks, depression, panic attacks, divorce, suicides, murders, stress and levels of anxiety and discontentment have all increased. As a society we have all sped up. We raise children with the same dizzying speed and bad example with which we ourselves work, live and play. We saddle them with weekly multiple tasks and social/sports activities: soccer, ballet, cheer, football, rehearsals, etc. Yet, do we ever sit down with them and appreciate what they have or what they do, before "rushing" off to the next thing? When do they have time to study or to sit down and read a good book?

As a kid growing up in the seventies, life's pace was a heck of a lot slower and because of that there was more time to spend with family and friends. My parents made twice a year treks to Tijuana, Mexico to a mission where we would donate our used clothing. Six kids of varying ages accumulate a lot of clothes and my mom and dad made these trips an "appreciate what you have" life learning lesson for all of us. We, in fact, used to look forward to going there. What child now-a-days would look forward to such a small but hugely important life lessons? Instead, we give tend to give them "things" we didn't have and turn out some pretty spoiled kids. Slow the pace down for them and in your world. Appreciate what you have and teach them to do that in their lives.

Therefore, as you go about applying all that I have covered keep that in mind and at the forefront of your plans, goals and implementation. The mission here is not to engulf your life with crazy activity and endless "To Do" lists, that sap your spirit and mind late and keep you up, but to create a life of balance and harmony --- a life where you slow down the pace and appreciate the pace of passion.

To apply *The Secrets* we must:

Have Faith.

It is in life's darkest moments that God will sometimes reveal to you the purpose for each storm. Sometimes it does not happen in the middle of the storm, when you are being lashed about and the waves keep rolling in trying to knock you out of your boat. But cling to hope and faith that God will never leave you nor forsake you.

It is in these moments of despair, difficulty and trying times that we find our purpose, where passion as a compass will lead us to the shores of promise of a better day. No matter what, we are still made better and stronger by the storms of life or business tidal waves, only when we are open and willing to see the lessons from these experiences.

Learn from yesterday,
Live for today,
Hope for tomorrow.

~ Anonymous

Believe.

Believe in yourself. A lack of self-esteem is the doom of your passionate desire to succeed at what you choose to do. Have a burning desire and faith that you can and will be successful in your goals.

Believe in yourself. Prayer, faith and positive affirmations are the keys to unleashing the power within your conscious and subconscious mind, and the hope in your heart and soul. If you don't believe in yourself and your dreams, projects, or goals, how in the world will you be able to connect with others? You'll never convince anyone else to believe in them if you don't first believe in them with all your heart.

Act NOW!!

Set clear goals, plans and take whatever steps each week to move a little closer to the goal and the implementation of your plan. Great success is the result of a great many small steps. It doesn't require taking huge, scary leaps; it only requires following a plan and taking measured and appropriate action steps.

Do It For You.

Make a list of the reasons why you have not acted and the nonsense excuses playing in your head that keep you from living a life of passion and purpose. It will make you aware of your inner-voice and its limiting beliefs. Identify them, conquer and banish them from your mind. Passion-driven people have trained themselves to release doubt from their minds. They have faith in themselves and in their action plans, despite any obstacles.

Dream — but Dream BIG Dreams.

Within your deepest desires and highest dreams are the keys to your happiness, success and purpose, look for them. God has placed them in your being. Your heart, soul, spirit and mind know only those limitations you have imposed upon yourself through your own limiting beliefs — they can be removed and new positive uplifting ones placed in your inner soul, mind, and heart. Ask for them.

Unleash!

It's time to get on with it. Life is too short to wait to fulfill and unleash the passion, purpose and dreams you have for you, your family, your spiritual life, your business life, life in general, when you think "it will be just right."

For he who has no course planned,
No wind shall be favorable.

~ Sailor's Creed

The part of unleashing involves taking your dreams and creating action plans. Just as the captain of a ship plots a course *before* he leaves the port, as he has a destination in mind, do the same with your life. Do not meander aimlessly through life. All that will happen in later years will be broken dreams, dashed hopes, thoughts of having missed the mark and purpose in your life.

Take your imperfections and just get on with it. Get your tennis shoes and start the journey! If you get too tired because you didn't train, well slow the pace until you catch your breath and keep on walking. For heaven's sake: don't quit the race. Life is nothing but a journey, not a destination.

Success in *The 9 Key Areas of Life*™ is the same thing: a journey not a destination. You made a small fortune in business? Great! Now look for ways to give some of it away. You have a great Spiritual Life? Wonderful, now seek to make the lives of others better by service to your community. Still too young to figure out what you want to do in life? No problem, for now, love and connect with family more often than you do now in order to create memories that will last everyone a lifetime. Retired and bored? Ask yourself how can you can take your wisdom and experience in life and mentor, inspire and teach younger generations.

I could go on and on, but you get the idea. The idea is to create tuning points, changes in your life and implement plans that will place you on the road towards making a difference; a difference for you and for the world.

Observation/Reflection: In what areas of life do you need to go to the next level, slow down and live life at the pace of passion? Take time to smell the flowers along each moment of the journey. With each relationship and contact you have with family, friends, and even strangers actively listen and involve yourself in the moment with them.

Rocky Times

The Bridge Over Rocky Times
May Not Be What We Expect it To Be.
It May Be Shaky and Unsteady.
However, With Courage
We Grab a Hold of It and Cross Over,
Knowing That on The Other Side
Is a Better Place,
A Better Life to See, and
A Better Person to Be…

CHAPTER THIRTY

The 16th Secret: The Power of Living Passionately Inspired - A New Life

---

It's not the years in your life that count,
It's the life in your years.

~ Abraham Lincoln

The Secret to a Life of "G.R.O.W.T.H." We need to place certain things in our lives in order for us to be productive, balanced, harmonious, and passion-driven individuals.

In each of the 9 key areas of a Passion-Driven® Life we need to have or implement the acronym: "G.R.O.W.T.H."

I cannot claim originality in it. John Childers, a mentor of mine, first introduced it to me and they stand for the following in their order of importance in our lives:

G	od who gives us faith (Needs to be always first).
R	elationships that matter to us and are healthy (Family and friends).
O	utlook that is always positive (Faith and hope gives us this).
W	ealth to enjoy it and use it for a greater good in the world.
T	ime management (A balance in all areas of life).
H	ealth so we can live well and appreciate life fully (A healthy life).

Placing all these in correct order will, no doubt, ensure not that we live a life well-lived but that we leave a lasting and memorable legacy. That we teach the wisdom we learned to future generations, and in the process live a life worth celebrating!

Now go run the race of life to the finish. Create a life of Spiritual GROWTH, a Life of personal GROWTH, a Life of family GROWTH, and a Life filled with Love GROWTH.

In all, live a life with purpose, hope and passion as we do those things which we admire, enjoy, do well, and do with love. Then and only then can we live a life that is fruitful, empowering, and "H.A.P.P.Y."

The Secret to Living a H.A.P.P.Y. Life

There are many things we can choose to do in life. The most important is the attitude we bring to life on a daily basis. Attitude is what will allow us to overcome the obstacles that come across the road and our life-long journey.

Attitude will reflect the purpose and passion in our lives. Live a "H.A.P.P.Y. Life" reflects an attitude that stands for:

H	ope that never fades.
A	live with purpose while achieving dreams.
P	assion-driven, Prayer-driven, and Possibility-driven.
P	eace in your heart and soul. Prosperity and abundance in giving.
Y	ears of legacy and love building.

101+ Passion-Driven® Things to Do in Life

There is no shortage of people who live life quite mundanely, without passion or purpose. Now that you are not one of those individuals and you know the secrets that open a new life to you, I want to give you a final challenge: LIVE. LIVE. LIVE!!

Don't wait until you retire. Don't wait until the kids leave the house or get married. Live without Excuses! Don't wait until you've built your business empire. Live Now and Live for Today, with the hope and passion that tomorrow will bring more blessings. Yet, don't put it off. Live life as if your days are now counted --- they are indeed.

Another typical thing I've heard through the years from retirees, the terminally ill or plain passionless folks is that it takes "too much money." Living the good life, as one person I know who is eighty-three has told me repeatedly, "is only for the rich." She's lived in a scarcity mentality her entire life and cannot see the possibility or hope of doing things for the sheer joy and passion.

To help you along in your new life, here is a list of "101+ Passion & Legacy Building Things To Do in Life." Some are simple, others are silly, and some require travel in your local area, others some travel outside the country. Some can be done with family, for family and without family. It doesn't matter what you choose, the important thing is for you to get start living life abundantly, building a legacy you can leave behind, and a life you are passionate about it! It is by no means complete but it gives you an idea and a place from where to launch your new life.

The 101+ Passion List

1. Audio record favorite portions of Bible and make it a part of your estate.
2. Record or video your family history/genealogy.
3. Take your children/grandchildren to where you born.
4. Take your children/grandchildren to where you were raised.
5. Create scrapbook albums.
6. Visit the Grand Canyon Arizona (USA).
7. Volunteer at church.
8. Volunteer at a school.
9. Volunteer with SCORE (Service Corps of Retired Executives).
10. Take up photography.
11. Take up swimming.
12. Take a computer class.
13. Visit the local museum(s).
14. Go snorkeling.
15. Take a pottery class.
16. Write your memoirs.
17. Publish your memoirs.
18. Take an art class.
19. Join FaceBook, Twitter or MySpace.
20. Host a large extended family get-together.
21. Take a train across Canada, USA or Europe.
22. See London, England.
23. Go on a trip with World Vision or Feed the Children.

24. Add charities to your will/estate.
25. Help build a house with Habitat for Humanity.
26. Scream at the top of your lungs from a mountain top (out of joy and not despair).
27. Teach & pass on family recipes.
28. Pass on family heirlooms *before* you die.
29. Invite a stranger to a meal.
30. Invite a homeless person to a meal.
31. Give away at least 10% to church or charities.
32. Attend college course with granddaughter/grandson.
33. Write your own eulogy.
34. Write a novel and publish it.
35. Write poetry and publish it.
36. Create a nature photo album.
37. Meet the President.
38. Help raise grandchildren.
39. Raise children to love God.
40. Visit the children you sponsor through Feed The Children, etc.
41. Serve Thanksgiving Dinner at a homeless shelter.
42. Join a prison ministry.
43. Join a church youth group even though don't have young kids.
44. Preach a sermon.
45. Volunteer at a hospice.
46. Volunteer at a handicapped workshops.
47. Volunteer at a pet shelter.
48. Visit children in the hospital.
49. Ask for forgiveness.
50. Accept forgiveness.
51. Visit a cemetery and reflect on importance of life.
52. Ask God into your life.
53. Spend the "dash" between year born and year died with complete meaning.
54. Be authentic.
55. Watch American Film Institute's 'Top 50" films of all-time.
56. Buy items at a charity.
57. Give one month's wages to charity.

58. Plant a tree.
59. Sail around the Caribbean.
60. Take gifts to the poor in another country.
61. See five operas in one year.
62. See a play in Times Square New York (USA).
63. See a play in London, England
64. Pray for 1 hour in one sitting.
65. Go swimming with sharks, dolphins, or manta rays.
66. Camp under the stars for a day or a week.
67. Cook meals and desserts for local police or firemen.
68. Take a week vacation on a houseboat.
69. Volunteer to wash dishes at a food shelter.
70. Go view a multi-million dollar house for sale.
71. Go fishing at the pier, lake, or river by yourself.
72. Send the President an opinion or thank you letter.
73. Visit the United Nations building.
74. Be nominated into the Who's Who.
75. Take the next 5 birthdays off from work.
76. Sit at the beach or mountains and watch a sunset alone.
77. Build a sandcastle at the beach.
78. Play badminton at the beach.
79. Learn to play bridge.
80. Write letters to your grandchildren and point out something special about each of them.
81. Fast for 48 hours and meditate and pray.
82. Go the airport in a limousine.
83. Donate blood at least 5 times during lifetime.
84. Create care packages for the military.
85. Create food care packages for the needy.
86. Walk or run a marathon.
87. Bike for 50 miles.
88. Read the great works of literature.
89. Start a journal.
90. Buy tickets for a sports game and donate them to disadvantaged children.
91. Send opinion letters to at least 5 major newspapers.

92. Take up gardening.
93. Cut the lawn of a widow for a year.
94. Organize a free widow's or single mom's "Handy Man Crew."
95. Buy Thanksgiving turkeys for 10 people.
96. Buy a Christmas tree for a poor person.
97. Donate toys and clothes for Christmas to the poor.
98. Frame your children's first art.
99. Video or record your child speaking.
100. Volunteer with the Boys Scouts.
101. Volunteer with the Girl Scouts.
102. Drive a sports car at 150+mph.
103. Volunteer for a political candidate.
104. Volunteer for a Christian revival rally.
105. Volunteer to deliver gifts to the needy.
106. Become a Big Brother volunteer for inner city youth.
107. Become a Big Sister volunteer for inner city youth.
108. Have a picnic under the stars.
109. Stay at a 5-Star hotel at least one night.
110. Volunteer to go to a mission's trip to third world country.
111. Dive the Great Barrier Reef.
112. Watch children on a merry-go round.
113. Be an organ donor.
114. Get up, smart up, and live up --- read all the classics of literature.
115. Take your family on an exotic vacation to a fantasy place.
116. Go sightseeing and traveling along historic highway routes & towns.
117. Call a talk-show and voice your opinion.
118. Start a unused clothing collection in your neighborhood, then take it to the local shelter, rescue mission or church.

There are so many things that we can do for ourselves, our family, and our community. **For the baby-boomers life should be thrilling and an everyday adventure rather than continuous drudgery so many have made it. You have been gifted with talents, knowledge, experiences, and wisdom. It is your responsibility to give to the world those as gifts of legacy.**

I want to share with you a compilation of thoughts that I want you to take from our time together. Remember that having and unleashing passion is not a goal or destination, but a process along the journey of life.

My Thoughts

Love God fully.
Love unconditionally and much.
Laugh much more often than you cry.
Let go...
Trust God,
And trust yourself.
Let go ...of past hurts.
Learn to forgive others.
Let others praise you.
Learn to forgive yourself and,
Let go of your disappointments.
Bask in accomplishments; but don't stop there,
Continue onward creating new ones.
Give your wisdom, talents, love, and money to others,
So they too can benefit from them.
Live well.
Live with love and respect for yourself;
Live with love and respect for others.
Don't take yourself too serious,
Remember the less fortunate, the down-trodden.
Life sometimes takes many strange turns
And you make end up being one.
Encourage everyone you come into contact with.
Live in such a way that you reflect
And live these virtues in your journey of life.

≈

<u>Endless Joy Ahead</u>

The Passion-Driven® Life
Is Yours and Ahead of You,
Alive With
Endless Possibility,
Endless Joy,
Endless Blessings,
Endless Love, and
Endless Meaning.
Enjoy the Ride,
Enjoy the Scenery.
Live the Experience,
Make It Worthwhile,
Please God,
Live It Abundantly,
And Surprise Yourself…

CONCLUSION

The 17th Secret: The Power of Life Changes ---
Creating Your Turning Points

Inside every soul,
There is a beautiful journey
Waiting to be started,
And a heart,
Longing for its beginning.

~ Louis F. Vargas

The following was written by fellow Colombian Nobel laureate, Gabriel Garcia Marquez, as he began a slow decline in health due to cancer. It has been edited, yet it goes straight to the heart of the matter of living passion-driven and making a difference in life.

The Puppets Last Goodbye

If God allowed me one more piece of life,
I would take advantage of that time as best I could.
I would probably not say everything I think, but definitely think
    all I say.
I would value things not for what they are worth...
I would continue where others have stopped.
If God allowed me one more piece of life,
I would wallow in the sunlight, leaving uncovered,
Not only my body but my soul.
I would prove to men how wrong they are to think that they
Stop falling in love as they get older,
Since they actually start getting older as soon as they stop falling
    in love.
So many things I have learned ...

I have learned that everybody wants to live at the top of the
    mountain,
Forgetting that is how we climb is all that matters.
I have learned that a man has the right to look down on somebody,
Only when he is helping him to get up.
Always tell what you feel and what you think.
If I knew that today would be the last time I will see you…
I will embrace you strongly to be the guardian of your soul.
If I would know that these would be the last minutes that I will
    see you…
I would say, "I love you", and wouldn't assume you would know it.
There is always morning, where life gives us another opportunity.
Keep always close to you, your dear ones, and tell them how much
    you need them
And love, and take care of them.
Take the time to say, "I'm sorry", "Forgive me", "Please", "Thank
    You",
And all the nice and lovely words you know.
Nobody would remember you if you keep your thoughts secret.
Force yourself to express them.

~ Gabriel Garcia Marquez

**Decide today that your life will change for the better. Decide
that with God's providence, it is in your hands to create *your turning
points in life*. It is possible to live life with total prosperity, total love,
total commitment, and total passion. You need a support system of
like-minded, inspired and passion-driven people to spur you on.**

**The secrets, steps, strategies, keys and principles which I
covered in this book need to be worked on with dedication, drive
and commitment. To accomplish that there are learning tools are
crucial to that life long process of living life with purpose, passion,
and prosperity.**

More important, however, is that success in life is not defined
exclusively on becoming wealthy but by the intangible factors of love,

sharing, being a part of someone's life; teaching, listening, and being a true friend, legacy building and empathy for the hurt someone has in their life.

There are free resources for you to be able to begin the journey or expand your current success journey into having a more balanced life. Without any more excuses create your turning points. Log onto: www.ThePassionDrivenLife.com.

To everything there is a season,
And a time to every purpose under heaven.

~ Ecclesiastes 3:1

Keep in mind that the attainment of "money success" should not be the only all-encompassing drive and purpose for your life. That is not wealth in my book. There are the usual late night infomercials and the internet bombardments of get-rich systems promising us that we can a fortune doing this or that, putting aside whether or not they are true, my question is this, "And then what will you do with it?"

Life is more than accumulating money in a bank account. It is about loving God, loving you, loving others, loving life, creating great relationships, great times, and living life with every breath you have to its absolute fullest. If we manage to be blessed, and as a result of our labor and wisdom, we manage to create a fortune, then we are under obligation to do something with it besides pleasure ourselves. If there is one lesson I learned about money is that it can come just as easily as it can go.

You now know the secrets, have the tools and the knowledge. Implement and use them to forge an amazing journey of passion and purpose. Live life head-on. Move on. Make your life count. Gain perspective and insight on how you can make a difference.

Real worth and value is tied to the love we give, the treasures we share with others, and the lives we can change or influence by living life with passion, by living it in the small details and moments that may seem insignificant at first, but at the end of it all can make all the difference in the hearts and souls of the men, women, and children whose lives we touch.

Be bold. Thank God for life and its blessings --- good and bad--- it all has a purpose, we just don't realize that there is good that can come from bad. Remember the stories of Brenden, Michael, Estella, Ron and Rick. Though handed some seemingly bad lemons in life they went past that, and created memorable legacies of love, sharing, compassion, and possibility. Each lived "out loud" and on fire for life. Make a difference. Love. Embrace life and its beautiful journey. Enjoy the amazing scenery and the exhilarating moments you will create along the way.

Being passion-driven will allow you a new perspective and a new life journey. Make it happen and enjoy the ride --- no excuses, no matter what life throws at you, despite the inevitable bumps, wrong turns and obstacles that come along the way along the road in the valleys. When they pop up --- and they will --- steady your course with prayer and persistence. And then move on with unyielding passion up the mountain.

♥

Do all the good you can,
By all the means you can,
In all the ways you can,
At all the times you can,
To all the people you can,
As long as you can.

~ John Wesley

AFTERWORD

The Final Secret: The Power of Passionately Living in The Valleys of Life

---

Being on the mountaintop is wonderful,
But we don't live on the mountaintop;
We live in the valleys of life.

~ Dudley C. Rutherford

The process of transformation in life is not easy nor is it accomplished in just one weekend or by reading just one book. Anything that promises that is pure folly and not reality. They can, however, serve as a tool to guide you on a new journey and a new direction in your life. During the period of writing this book many transformations and crises have arisen personally and in business for me. Guess what? --- It is what it is, so I embraced them, faced the challenges and made changes where I needed.

Change and transformation is a gradual process in our lives. There are baby steps we must take to begin the process --- small changes in the beginning that later will make a difference.

It is like a large ocean liner or jetliner whose captains change direction in a gentle and slow manner. They decide on a new course and move the mechanisms slightly. The ship or jet, thereafter, immediately responds and gradually heads in a different direction. Do the same in your life --- immediately decide to change, take actions intended to change directions, work at it diligently, implement gradually, and then you'll see changes.

If you would like to accelerate it a bit more, do it if that fits your style, however, don't be in a rush to live your life at the speed of light --- instead live life at the speed of passion: embracing what is important in life and the decisions that make a difference.

Just like the ocean liner or jet example, we must make turns and make bold decisions to change our circumstances and rise above our crises. Then we move gradually onward. Once in awhile the change is almost immediate. If it does not occur for you, however, do not despair. Continue onward with prayer, patience and persistence, and over the course of time you will see change.

Patience is indeed a virtue when it comes to change in our life. Before we can begin a new chapter in our lives and a positive change, you must look at yourself in a positive light filled with possibilities. You must first love yourself in a positive manner and seek to be the change you desire. Loving God, seeking spiritual enlightenment, acceptance of you, and asking for wisdom is one the most crucial keys to loving yourself.

Loving yourself will allow you to be in a state of mind and spiritual readiness to accept change. Be and do that and the outcome or direction of the things you set out to do will be greater than you ever could have imagined. Love will allow you to embrace your personal failures as well as your successes. Love will enable you to view your inner and outer worlds differently, and to accept God's blessings and wisdom.

My friend and über-mentor Donald F. Ford, a jovial, kind-hearted and effervescent man of seventy-four years who took up the hobby of racing Z01 Corvettes at speeds of more than 165 miles per hour only four years ago, has experienced life in the highest of highest mountaintops financially, as well as lived it in the lowest of lowest valleys in life both personally and financially, constantly recites the Vince Lombardi quote: "Winners never quit and losers never win!" to encourages others. This is so true. With the choices we make in the "now", we shape, ensure and most likely win our victories in the future. Therefore, never quit.

We must leave a legacy to our children and our world that reflects love. That is what *The ComPassion Project* is all about. We must live to enjoy life, not to work until we no longer have a life. And yes, I know of the terrible things that happen to so many nice, caring and loving people in life. That's the thing with living life --- you have mountaintops and you have many valleys.

I don't understand why great mothers, fathers, sons, daughters, family or friends are stricken by terminal illnesses or accidents, die so young and leave behind broken hearts and many unfulfilled dreams.

I've had to experience that in my life with family and friends far too many times already, and each time it hurts. I just read Ron Pausch's *The Last Lecture*. His short life and terminal cancer battles resonated with a message of living with passion, meaning, family love, and without excuses.

I don't understand why hope leaves the souls of men and women, and they decide to meander through the rest of life abusing alcohol or drugs --- escaping the demons of past and avoiding future ones. I've seen that in my family and it's happening daily in every town and city in our world. I don't understand in the extreme cases why some people decide to take their own lives. I've lived through that with a family member and a friend, and it's not pretty.

I don't know why other people lose their sanity --- literally --- from one day to the next and live in a make-believe world. My nephew (Vince), a college friend (Tom) and a lawyer I employed at one time (Mark) were all smart, handsome and possessed brilliant minds, yet due to mental illness they slowly slipped into a world in which only pain and disorientation exists. The only thing I could share with them was respect and love. Nothing else stuck to their minds, but their hearts receive it openly. We tend to do too much sometimes with people who are hurting and we can't seem to reach them emotionally or spiritually. All they may want or ever need is just respect and love; their heart will pick up the message.

I don't understand why faith, hope and possibility leave the souls of individuals and they decide to merely exist in life, not really *live* life. And I don't understand why bad things happen to seemingly good people in the world.

There are many things I don't understand and many questions to which I do not pretend to know the answers. However, I do know about: rising up out of the ashes of life, never quitting, selfless service, and that the possibility to change direction in life exists.

Above all, I know about faith, hope, grace, peace, and the power of purpose and passion found through a relationship with God. I also know that through that relationship we can overcome all kinds

of things that will pop up out of the *Pandora's Box* known as life --- crises, storms, obstacles, evil, and difficulty. At the bottom of that *Box*, however, is found hope --- so cling to God; hope will eventually pop out of *Pandora's Box* and into your life while you're still in the valleys of life.

It is in the valleys of life where our character and our faith are tested. It is in the valleys of life that we can reach out to others and where we can have the most impact. In the valleys of life is where we *choose* to rise above the tide of tough times and crawl and claw, if need be, up the mountain.

And in the valleys of life is where God most assuredly and reassuringly holds our hands and gives us the comfort we so desperately need. It is where He gives us the hope of a better tomorrow and opens up doors of possibility to us. He points the way --- if only we just listen, learn, observe and with faith choose to walk through the doors of opportunity.

I also do know this: take your experiences and moments while in the valleys of life and learn from each moment --- whether good or bad. From the valleys of life cherish each moment of happiness; never forget the moments of laughter, nor the moments of tears, and hold onto the dreams which propelled you forward. And allow each and every instance of being in the valleys of life not to be ones of constant despair but of hope. All these will mold you into a better person, if you choose to allow that process of transformation to take place.

As for business, capitalism of course is designed and geared to make a profit. However, I propose it needs to be values based capitalism instead of the kind of greed we have witnessed. Incredible customer and social value and world-class service should be given in exchange for money. Unfettered greed, much as we have seen in the speculative trading markets generates nothing more than a disdain for capitalism. When I was on Wall Street I was told and did learn that sharks never go after each other, they go after easy prey. I believe one of the reasons what happened to our economy is that kind of mind-set.

There are alternatives to capitalism such Paul Newman and billionaires Sir Richard Branson and Bill Gates, among many others, reflect and espouse --- wealth that carries with it ethical and social responsibilities. That is a choice business people and entrepreneurs alike must implement with a purpose and a passion to make a difference.

In business if you place quality and service above all else, and continually ask, "How may I/we help you, even if you decide not to buy anything from us?" you will not have customers but rather raving clients beating at your door. Do that first instead of thinking of your pocketbook and business will follow like bees to honey.

As entrepreneurs and business people we must follow our passion for what we do and do the right thing, while at the same time we must live and work at the speed of passion, and not let work or our business totally engulf our being 12, 14, or 16 hours a day, week in and week out, as it did me at one time. It can be a fast-track to the grave and sour our relationships.

As for the Baby Boomer generation, in North America alone a baby boomer turns 60 every 8 seconds --- that's a total of 4 million baby boomers annually ready to re-evaluate their lives, chart new courses and weigh options as to what dreams to unleash for the future. These years post-retirement should not be a time of sour reflection upon the youth and years gone by. Instead, they should be treated as years filled with amazing opportunity to learn and share new things, to share passions, wisdom, and experiences. It is a time to create new meaning in your life, just like Josefina did, and to make your golden years your Power and Passion Years!

In all, I do know that living a life of passion, with divine purpose, with meaning in all the nine areas of life, and a life that makes a difference is more important than merely living day-by-day striving in your mind to keep your head above water, and without having anything to look forward to, or to share or to leave as a legacy for future generations.

I do know that the secret to success in our personal life and business life is to do what we love, be and do what we believe in, live what we do, and to leave things better than how we found them.

I do know that life is about appreciating and absorbing each relationship, each moment, and each day and each year, rather than constantly living in our own little world, totally self-absorbed in ourselves without impacting or making a difference. As we have seen there is more to life; it is not all about you, your business or your career. Reach out and have that "final chocolate" in your life.

<u>*A Chocolate a Day Keeps the Blues Away*</u>

Life's so short, my friend, I hate missing out on something good.

This year I realized how old I was --- 80. I haven't been this old before.

So, before I die, I've got to try those things that for years I had ignored:

I haven't smelled all the flowers yet.

There are too many books I haven't read.

There are more fudge sundaes to wolf down and kites to be flown.

I've not laughed at all the jokes.

I've missed a lot of Broadway hits, potato chips and cokes.

I want to wade again in water and feel ocean spray on my face.

I want to sit in a country church once more and thank God for His grace.

I want peanut butter every day spread on my morning toast.

I want un-timed long distance calls to the folks I love the most.

I haven't cried at all the movies yet, or walked in the morning rain.

I need to feel wind in my hair.

I want to fall in love again.

So, if I choose to have dessert, instead of having dinner,

Then should I die before night fall,

I'd say I died a winner, because I missed out on nothing.

I filled my heart's desire.

I had that final chocolate mousse before my life expired.

~ Anonymous

What's important in life is a question that we constantly don't ask ourselves. However, that is a question which Cindy Sigler Dagnan was forced to ask herself when, at only thirty-nine years young, a tumor was found during a routine medical examination and which forever changed her life.

In Cindy's own words, *"I was seized by fear. I sobbed about the possibility of not growing old with my husband. I thought of all the moments I might miss out on and the storehouse of information I wanted to pass on to my young girls...I noticed what I'd forgotten or never taken time for: the smell of dryer sheets, the warmth of clean laundry, the chalky gray of a sky before rain. I quickly discovered what was important to me --- the depth of my faith and the joy of second chances... There is grace and laughter in second chances. Facing our mortality leaves us with choices: to lose our breath giggling, to eagerly unwrap the gift of each moment, to grab onto what's really important, to leave an intentional legacy and exit this life laughing."*

For Cindy Sigler Dagnan her life was turned on its head with news about her medical condition. After her surgery she learned that the mass which had been removed was not a lymphoma, and that she had been granted a second chance at living. Though she endured dark nights in her soul as she wandered through the lowest point in the valley of her life, she thanks God for the gift of a second chance at life and now embraces it with new meaning, purpose, vigor and unfettered passion.

If you remember one thing from our journey together, I hope, it would be that living life with passion while in the valleys of life can be just as rewarding as making it to the mountaintop. Once there, never forget the lessons learned and pass them on to others. It is our obligation and an act of love. Continually ask and remind yourself, "What is really important in life?" Measure your worth and impact in life through love from the heart and inspiration on souls; not by pluses or minuses on bank statements.

In your life: Believe. Connect. Inspire. Grow. Celebrate. Unwrap the wonderful and blessed gift of each moment of life and infuse it with purpose and passion. Persevere in the valleys of life where others would quit, and never believe you are alone in your journey, never cease to believe in yourself, never stop believing, and never give up on Divine power. Individuals who are passion-driven have balance in all areas of life, live longer, are happier, have a keen sense that they matter in life, and are more fulfilled by their role in it. They *choose* passion and its pace, and fully unleash their purpose with every ounce of energy in their being.

In the process they inspire others to do the same, to never give up, to fight and overcome as they make it through their dark valleys of life, and they inspire people to create meaning in their own lives, and to live life with unyielding passion, no matter what comes their way.

Remember to inspire your life and infuse your mission with passion. Persevere in the valleys of life where others would quit, and never believe you are alone in your journey. God is not going to desert you in your times of trials. Be, "Firm, strong and go onward." Passion --- pass it on.

Ripples

Thank You...
For Being a Part of This Journey.
For Opening up Your Soul.
For Making a Difference
In Your Life.
And Thereby Creating "Ripples"
Which Will Radiate
Deep From Within Your Soul
And Touch
The Souls of Others...

www.ThePassionDrivenLife.com

A Special Invitation ...
THE ComPASSION PROJECT
TRANSFORM THE WORLD & MAKE A DIFFERENCE

If your actions inspire
Others to dream more,
Learn more,
Do more
And become more,
You are a leader.

~ John Quincy Adams

Dear Friend,

My hope is that through this journey together you have renewed and filled up your spirit, soul and mind with insights, purpose, empowerment and passion as to what is possible in life for you, and how you can make a difference in key areas. Gratefully unwrap the gift of life each day.

Help us out and be a part of a worthy cause. **Our goal**, through our partnership with Feed The Children, is to monthly feed, clothe and care for **1,000 poor and needy children.** That is the mission of *The ComPASSION Project.* 10% of all sales will be donated towards that cause.

If your heart and soul has embraced and been taken in with the message of this book, keep it going. Inspire others; get the word out on the book and the Project. If you know of someone who can be inspired by "The Passion-Driven Life" and would like to send it as a gift, please log onto: www.ThePassionDrivenLife.com. *You'll receive* free *power-packed educational materials, normally sold for $127, as part of a limited promotion for this book.*

Please e-mail us to share your story of hope, passion, soul inspiration, of you overcoming obstacles or making a difference in the lives of others so it may considered in the next book series.

Buy some books to give away to your local school, church, synagogue, hospital, college/university or any place where people are searching to transform their lives. If you have a newsletter, blog, web site, or social media account recommend this book. Write a book review on www.Amazon.com, www.BarnesandNoble.com, your local newspaper, or your favorite magazine.

THE PASSION-DRIVEN® LIFE CHARITIES

You can give without loving,
But you cannot love without giving.

~ *Anonymous*

In partnership with *Feed The Children* (FTC), the author will donate percentage of royalties from this book to FTC; a non-profit charity that feeds, clothes and provides medical necessities for children in 119 countries. They encourage the heart and mind, bring faith and hope to the soul, and plants seeds of love. By investing in this book you become an ambassador of hope and love.

In addition, the publisher, Morgan-James Publishing, will also donate a percentage of sales proceeds from this book to *Habitat for Humanity*, a non-profit charity that builds low-income housing and seeks to eliminate homelessness around the world. *Habitat for Humanity* information can be viewed on their website www.habitat.org or by calling 1-800-422-4828.

I encourage you to search your heart and sponsor a poor and hungry child via sponsorship through *Feed The Children*. For only about $1 per day you really can make a permanent difference in the world. Please visit their website www.feedthechildren.org or call toll-free at 1-800-627-4556 to enroll.

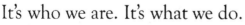
It's who we are. It's what we do.

BIBLIOGRAPHY

Alexander, Prioleau. *Want Fries With That? A White-Collar Burnout Experiences Life at Minimum Wage.* New York: Arcade Publishing Group, 2008

Hill, Napolean. *Think and Grow Rich.* New York: Penguin/Hawthorn Books, Inc. 1937.

Honore, Karl. *In Praise of Slowness: How a Worldwide Movement is Challenging the Cult of Speed.* New York: HarperCollins Publishers, Inc., 2004.

Mayes, Frances. *Under The Tuscan Sun: At Home in Italy.* New York: Broadway Books, 1996.

Pink, Daniel H. *A Whole New Mind: Why Right-Brainers Will Rule The World.* New York: Penguin Publishing Group, 2005.

Rutherford, Dudley C. *Romancing Royalty.* Porter Ranch: Joy Comes in the Morning Productions, 2005.

The Holy Bible, New International Version. Grand Rapids: Zondervan Publishing, Inc. 1973.

Warren, Rick. *The Purpose-Driven* Life: What On Earth Am I Here For?* Grand Rapids: Zondervan Publishing, Inc., 2002.

MEET THE AUTHOR

I slept and dreamt that life was joy.
I awoke and saw that life was service.
I acted and behold, service was joy.
~ Rabindranath Tagore

Louis F. Vargas is an immigrant who grew up on the wrong side of the tracks in Los Angeles. Despite majorcrises and difficulties in life, he rose up to become a Wall Street stock-broker and municipal bond trader. He's started successful businesses in various industries, including an *Inc. 500* company. He is now CEO of NMCC Corporation, a business and management consulting company, and founder of *Passion-Driven® Enterprises*, a personal and business development education and training company.

He is a sought out business consultant, speaker, and expert in strategic branding and leadership, as well as strategic marketing, planning, and sales maximization. As an executive business coach and consultant he inspires innovation and high-performance in both management and employee teams.

Mr. Vargas was inducted into *Who's Who in America*, is an *Inc. 500* Biznet adviser, volunteers with Junior Achievement, and a member of several business associations.

He has a B.A. degree from USC in international relations, philosophy, & political science, and completed post-graduate work in public administration and real estate development. He lives in Southern California, is happily married and passionate about his family life.

To book Mr. Vargas as a speaker, business consultant, or coach, log onto: www.StrategicBusinessMaximization.com.

WHAT'S NEXT?

It's now time to take action and put wheels on your dreams; connect with like-minded mentors, leading achievers and passion-driven individuals who have the inside track to success and an abundant and balanced life. How?

For a limited time, as part of the book promotion, on the web-site **www.PassionDrivenSoul.com** receive **FREE** Life Success tools (valued at $775.00) that I've used through the years with corporate clients to sky-rocket their success, and bring balance, direction and value to individuals lives. The success tools and bonuses are yours when you test-drive membership in the *Passion Driven Soul Success Network.* You'll receive:

- ✓ **BONUS #1: The Passion-Driven® Life Assessment Test;**
- ✓ **BONUS #2: The Passion-Driven® Life P.L.A.N.S.™ Program;**
- ✓ **BONUS #3: The Purpose & Passion-Driven® Goals Setting Guide;**
- ✓ **BONUS #4: Passion-Driven® Business Development Survey;**
- ✓ **BONUS #5: The breakthrough *40 Days to Success Program*;**
- ✓ **BONUS #6: The classic book *Acres of Diamonds* by Dr. Russell H. Conwell;**
- ✓ **BONUS #7: The timeless success book *As a Man Thinketh* by James Allen;**

Plus as part of your membership:

- ✓ **Access to cutting-edge monthly information and interview sessions from top experts, thinkers, movers and innovators in the Business & Career, Personal Development & Growth, Relationships & Love, Health, and Spiritual fields.**
- ✓ **Monthly tele-conference and coaching calls with me and renowned experts.**
- ✓ **VIP tickets and discounts to summits and trainings.**

These tools if used in conjunction with *The Passion-Driven Life* will create needed changes and propel your new life forward. Change your world, change the world....

Unleash the ***power and purpose of your dreams*** and lead the life you long for. TAKE ACTION before the offer ends! Log onto: **www. PassionDrivenSoul.com.**

Notes/Inspirations

Notes/Inspirations

Notes/Inspirations

BUY A SHARE OF THE FUTURE IN YOUR COMMUNITY

These certificates make great holiday, graduation and birthday gifts that can be personalized with the recipient's name. The cost of one S.H.A.R.E. or one square foot is $54.17. The personalized certificate is suitable for framing and will state the number of shares purchased and the amount of each share, as well as the recipient's name. The home that you participate in "building" will last for many years and will continue to grow in value.

Here is a sample SHARE certificate:

THIS CERTIFIES THAT

YOUR NAME HERE

HAS INVESTED IN A HOME FOR A DESERVING FAMILY

1985-2005

TWENTY YEARS OF BUILDING FUTURES IN OUR COMMUNITY ONE HOME AT A TIME

1200 SQUARE FOOT HOUSE @ $65,000 = $54.17 PER SQUARE FOOT
This certificate represents a tax deductible donation. It has no cash value.

YES, I WOULD LIKE TO HELP!

I support the work that Habitat for Humanity does and I want to be part of the excitement! As a donor, I will receive periodic updates on your construction activities but, more importantly, I know my gift will help a family in our community realize the dream of homeownership. I would like to SHARE in your efforts against substandard housing in my community! (Please print below)

PLEASE SEND ME _____ SHARES at $54.17 EACH = $ $_____

In Honor Of: _____

Occasion: (Circle One)   HOLIDAY   BIRTHDAY   ANNIVERSARY

      OTHER: _____

Address of Recipient: _____

Gift From: _____ *Donor Address:* _____

Donor Email: _____

I AM ENCLOSING A CHECK FOR $ $_____ PAYABLE TO HABITAT FOR HUMANITY <u>OR</u> PLEASE CHARGE MY VISA OR MASTERCARD *(CIRCLE ONE)*

Card Number _____ Expiration Date: _____

Name as it appears on Credit Card _____ Charge Amount $ _____

Signature _____

Billing Address _____

Telephone # Day _____ Eve _____

PLEASE NOTE: Your contribution is tax-deductible to the fullest extent allowed by law.
Habitat for Humanity • P.O. Box 1443 • Newport News, VA 23601 • 757-596-5553
www.HelpHabitatforHumanity.org